MARGUERITE BOURGEOYS AND THE
CONGREGATION OF NOTRE DAME, 1665–1700

McGILL-QUEEN'S STUDIES IN THE HISTORY OF RELIGION

Volumes in this series have been supported by the Jackman Foundation of Toronto.

MARGUERITE BOURGEOYS

AND THE CONGREGATION OF NOTRE DAME, 1665–1700

Patricia Simpson

McGill-Queen's University Press
Montreal & Kingston · London · Ithaca

Legal deposit fourth quarter 2005
Bibliothèque nationale du Québec

Printed in Canada on acid-free paper that is 100% ancient forest free
(100% post-consumer recycled), processed chlorine free

This book has been published with the help of a grant from the
Congrégation de Notre-Dame de Montréal.

McGill-Queen's University Press acknowledges the support of the Canada Council
for the Arts for our publishing program. We also acknowledge the financial support
of the Government of Canada through the Book Publishing Industry
Development Program (BPIDP) for our publishing activities.

LIBRARY AND ARCHIVES CANADA CATALOGUING IN PUBLICATION

Simpson, Patricia, 1937–
Marguerite Bourgeoys and the Congregation of Notre-Dame, 1665–1700 /
Patricia Simpson.
(McGill-Queen's studies in the history of religion ; 42)
Includes bibliographical references and index.
ISBN 0-7735-2970-5

1. Bourgeoys, Marguerite, Saint, 1620–1700. 2. Congregation of
Notre-Dame – History.   3. Nuns – Québec (Province) – Biography.
4. Christian saints – Quebec (Province) – Biography.   I. Title.   II. Series.

BX4700.B76S542 2005   271'.97   C2005-904608-2

Set in 10.6/13 Sabon with Trajan Pro and Weiss
Book design & typesetting by zijn digital

CONTENTS

ACKNOWLEDGMENTS

The author wishes to express her gratitude to Joyce Roberts for assistance with research, for technical aid, for reading the manuscript, and for providing encouragement and advice about the manuscript at all stages; to Danielle Dubois for reading and making suggestions about the manuscript; to Rachel Gaudreau for assistance with the preparation of the illustrations; to Florence Bertrand, Raymonde Sylvain, Rolland Litalien, and Marc Lacasse, of Montreal, and to Marie Marchand, Pierre Lafontaine, and Jeanne D'Arc Boissoneault, of Quebec, for help with archival research; to Elizabeth Hulse for her invaluable editorial assistance; also to the members of the general administration of the Congrégation de Notre-Dame of Montreal for their continued confidence and support.

NOTE ON TRANSLATION
AND NAMES USED

All the original sources and most of the secondary works relating to the life of Marguerite Bourgeoys are in French, and few of them have been translated into English. Where a suitable translation is available, it has been used and is cited in the bibliography and notes. Where no such translation is readily available, the one provided is the author's own.

The names of many of the persons who appear in this work were spelled in a variety of ways in documents of the period. In the case of Marguerite Bourgeoys's contemporaries, the names of persons mentioned in the text appear in the form in which they are most frequently found in her writings and in other well-known works of the time. The names of the early sisters of the Congrégation de Notre-Dame de Montréal are given in the form in which they were signed or, if no signatures have been found, in that in which they appear in the *Histoire de la Congrégation de Notre-Dame de Montréal*. Other names are spelled as in the *Dictionary of Canadian Biography*. Several different Congrégations de Notre-Dame are mentioned in this work, but "the Congregation" (capitalized) refers always to the Congrégation de Notre-Dame de Montréal, the community founded by Marguerite Bourgeoys.

A small box made of stillborn calfskin that belonged to Marguerite Bourgeoys and was perhaps the one containing her papers and articles that was accidentally left behind at Quebec at the beginning of her second return to France in 1670–72. It must have continued to be used in the Congregation after her death, since the lock and handle were replaced during the eighteenth century. (Photograph: Bernard Dubois; Musée Marguerite-Bourgeoys)

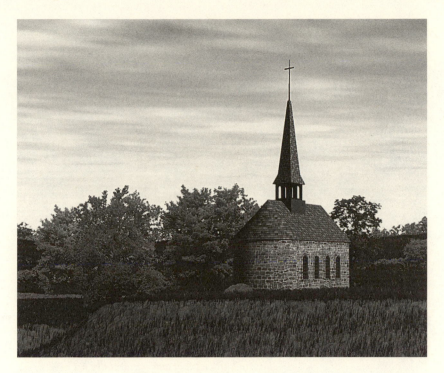

Marguerite first began to plan a chapel of pilgrimage dedicated to the blessed Virgin in 1655. After many delays, the chapel, Montreal's first stone church, was completed in 1678 and dedicated to Notre-Dame-de-Bon-Secours. It was destroyed by fire in 1754, and the present chapel erected over the original foundations in 1771. Using information from historical documents and from recent archaeological discoveries, this computer-assisted projection pictures the chapel as it might have looked in its natural setting about 1680. (Virtual historic reconstruction: Omar Bakat, GRAPH Architecture Inc.; Musée Marguerite-Bourgeoys)

Foundation of the 1678 chapel uncovered in the archaeological explorations below the present chapel in 1996–97. This photograph of the foundation of the apse shows the holes left by stakes when the wooden palisade surrounding the town was extended to take in the Faubourg Bonsecours and the apse became part of the fortifications. (Photograph: Rachel Gaudreau, Musée Marguerite-Bourgeoys)

Statuette of Virgin and Child in oak given to Marguerite Bourgeoys by the Baron de Fancamp in 1672 for the chapel of pilgrimage whose construction she had begun in Montreal. Already a century old at the time of its presentation, the statuette has survived both fire and theft and is now preserved in Notre-Dame-de-Bon-Secours chapel in Montreal. (Photograph: Rachel Gaudreau, Musée Marguerite Bourgeoys)

*Lead commemorative plaque placed under the first stone of the foundation of
Notre-Dame-de-Bon-Secours chapel on 30 June 1675*

Brass engraving with image of Virgin and Child described in the documents as "copper medal of the Blessed Virgin" and placed with the commemorative plaque in 1675

Both of these objects were rediscovered in 1945 when a wall in the crypt of the present chapel was pierced to provide a fire exit. They had been recovered after the fire of 1754 and placed with the commemorative plaque of the 1771 chapel. (Photographs: Pierre Fauteux, Ville de Montréal)

Holy water font in glazed earthenware, one of the few artifacts recovered during the archaeological excavations beneath Notre-Dame-de-Bon-Secours chapel in 1996–97. Such articles of devotion were important in the seventeenth-century; the rule drawn up for the Congrégation de Notre-Dame by Bishop Saint-Vallier specified that each sister must have a holy water font in her room. This one has obviously been broken and repaired. (Photography: Pierre Fauteux; Collection of the Ministère de la culture et des communications du Québec, Ville de Montréal)

The Maison Saint-Gabriel. Marguerite Bourgeoys first received a land grant at Pointe-Saint-Charles in 1662. This property was added to over time, and the farm established there helped support the work of the Congregation until the first quarter of the twentieth century. It is now a museum recalling especially the work done by the Congregation with early female immigrants to Montreal. (Photograph: Pierre Guzzo)

Stone tower in the grounds of the Grand Séminaire on Sherbrooke Street in Montreal. All that now remains of the Mountain Mission established by the Sulpicians in 1676 is two stone towers that were part of the fortifications erected in the 1680s. The sisters of the Congregation taught in one of these and lived in the other. (Photograph: Abla Monsour)

Painting of the Child Jesus known in the Congrégation de Notre-Dame as
"Marie Barbier's Child Jesus." Marie Barbier, the first Montrealer to enter
the Congregation and Marguerite Bourgeoys's sucessor as superior, had
immense devotion to the Child Jesus and reportedly kept an image of him
over the oven where she baked bread. Edward O. Korany, who restored the
painting in 1966, thought it unlikely that the painting was the work of either
Marie Barbier or Pierre Le Ber. He found that it had been exposed to high
heat and there was soot in the cracks, suggesting that it survived one
or more fires at the Congregation as well as Marie Barbier's oven.
(Photograph: Bernard Dubois; Musée Marguerite-Bourgeoys)

Painting of the Holy Family by unknown artist. The painting, obviously imported from France, was given to Marguerite Bourgeoys by Gabriel Souart, Montreal's first parish priest, at the time of the founding of the Confraternity of the Holy Family in 1663. (Photograph: Norman Rajotte; Musée Marguerite-Bourgeoys)

Pall embroidered by Jeanne Le Ber, the religious recluse. She spent her time in prayer, making clothing for the poor, and creating beautiful embroidered vestments and altar ornaments. (Collection Maison Saint-Gabriel)

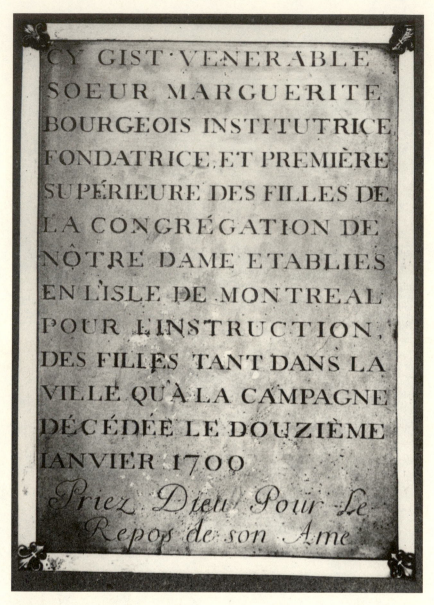

CY GIST·VENERABLE
SOEUR MARGUERITE
BOURGEOIS INSTITUTRICE
FONDATRICE, ET PREMIÈRE
SUPÉRIEURE DES FILLES DE
LA CONGRÉGATION DE
NÔTRE DAME ETABLIES
EN L'ISLE DE MONTREAL
POUR L'INSTRUCTION
DES FILLES TANT DANS LA
VILLE QU'À LA CAMPAGNE
DÉCÉDÉE LE DOUZIÈME
IANVIER 1700
*Priez Dieu Pour Le
Repos de son Ame*

Copper plaque erected by François Dollier de Casson to indicate Marguerite Bourgeoys's burial place in Montreal's original parish church. The plaque underlines what was distinctive about the community she founded: because its members were uncloistered, they were able to go out and teach girls in the country.

Two sides of a reliquary that are evidence of the fate of Marguerite Bourgeoys's writings. This reliquary must have been created after the burning of the Congregation mother house in 1768 and before the 1830s, when Étienne-Michel Faillon put a stop to this practice and made an attempt to recover the fragments of her writings that had been distributed as relics. It contains ashes of her heart, as indicated by the heart symbol and the words "Cendres de la coeur de la vénérable Sr Marguerite Bourgeois." On the reverse side are the words "l'ecriture de la vénérable Sr Marguerite Bourgeois," and in the centre is a fragment of paper bearing the words "St gabriel" in Marguerite Bourgeoys's handwriting. (Photographs: Bernard Dubois; Musée Marguerite-Bourgeoys

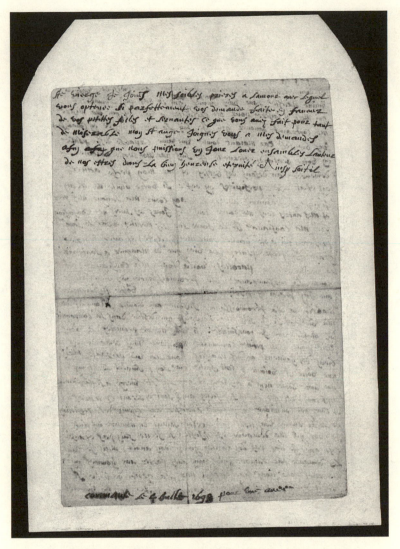

Autograph copy of a prayer composed by Marguerite Bourgeoys and dated 4 July 1693. Addressing the "eternal and all powerful God," she asks for the Congregation not wealth, honours, or pleasures in this life but a faithful fulfillment of the will of God after the example of Jesus and his mother. She then asks for the eternal salvation of all the present and future members of the Congregation, as well as of those who assist them to advance on the road of perfection. This is the only sustained piece of the founder's handwriting still in the possession of the Congrégation de Notre-Dame. (Photograph: Murielle Boisvert; Congrégation de Notre-Dame)

MARGUERITE BOURGEOYS AND THE
CONGREGATION OF NOTRE DAME, 1665–1700

INTRODUCTION

This book takes up the life of Marguerite Bourgeoys in 1665, a watershed year in the history of Montreal and of New France. It saw the departure of Paul de Chomedey de Maisonneuve, Montreal's founding governor and its defender during the early years of the settlement's existence, when it had stood so often on the brink of extinction; the year also saw the arrival of the Carignan-Salières regiment, sent at last to confront the Iroquois threat to New France. The dispatching of this force to the New World reflected a new concern on the part of the royal government in France for its North American colonies, an interest that would bring great changes to all of New France, but particularly to the tiny, vulnerable missionary settlement of Ville-Marie on the island of Montreal. These changes would profoundly affect the life of Marguerite Bourgeoys, who had arrived there twelve years before.

Marguerite had left her native city of Troyes in 1653 to journey to Montreal at the invitation of de Maisonneuve, who was, like her, a native of the French province of Champagne. The founding of Montreal was an outcome of the great spiritual renewal in seventeenth-century French Catholicism that involved both men and women from all classes of society. The object of the settlement on the island at the confluence of the St Lawrence and Ottawa Rivers was the evangelization of the Native peoples of the New World. This purpose was intended to be attained, at least in part, by presenting the example of a Christian community that would resemble the early church. The founders' plans had included the establishment of a hospital and a school in the colony. The first of these objectives had already been fulfilled by Jeanne Mance, Montreal's first hospital administrator and nurse, who had been co-leader and bursar of the founding expedition. Marguerite Bourgeoys's role in Montreal was to be that of teacher of the children, both French and Native. At the time of her departure for Canada, she was thirty-three years old and already had considerable teaching and administrative experience.

For five years Marguerite was unable to accomplish her primary mission, the opening of a school. During this time, she went from house to house teaching the women to read and write, accepted the care of the first child born in the settlement to survive, and helped Jeanne Mance at the hospital; she also ran the household of the governor at the fort, where she lived and performed whatever other services she could for the tiny and beleaguered population. She involved the first Montrealers in the building of a chapel of pilgrimage on the banks of the St Lawrence not far from the fort. This was a time when she established lasting friendships not only with the leaders of the colony but also with the ordinary settlers.

By 1658 a sufficient number of children had survived to make a school feasible. In January of that year Marguerite Bourgeoys was given a stone building on the common near the river, a structure that had previously been used as a stable. She had a chimney installed, enlisted the aid of the children in eliminating traces of the former inhabitants, and there opened Montreal's first school on 30 April 1658. Later that year, she returned to France to seek companions to help with her work. Those who joined her took up residence in the stable school, where they not only taught the children but also received and gave a temporary home to young women who came from France in the hope of finding suitable husbands in the New World. At first, the prospective brides were recruited by the Société de Notre-Dame de Montréal. Later they were sent by the royal government in France; these women are known as the filles du roi. During that time, at least one of the first companions of Marguerite Bourgeoys began to travel to outlying settlements to give religious instruction to the children. Circumstances demanded that Marguerite and her companions teach both the boys and the girls, although that was not the custom of the time. *Marguerite Bourgeoys and Montreal, 1640–1665* is the story of those years, a period of constant danger in all of New France and particularly on the island of Montreal, then the western outpost of French settlement.

Throughout this early period, Ville-Marie retained its missionary purpose, even though hostilities between the French and the Iroquois not only kept the settlement's continued existence in peril but rendered all but impossible any attempt to realize that purpose. It ended with the departure of Montreal's first governor, an event that was, at least in part, a consequence of the rivalry between Quebec and Montreal that had existed since the founding and had sometimes helped to exacerbate the problems of the early years. De Maisonneuve's departure coincided with the arrival of the Carignan-Salières regiment, the reinforcements for which he and so many other colonial officials had so long been pleading in vain.

The regiment affected life in New France in many ways. By putting an end to the Iroquois threat at least for a time, its members made settlement safer and enlarged the area in which this could take place. The large number of soldiers who stayed in the country at the end of their tour of duty, especially those who married and established families, gave a much needed boost to the European population. However, neither they nor the women sent by the royal government between 1663 and 1673 came with a missionary purpose. Whatever may have been the motives of the settlers who had earlier been recruited for Montreal, the new population undoubtedly came, as most other immigrants to North America would across the centuries, in the hope of a better life. The authorities in France who had sent them were far more interested in the economy of the colony and the enrichment of the home country than in missionary endeavours, as their policies reflect.

If the policies of the French government would eventually bring to an end the dream of an ideal Christian community on the island of Montreal, they were also to have a considerable influence on the realization of another dream with which Marguerite Bourgeoys had come to Canada. This was her hope to establish a religious community of women, who, unlike the traditional communities of the time, would not be confined to the cloister but would live among and like the "little people" of their time. In 1640, thirteen years before her departure for Canada, when she was just twenty years old, Marguerite had had a spiritual experience she called a "touch" of grace. In response, she says, "I gave myself to God." When her attempts to enter the traditional contemplative women's religious communities of the time were repulsed, she became a member of an extern, outreach group established and directed by the cloistered

Congrégation de Notre-Dame, founded by Pierre Fourier and Alix Le Clerc. Fourier himself had been a pioneer in the invention of methods for teaching the children of the ordinary people and the poor. Eventually, Marguerite became the prefect of this group of women; they worked among the poorer people of Troyes, whose children were unable to attend the school conducted in the convent. Under her leadership, this association came to number four hundred members.

At the same time, she and two other young women attempted to begin a new kind of religious community, whose model would be Mary, the mother of Jesus. Mary, Marguerite believed, had worked alongside the Apostles and the other disciples, both men and women, in the early Christian church. This community would not be cloistered but would work for, with, and among the ordinary people. The idea that a religious community of women could live outside a cloister was, of course, very controversial at this time. Marguerite's first attempt failed when one of her companions died and the other married. In accepting to leave alone for New France, she might have seemed to be abandoning the dream of such a community. However, her spiritual director encouraged her with the hope that "what God had not willed in France, He might, perhaps, bring to pass in Montreal."

An uncloistered community, the Congrégation de Notre-Dame de Montréal, did indeed come into existence, and this is the story of how it did so between 1665 and 1700, the year of Marguerite Bourgeoys's death. It is also an account of the geographical, economic, and religious circumstances that made the Congregation possible. A key factor in the community's development and survival was the fact that it was created in the New World in a pioneer society. Also of crucial importance was that it was founded in Montreal, where the Sulpicians exercised both religious and civil authority.

Neither Bishop Laval, New France's first bishop, nor his successor, Bishop Saint-Vallier, was able to understand Marguerite Bourgeoys's inspiration for a community of uncloistered women. However, given the problems of their immense and thinly populated diocese, they counted on the services of the sisters of the Congregation. Only women who could travel, only women who were able to stay and even to live in the homes of the settlers, could bring religious instruction to even a few of the far-flung hamlets. For this reason, Laval and Saint-Vallier tolerated and even, at times, encouraged a way of life they saw as a solution to temporary problems.

While the bishops sometimes had mixed feelings about the little community in Montreal, the secular authorities were uniformly enthusiastic, as their reports back to their superiors in France repeatedly indicate. In the Congregation they found a group of women who were self-supporting and who, far from being a burden on the public purse, were offering free education to the girls of the colony. The sisters were also encouraging and teaching the techniques of survival to women who had arrived in New France ill-prepared for the harsh conditions that awaited them. Not only did they give religious and moral instruction, but they taught people how to earn their own living. This fact ensured the moral, if not always the practical, support of officials concerned with the economic life of the colony.

The survival of the Congregation also owed a great deal to the encouragement of the Sulpicians, who had replaced the Jesuit missionaries in Montreal in 1657. They were not a religious order but an association of priests founded in Paris by Jean-Jacques Olier, one of the leading members of the Société de Notre-Dame, which had organized the founding of Montreal. In 1663 they had become seigneurs of the island when they assumed the debt of of the Société de Notre-Dame. While a few among their number would cause Marguerite Bourgeoys immense suffering in the last decade of her life, they were, on the whole, an unfailing support to the Congregation without which it could not have survived in the first century of its existence.

The Congrégation de Notre-Dame de Montréal obtained civil recognition in the form of letters patent granted by Louis XIV in 1671. In 1698, less than two years before the death of the founder, the community accepted a rule drawn up by Saint-Vallier, the then bishop of Quebec, and pronounced public vows for the first time. This official recognition on the part of the church gave the new group a greater degree of security. How much of Marguerite's original vision for the Congregation had to be sacrificed in the struggle for ecclesiastical approval is another question.

The first source of information about these years in the life of Marguerite Bourgeoys is, of course, that miscellaneous collection published as *Les écrits de Mère Bourgeoys* and in English translation as *The Writings of Marguerite Bourgeoys*.[1] Several earlier biographers are also helpful. Charles de Glandelet, the first of these, actually knew Marguerite during much of this period since he arrived in Canada in 1675. He was even more closely acquainted with Marie Barbier, the first Montrealer to enter the Congregation and Marguerite Bourgeoys's successor as superior of the community in 1693. His unpublished account of Marie Barbier's spiritual life gives some insight into the founding of the first missions of the Congregation in the Quebec area. Michel-François Ransonet's 1728 biography adds little new information but illustrates the process of legend-making already at work.

Étienne Faillon's biography of 1853 and his other works on the history of Montreal, written with full access to Sulpician records in Paris and in Montreal, remain invaluable to anyone studying this period. The work of another, earlier Sulpician biographer has tended to be devalued in later years. In his 1942 biography, Albert Jamet was especially distrustful of Étienne Montgolfier, who began his life of Marguerite Bourgeoys about 1770. Without doubt, there are mistakes and misunderstandings in his work, but Montgolfier certainly knew the importance of returning to the sources and must have made use of written documents that have since disappeared.[2] He also had access to a considerable oral tradition. When he arrived in Montreal in 1751, it was still possible to talk with sisters who had actually known and lived with Marguerite Bourgeoys. Lydia Longley, who died in 1758, Madeleine d'Ailleboust, in 1759, and Madeleine Chesnay La Garenne, in 1760, were all members of the Congregation before her death. Although Montgolfier's work must be used with caution, it still has a certain value, particularly when it is the only source of information about certain events.

Perhaps the most important source of all for the understanding of events in the last decade of Marguerite Bourgeoys's life is the letters of Louis Tronson, the Sulpician superior in Paris from 1678 to 1700. Throughout his years as superior, he had his secretary make copies of all his letters in large notebooks annotated for easy reference. These letters, often models of moderation, wisdom, and tact, are so detailed that it is usually possible to deduce the contents of the letters to which he is replying. They are the main source of information about the crisis provoked by a "visionary" in the Congregation in the 1690s and the reaction of the community to the rule presented to them by Bishop Saint-Vallier in 1694.

The loss of records and archives of the Congregation in the fires of 1683, 1768, and 1893 means that much of its history must be reconstituted from other documents, civil and religious. The Congregation archivists and those they enlisted to help them devoted great efforts to do so, especially Sister Sainte-Henriette, the author of the monumental nine-volume history of the Congregation published at the beginning of the twentieth century. In the second half of the twentieth century, Mary Eileen Scott continued to seek out documents relevant to the Congregation in both French and Canadian archives. For the period covered by this book, such records are the registers of births, marriages, and deaths in Notre-Dame, Montreal's first parish, as well as the parish accounts and the minutes of wardens' meetings. They include documents related to the sale and exchange of property, to marriage contracts, to wills and inventories, and to civil disputes in what was a very litigious society, drawn up especially by Bénigne Basset and Claude Maugue, his successor as court clerk. There are even inquiries into accidental or suspicious deaths and testimony in criminal cases which cast light on events in the early Congregation. Reports sent to the ministry of the Marine by the governors and intendants of New France contain several laudatory descriptions of the work of the Congregation. There are also helpful details to be found in the censuses conducted in 1666, 1667, and 1681.

The records of two other seventeenth-century Canadian religious communities are also useful. The first of these is the annals of the Hospitallers of the Hôtel-Dieu in Montreal, where Sister Marie Morin's *Histoire simple et véritable* was begun in 1697. Perhaps no one outside the Congregation knew the community more intimately than Sister Morin, who had become so close a friend of first members of the Congregation. The other is the *Les annales de l'Hôtel-Dieu de Québec*. The sisters there appear to have formed a warm relationship with the sisters of the Congregation.

In the end, however, much of the early history of the Congregation cannot be known from documentary evidence. The lives, for example, of those sisters who never held office and had to sign legal documents or appear in any kind of litigation did not leave recorded traces, except perhaps of their baptism and their burial. In presenting what was once oral tradition in the Congregation or in other sources, I have tried to identify it as such.

Much of what remains of the writings of Marguerite Bourgeoys was set down in the difficult final years of her life and reflects the inner conflict and anguish of that time. Unless the statements she made then are seen in that context and used with care, they can cast a shadow over the earlier years and over the face of a younger and happier Marguerite. Yet there is evidence in the observations of some of her contemporaries both inside and outside the Congregation that her gentleness, her kindness, and her joy, once among her most striking characteristics and surely those that attracted others to her, continued to the end. The thirty-five years described in this book were, for Marguerite Bourgeoys, years of hard work and struggle, of difficulties and contradictions, even, at times, of catastrophe. They were also years of new beginnings, of courage, of hope, and of the laying of firm foundations on which future generations could build. At the close of *Marguerite Bourgeoys and Montreal* I suggest that Marguerite Bourgeoys transferred to the Congregation what had been the original ideal for Montreal: "O my dear sisters, let us revive at least among ourselves the true spirit of cordiality and love which formed the glory and the beatitude of the first Christians." In the midst of all the problems that plagued her during the last decade of her life, in a country plunged into a brutal war, she had the consolation of seeing women from all the warring factions – the French, the Canadians, the Iroquois, and the English colonists – able to live and to work together in the Congregation. Her life demonstrates that she never wavered in her conviction that education can make a difference in the individual and in society, that the enemy is ignorance, and that if people can be brought to understand, they can be brought to reconciliation and peace.

CHAPTER ONE

A NEW SOCIETY TAKES SHAPE
1665–1670

*At the insistence of the sisters, I found myself forced to build
at the end of the land ... which served as our property,
including lodgings for the men and boarders.*[1]

In 1665 Montreal had seen what was to prove the final departure of
Paul de Chomedey de Maisonneuve, its founder and first governor.
He had been its defender not only against the attacks of the Iroquois but also, and from the very moment of his arrival in Canada
in 1641, against the misunderstanding and, at times, hostility of
officials at Quebec. In him, Marguerite Bourgeoys had lost the
fellow countryman who had first persuaded her to come to Ville-
Marie and then had become a close and trusted friend. Never again,
under the French regime, would Montreal enjoy the kind of administrative independence it had been able to exercise at least part of
the time in its first decades of existence, though it continued to have
its own governor until it became a part of the general administration of the colony. The regret Marguerite undoubtedly felt at the
departure of de Maisonneuve in what seemed to his supporters to
be unjust and ignominious circumstances[2] had to be set aside as she
responded to the opportunities and needs opened to her by changing conditions, not just in Montreal but in all of New France, which
was on the threshold of dramatic transformation.

In the autumn of 1665 Marguerite Bourgeoys was forty-five
years old. Twelve years earlier she had accepted the risk of leaving
her home in one of the oldest cities in France to teach the children

in a tiny, newly founded settlement on an island in the St Lawrence River, whose continued existence was, at best, precarious. Her decision to accept the invitation of de Maisonneuve had been difficult because it meant leaving work among the poor of Troyes, at which she was very successful, to participate in a project whose prospects were, at that moment, very dim. Marguerite had started on the long and difficult journey with no other material luggage than a small bundle of immediate necessities. She did so in the belief that if God willed her involvement in the missionary project that Montreal was intended to be, God would provide.

Although she was forced to leave for the New World without companions to share her work, Marguerite Bourgeoys also carried with her the hope that she would one day be part of a new kind of religious community for women. This community would not be cloistered but would follow what she believed was the example of Mary, the mother of Jesus, and the other women disciples in the early Christian church. Meanwhile, she showed a remarkable talent for friendship and for the creation of a kind of community among the members of any group of which she became a part, whether aboard disease-infected ships, in the Montreal shed at Quebec, or in the beleaguered fort in Montreal. Marguerite would one day urge the members of the community she founded to become skilful in all kinds of work in order to be useful to others. She began by examplifying this counsel herself.

By 1665 Marguerite had three companions to live in community with her and help in various ways in the many tasks that fell to them in a pioneer settlement. The oldest of these was Catherine Crolo, who was a year older than Marguerite and a friend from the time when both had worked among the poor of Troyes. According to Sister Morin, Catherine was an indefatigable worker who undertook the heavier labour of the community, seeing herself as "the servant of all and the donkey of the house."[3] Marie Raisin and Anne Hiou, both now in their late twenties, helped to teach the children and the women of Ville-Marie and perhaps of other settlements. The three had bound themselves by civil contract to live in community and to teach the children of both the French settlers and the Native peoples.

At this time the Congregation was still lodged in the stone building known as the stable school because of its former purpose. The lower storey was both the daytime living quarters and the schoolroom, while those living in the house slept in what had been a dovecote above. In 1662 Marguerite had also bought a small nearby house, where she had begun to lodge filles de roi the following year. Besides teaching the children who came to the school, the sisters "worked day and night" sewing and making clothes "so as not to be a burden to anyone and to support themselves."[4] They also gathered the older women for devotions and religious instruction on Sundays.

Although the freedom of the sisters to travel and to go out among the people was an essential aspect of Marguerite Bourgeoys's idea of uncloistered religious life, equally important at this time was their freedom to take others into their house. The *maison de la Congrégation*, as the former stable was already called in Montreal, did not just play the role of school. From the day in 1653 when she had begun to care for the young Marie Dumesnil, Marguerite had looked after the young women coming to New France in the hope of marrying and settling there. In 1663 she had walked down to the shore to meet the first filles du roi to arrive in Montreal, insisting that the house of the Blessed Virgin must be open to all women. There would have been several such women living with the Congregation in the autumn of 1665: of the eleven who arrived in 1665, four married in November, one in December, two the following January, three in March, and one not until the next July. Besides the women who lived with the Congregation until they found husbands, the sisters sometimes also had charge of young children for a variety of reasons. As well, their house was frequently used for public occasions: marriage contracts were signed there with numbers of witnesses and guests in attendance; the dead were waked there on the eve of burial.

If life was crowded and busy in the stable school, there was also the happiness and shared laughter that come from the comradeship to be found among a group facing difficult circumstances together. No doubt, the personality of Marguerite Bourgeoys herself was an important factor in encouraging and inspiring this group, holding it together and giving it an esprit de corps. In 1663 her companions had reacted with dismay to her decision to live with the filles de roi in the small house she had prepared for them. Perhaps their feelings were due more to the loss of her presence in the main house than to a fear of undertaking even more responsibilities.

At this time, the situation in Montreal was still such that the little group had to draw up the outside ladder after they climbed it to their sleeping quarters each night. This must have been a constant reminder to them of the danger they faced at all times, the possibility of an Iroquois attack. But in 1665 that threat was about to be brought to an end, at least for several decades. Impressed by the success of the Dutch and the English in deriving wealth from their overseas colonies, Colbert, the French king's most powerful minister, had determined to emulate them. It was with this end in view that New France had been removed from the possession of the Compagnie des Cent Associés in 1663 and the Compagnie des Indes occidentales had been created. To further Colbert's economic ambitions for the colony, the reinforcements for which several previous governors, the Jesuits, and Bishop Laval had for so long pleaded in vain were finally sent to quell the Iroquois menace once and for all.

Certainly, by the autumn of 1665, Montreal was aware of the exciting events that had taken place in Quebec during the past few months. On 26 February 1664, Alexandre de Prouville de Tracy, an experienced and highly respected soldier, had set sail from France for the French possessions in the New World with the imposing title of viceroy in command of all French forces in America on both land and sea. After a first stop in the West Indies, he had arrived at Quebec with a contingent of four companies on 30 June 1665, to the immense relief and joy of all New France. The entire Carignan-Salières infantry regiment, which had previously seen service against the Turks in Hungary, had been sent to New France for the campaign against the Iroquois; four companies arrived before Tracy, eight in August, and eight more in September – in all, over 1,200 men.

The excitement of the struggling colonists at such an unprecedented show of strength made this an unforgettable time. If anticipation of the eradication of the Iroquois menace was insufficient to impress all the settlers, the pomp and ceremony that surrounded Tracy's arrival and every public appearance must have done so. As church bells pealed, the viceroy was formally received by Bishop Laval arrayed in full pontifical vestments and surrounded by his clergy. Tracy entered into the spirit of the occasion by refusing the cushion offered him and kneeling on the bare floor for the singing of the Te Deum, despite the fact that he was ill and weakened by fever. Wherever he went, he was preceded by an escort of twenty-four guards wearing the king's colours and by four pages; six lackeys followed him, and he was surrounded by a large number of richly dressed officers and accompanied by his aide, the Chevalier Alexandre de Chaumont.[5]

The arrival of the regiment at Quebec was not an unmixed blessing for the people of New France. Marie de l'Incarnation wrote to her son that because the ships were so loaded with men and baggage, they failed to bring the local population their regular supplies from the mother country: "We will be greatly inconvenienced," she wrote, "but we must suffer a little with the others."[6] An outbreak of disease among the arriving soldiers also had serious consequences. Though the men had remained in good health during most of the voyage from France, the situation changed just before they landed. The sisters at the Hôtel-Dieu in Quebec were worked almost to death by the large number of patients who now demanded their care, and the parish church had to be transformed into a temporary annex to the hospital. When the church was full, some of the patients even had to be cared for in neighbouring houses.

But at least in the first days after its arrival the regiment was seen by the religious authorities and communities at Quebec as an unmixed blessing. Marie de l'Incarnation saw an army filled with "faith and courage" growing in awareness that it had come to fight "a holy war that concerned only the glory of God and the salvation of souls."[7] The conversion to the Catholic faith of several Huguenots among their number seemed to confirm the piety of the new reinforcements. The epidemic and the arrival so late in the year prevented the regiment from immediately beginning a campaign into Iroquois territory, but the work the men were put to would have brought them into contact with Montreal. They began the construction of a series of forts along the Richelieu River and Lake Champlain to protect the advance of the troops when such a campaign would begin. Alarmed by news of these happenings, some of the Iroquois tribes made an attempt through Garakontié, the Onondaga chief, to renew peace with the French and, in the process, to demonstrate that they too appreciated the importance of ritual and ceremony.[8] These peace efforts were ultimately unsuccessful, but they did have one immediate benefit for Montreal: an exchange of prisoners brought about the release of Charles Le Moyne, one of its leading citizens, who had been captured by the Iroquois the previous summer.

In January 1666 Daniel de Rémy de Courcelle, the new governor of New France, who had arrived the previous September, led an expedition into Iroquois territory in what is now up-state New York. This expedition was a fiasco. Neither the soldiers nor their commanders had any experience of Canadian conditions; nor were the commanders open to local advice, a frustration that Canadians were often to endure in their dealings with European officials. Faillon suggests that Tracy could have benefited significantly from the advice of de Maisonneuve, whom he had, instead, banished to France.[9] Disaster was occasioned not by encounters with the Iroquois, of which there were none, but by the Canadian winter, for which the French soldiers were totally unprepared. Courcelle had become impatient and started out before the arrival of the Algonquin allies, who served not only as guides but also, by hunting along the way, as provisioners to the French army. As a result, some of the soldiers starved to death, others froze, and the entire group lost its way and had to seek help at the Anglo-Dutch settlement at Corlaer (now Schenectady). The remnant of the French army regained Quebec on 17 March. Futile though it was in most respects, this expedition, because it had penetrated so deep into their territory, impressed the Iroquois to the extent that they joined in peace negotiations the following summer, but the French continued to be uneasy about the behaviour of the Oneidas and the Mohawks.

In early September 1666 the decision was made to send a large expedition into Iroquois territory. About thirteen hundred men participated in the venture, including 110 members of the Montreal militia, under the command of Charles Le Moyne, and 100 Huron and Algonquin allies. François Dollier de Casson, the future seigneur of Montreal and author of its first history, had just arrived in New France for the first time and was one of the four chaplains who ministered to this army. When they reached four Mohawk villages, they found them deserted, for it was not the practice of the Iroquois to enter into conflicts where their defeat seemed a foregone conclusion. The French burned the villages before they began their long journey back to Quebec, which they reached on 5 November. Although there had been no confrontation and the expedition certainly did not result in the decisive defeat of the Mohawks, it had at least achieved its immediate purpose. In July 1667 the Five Nations made their peace with the French and their Huron and Algonquin allies. Relations between the French and the Five Nations were not to be without further incident, but New France was never again to stand on the brink of destruction by the Iroquois. The same year saw the return of Acadia to French rule through the Treaty of Breda. The decline of the military threat from the Iroquois and the English left more energy and attention to be devoted to the economic prob-lems of New France.

Those problems were the special responsibility of Jean Talon, who arrived in Quebec in the late summer of 1665 to take up the post of intendant. Under Colbert's restructuring of the administra-tion, the intendant had vast powers: he was responsible for the civil administration of the colony, for overseeing the administration of justice, and for the colony's finances, including the development of the economy. But he was also responsible for the maintenance of the army and works of fortification. Talon had played no small role in the decision to send out the French expedition into Iroquois ter-ritory. Once peace was achieved, he could devote himself more fully to Colbert's economic plans for the colony.[10]

During Talon's tenure, immigrants flowed into New France at a previously unprecedented rate. Up to five hundred men a year were added to the population of the colony. Although the Carignan-Salières regiment had been posted to Canada for eighteen months only, four hundred of its surviving members chose to remain when the rest returned to France in 1668. The desire of the royal gov-ernment was that these men would settle and raise families, rather than be lured into becoming coureurs des bois by the promise of quick and easy revenues from the fur trade. Accordingly, about 150 young women of marriageable age were sent to the colony each year. Obviously, the previous experience of Marguerite and her Congregation with French immigrant women would be of consid-erable value here, not only in the reception and acclimatization of the women themselves[11] but in continuing service to the many fami-lies that now came into being as the result of increased immigration and of government policies intended to promote early marriage and large families.[12] The most important service the Congregation offered was, of course, that for which Marguerite had come in the first place, and for which she had enlisted her first companions: the free education of the children of the colony.

The fact that the Congregation was not perceived as a religious community by civil authorities whose outlook was formed by the traditional communities of the day was an advantage rather than a drawback. Colbert was hostile to the Jesuits, although they could have made valuable allies in the implementation of some of his schemes. They were as little eager as he to see the colonists become coureurs de bois, for they saw the presence in the wilderness of such men, often eager to throw off the restraints of civilized behaviour, as a detriment to the evangelization of the Native Peoples. In general, colonial officials tended to perceive the traditional religious communities as a potential economic burden, rather than an asset to the colony. Marguerite's secular sisterhood had already demonstrated its capacity to finance itself and its work. Its freedom of movement was an advantage as new settlements appeared. Because it had not yet acquired any canonical recognition, the state could not be called upon to step in if it ran into financial difficulties. All this made the Congregation very appealing to the secular authorities both in New France and in the home country.

Despite the departure of de Maisonneuve, Marguerite Bourgeoys must have shared in the atmosphere of hope and anticipation that was general among the people of New France as a result of the new royal policies. For the first time since her arrival in 1653, the peace meant that there was a real possiblity of reaching out to the Native population. The women who would arrive in increasing numbers until 1673 would need shelter, counselling, and education in the skills required for survival in their new environment. The children who would result from the unions they entered into would fill the school. Yet just at this promising and challenging moment, Marguerite's tiny Congregation suffered a considerable setback: the departure of Marie Raisin to enter the Ursuline convent in Quebec.[13]

Marguerite Bourgeoys had, in fact, recruited four companions in France in 1659. However, one of these, Edmée Chastel, had left the group in 1661 to become the servant-companion of Barbe de Boullogne, widow of Louis d'Ailleboust, and the two had gone to live in Quebec. Now the younger and more promising Marie Raisin, the second of the three companions Marguerite had recruited in her native Troyes, appeared to be lost to the group. Marguerite could not have helped but think back to her first attempt at uncloistered religious life in that city some twenty years before, and at its failure when one of her companions married and the other died. This time the situation was complicated by the obligation to fulfill the many responsibilities that she and her companions had already accepted in Ville-Marie.

Marie Raisin had been born in Troyes in April 1636, when Marguerite Bourgeoys herself was just sixteen, her mother still living, and the "conversion" of 1640 still in the future. Like Marguerite, Marie was baptized at the church of Saint-Jean-au-Marché, and since they lived not far apart, the two families would almost certainly have been known to each other. It is quite possible that Marguerite had known Marie from her birth, even before she knew Catherine Crolo, whom she seems to have met through the extern community of the Congrégation de Notre-Dame of Troyes. There are indications that Marguerite Bourgeoys had a great deal of confidence in Marie Raisin. Canada's first systematic census was announced by Jean Talon shortly after his arrival. It took place in the early months of 1666, and it places Marie Raisin at Trois-Rivières as school-teacher. This is the earliest documentary evidence of the early practice in the Congrégation de Notre-Dame de Montréal of what were known as *missions ambulantes*, or travelling missions. Even before the Congregation began to establish permanent missions outside Ville-Marie, its members went to other settlements where there were as yet no schools to prepare the young people for first communion. Marcel Trudel calculates that the census was conducted in the Trois-Rivières region between the middle of January and the middle of April.[14] It was in July that Marie Raisin arrived at the Ursuline convent in Quebec.

At this time, Marie was thirty years old and had been in Montreal almost seven years. Life in the school at Ville-Marie had been demanding, hectic, and no doubt exhausting. Life as an itinerant teacher would also have been all those things and more. If Marie Raisin was in Trois-Rivières in the late winter or early spring, she must either have spent the whole winter there or made a winter journey. In whatever season she travelled, the trip would have taken several days, with the nights spent camping on the banks of the St Lawrence or staying at some habitation to be found along the way. On arrival in Trois-Rivières, she, like later sisters on such missions, would have had to live in the already crowded household of one of the local families. Besides the physical hardships involved in travel and in accepting whatever living conditions were available, Marie Raisin must have had to cope with another deprivation, that of companionship.[15] She came from a cultivated family in France, a family of musicians and actors. Although surrounded by people all the time, she would have found few with whom she had much in common. Realizing the importance of companionship, Marguerite was later to send her sisters out two by two to the missions, and when it was not possible to do so, the sisters were usually accompanied by one of the young women from a confraternity they had organized. It is perhaps not to be wondered at that Marie Raisin began to long for the peace and fellowship of the cloister.

Marie's departure may also reflect her doubts and uncertainties about the radically different kind of religious life being attempted by the Congregation in Montreal. After nearly four centuries, it can be forgotten how strange and new in the seventeenth century was the idea of uncloistered religious life for women. In the Montreal outpost, Sister Marie Morin, who was its next-door neighbour, could appreciate Marguerite's Congregation from her cloister, but there is no evidence that this was true in the old capital. For many more centuries, life in the cloister continued to be held up in the Catholic Church as superior to other forms of religious life. Marguerite Bourgeoys herself is never mentioned in the voluminous correspondance of Marie de l'Incarnation. In references to the Congregation, the "Filles séculières," as they are called, tended to be perceived as a stop-gap whom the Ursulines would replace in Montreal as soon as conditions permitted.[16] One needs a great deal of inner certainty to persevere in the absence of social support. Ironically, her months in the quiet of the cloister seem to have given that certainty to Marie Raisin, for Marie Morin reports that Marie Raisin realized the cloister was not God's will for her, and in mid-November she made the painfully cold journey back to Montreal "to be reunited with her sisters at the Congregation." Her return was a source of satisfaction not only to the sisters of the Congregation but also to their neighbours at the hospital, for she was accompanied by Catherine Denis, who, unable to pay the dowry at the Hôtel-Dieu in Quebec, entered the novitiate of the Hospitallers of St Joseph at the Hôtel-Dieu in Montreal instead.[17]

It now seemed increasingly obvious to Marguerite Bourgeoys's companions that the stable school, with its one partitioned room downstairs and its converted dovecote, above was inadequate to the growing needs of the little community. Even with the addition of the adjacent building that Marguerite had bought in 1662 and to which she had first welcomed the filles du roi in 1663, they were hard-pressed for space in which to live, to work, and to house their varied and growing household. In 1663 there were about 70 girls and boys in Montreal aged between five and twelve years and therefore her potential pupils, for the boys' school would not open until 1668. By July 1666 that number had swelled to 129, 58 of them girls. That number was bound to grow in the immediate future for there were about 170 children under five years of age, 92 of them girls.[18]

The filles du roi continued to arrive yearly,[19] and although the number in some years was small (1664, 1666, 1669), in others it was higher – the eleven in 1665 already mentioned, for example, and thirteen in 1668.[20] In 1663 Marguerite had begun the practice of welcoming them into her household on their arrival in Montreal because "it was for the sake of families" and she believed that "the house of the Blessed Virgin" should be open to all women. Some of the women who arrived during the following decade already had relatives in Montreal with whom they might have stayed, but these were the exception; there is evidence that others continued to lodge at the Congregation until their marriages and that some of their stays might have been protracted. Although some women married within a couple of months of their arrival, others took longer to find or to settle upon a suitable match. The five women identified in the census of 1667 as "fille à marier habitant avec les filles de la Congrégation" must all have arrived the previous year. Of these, one married at the end of May 1667, two in November 1667, a third in February 1668, and a fourth not until March 1670.[21]

The return to New France of the Sulpician superior, Gabriel Thubières de Levy de Queylus, in 1668 relieved one pressure on the Congregation, for he finally opened a school for boys with Abbé Gabriel Souart in charge.[22] But when he threw himself enthusiastically into the project of educating Potawatami children who had been prisoners of the Iroquois, he entrusted another task to Marguerite and her companions. The Sulpicians took charge of the boys, but the girls came to live at the Congregation. Dollier de Casson, in his account of the year 1670–71, mentions "two girls with the sisters of the Congregation where they have learnt the French tongue and have been brought up in a European fashion, so that the bigger, who was the later baptized, is ready to marry a Frenchman."[23]

Besides the growing need for space for the school and for the reception of both immigrant and Native women, the Congregation also required living space for its workmen and was under growing pressure to open a boarding school, as some families in Montreal and the surrounding region did not want their daughters to have to make the long and difficult journey to the Ursuline boarding school in Quebec. For families in the outlying areas, a boarding school was somewhere their daughters could spend a few months preparing for first communion. Such a school in Montreal would involve less expense for the parents, who usually paid in kind. The insistence of Marguerite's companions on the necessity of building a larger house can scarcely be wondered at. What is puzzling, given her practical nature and the role usually played by common sense in her decisions, is her reluctance to do so. Nor did her uneasiness about the construction of a new and larger house disappear even after it was completed.

One reason for her hesitation was her commitment to living a life of poverty. For her, this meant living as Christ and as Mary, his mother, had lived:

The Blessed Virgin, whose daughters we are, embraced strict poverty and put aside all that was not absolutely necessary in food, clothing, linens and other things. Our Lord confirmed this by the poverty of His birth since He did not permit that any other house be found to shelter Him than a stable, no other cradle than a manger, and straw for His bedding. During the course of His life, He had nowhere to rest; He died naked on the cross. His first instruction on the mountain was this: "Blessed are the poor in spirit."[24]

Although Marguerite recognized that it must be "the mind and the heart that are poor," the former stable in which her work and her Congregation were born had powerful symbolic significance for her. They recalled the place where, she said, "The Blessed Virgin received kings and shepherds with the same love."[25] Despite all its limitations, she found its abandonment extremely difficult.

And Marguerite was not concerned only with the life lived by Jesus and Mary when they were on earth; she saw the life of Jesus continuing in the settlers around her: men, women, and children who, certainly in those early days, lived in considerable material poverty. Sharing in the poverty of Jesus meant sharing their poverty. All her life she would insist that conditions of life at the Congregation should not be better than those of the ordinary colonists around it. The best possessions of the Congregation were to be reserved for the use of the poor: "Whatever sheets we could get were for lending to the poor women in their need."[26] In these women she discerned the person of Christ.

There was still another reason for Marguerite's unwillingness to undertake the building of a new house at this time. In 1655 she had begun the construction of a chapel of pilgrimage dedicated to the Blessed Virgin under the title of Notre-Dame-de-Bon-Secours. Most of Montreal's tiny population of that time had participated in the project, from the governor to those poorer colonists for whom Marguerite had done sewing to compensate them for their labour. The work had been suspended on the replacement of the Jesuit missionaries by the Sulpicians in 1657.[27] When Marguerite returned with her first companions from the voyage of 1658–59, she was distressed to find that the building materials collected for the chapel had disappeared. Quite clearly the building of this chapel was exceedingly important to her. It was not something she had begun only to occupy herself because there were not yet a sufficient number of children old enough to open a school. The making of pilgrimages was an important devotional activity of the time, a symbol of the journey of life, a means of praying not just with the mind and heart but with the whole body.

Now, apparently, like her decision to go and live in the Charly house with the filles du roi in 1663, the chapel became a source of conflict between Marguerite and her companions. Clearly, they believed that the resources of the group should be directed to building more adequate quarters for themselves and their work, rather than the raising of a chapel of pilgrimage. Marguerite was learning again the price of living in community: "I no longer felt I was free to build this chapel." This time she capitulated to the wishes of the group: "At the insistence of the sisters, I found myself forced to build at the end of the land (about 100 feet long) which served as our property, including lodgings for the men and boarders. All that was at great expense." Then she adds, "but whenever I was in difficulty, I used to pray to the Blessed Virgin and to promise her that I would build her chapel. Immediately, I found whatever I needed."[28]

Besides beginning the construction of what became known as the *grand maison*, the "large house," Marguerite Bourgeoys was also developing ways to finance the work of the Congregation and perhaps also to help accommodate her growing household. Since 1662 she had held land in Pointe-Saint-Charles, two concessions obtained from de Maisonneuve, and a further piece bought from Urbain Boudreau. Her purpose in acquiring this land was the establishment of a farm that would support the Congregation and its work. For this, the land would have to be cleared and crops planted.

In keeping with the custom of the time, the land would have been worked by hired men, by *donnés* (persons who gave their services to a religious community in return for a guarantee of permanent support), or through an arrangement with neighbouring settlers. In all likelihood, there was no dwelling on this land before 1668.

In September of that year Marguerite bought an adjoining piece of land two arpents wide from François Le Ber and Jeanne Testard, his wife. On this land stood a house and outbuildings,[29] and there Sister Catherine Crolo took up residence. She was to run the farm until the house burned down in 1693. It is quite possible, even probable, that while continuing to live with her companions in what is now Old Montreal, Catherine had been going back and forth to supervise work on the farm since 1662, "by canoe in the summer, on foot in the spring and autumn, and on snowshoes in the winter."[30] The farm now consisted of about sixty-seven and a half arpents, or acres. Marguerite was to continue to add to it throughout her life, and the farm would be a major source of support for the Congregation and its work until the first part of the twentieth century.

Was the farmhouse also used to shelter some of the filles du roi until they found husbands? Although no documentary evidence has yet been found to answer this question, there are persuasive arguments that make it almost certain that the farm did indeed serve such a purpose. In the first place, there is the existence of a strong and persistent oral tradition. That tradition is supported by known facts: the reception of the filles du roi by Marguerite Bourgeoys and her companions; the growing problem of crowding at the stable school (the new house would not be completed until 1672); the large numbers of filles du roi arriving in 1668 and 1670. There was also another very good reason for housing these new arrivals at the farm. Marguerite Bourgeoys was motivated by the desire not simply to offer these women a temporary home but also to prepare them for the roles they must play as wives and mothers in pioneer households. About two-thirds of the filles du roi came from urban backgrounds. In the years 1669, 1670, and 1671, a high proportion of the recruits were from the Paris Hôpital général and came to New France to escape poverty and misery. Many were lacking in the strength, skills, and resources needed in the harsh and demanding world in which they had arrived. This was so much the case that it led to complaints and requests from Talon that the contingents be made up of young women from the country rather than the city.[31] Even a few weeks on a working farm might have provided the new arrivals who came from the institutions of Paris and Rouen with at least a basic preparation for the future. Their stay at the farmhouse of the Congregation would have given Catherine Crolo the chance to initiate them into some of the many skills on which the life and livelihood of themselves and their children would soon depend. The fact that the first sisters of the Congregation had themselves been urban women before their emigration to New France must have given them some sympathy with and insight into the problems of adjustment faced by these new arrivals.

As yet, however, the Congrégation de Notre-Dame de Montréal had no official legal existence. The time had come for that to change, and a major factor in bringing about the change was the approval of the civil authorities. Talon's criteria in appraising the religious groups working in the colony are implicit in his "Memo on the Present State of Canada" (1667). When he reports on the ecclesiastics of the country, he expresses special enthusiasm for the Sulpicians, by that time twelve in number, because they "are a charge neither upon the King nor on the country because of the property they bring to Canada, and that besides they do not cause the colonists the annoyance they feel at the conduct of others ... these Ecclesiastics live on their own revenue." While he describes the Ursulines in Quebec as "useful," he goes on to say that the hospital sisters at both Quebec and Montreal are "more useful" because they feed and care for the sick and wounded.[32] The work being done by the Congregation among the ordinary colonists of Montreal and the fact that the group was self-supporting could not fail to please the intendant. Marguerite Bourgeoys had absorbed the educational ideals and philosophy of Pierre Fourier and Alix Le Clerc through her work with the Congrégation de Notre-Dame of Troyes. These included the conviction that the education of the poor must enable them to earn a decent living. From its beginnings, then, the Congrégation de Notre-Dame de Montréal devoted itself not only to the religious and moral instruction of the settlers but also to providing them with the skills they needed to support themselves and to make a contribution to the society to which they belonged. In 1667 Courcelle and Talon made an official visit to Montreal, and the intendant visited every household in the settlement. On 9 October a general assembly of the colonists voted unanimous support for the application of the Congregation for letters patent.[33]

Though the civil officials were supportive of the Congregation, ecclesiastical authorities in both Montreal and Quebec were more ambivalent. Since his return to New France as superior of the Sulpicians in 1668, Abbé de Queylus had enjoyed surprisingly harmonious relations with Bishop Laval and indeed with the colonial authorities in general. As in his previous stay in Canada, Abbé de Queylus showed himself very sympathetic to the religious communities in Quebec. He planned to endow a hospice for ailing Natives in Montreal and to entrust it to the Hospitallers of St Augustine from Quebec, whom he had been prevented from establishing in Montreal in 1658.[34] He also turned a favourable eye on the Ursulines. On 25 September 1670 Marie de l'Incarnation wrote to the Archbishop of Tours: "There has been a plan to establish us at Montreal; but the business has been postponed for a time; and the Abbé de Quellus, who is the spiritual and temporal lord there for the Gentleman of Saint Sulpice, promises us his protection when things will be ready. We are not sorry about this postponement because we are not yet strong enough to undertake an establishment of this breadth. His grace our worthy Prelate, who undertakes nothing without prudence, is also of this sentiment."[35]

How these plans for the introduction of the Quebec communities, had they been carried out, would have affected the survival of the Hospitallers of St Joseph at the Hôtel-Dieu and the Congrégation de Notre-Dame in Montreal will never be known. Abbé de Queylus had to return to France to settle family business in 1671 and never returned to Canada. The Sulpicians who had spent more time in Montreal – Gabriel Souart, the first parish priest and a friend of the Montreal communities from the beginning, and Gilles Pérot, who had replaced him as parish priest in 1666 – were perhaps of a different opinion from their superior. Dollier de Casson, who succeeded de Queylus as superior, appears to have become a friend and confidant of Jeanne Mance. Their friendship might have begun even before she joined Father Souart in sending supplies to the starving garrison at Fort Sainte-Anne while Dollier was chaplain there in early 1667. As his *Histoire du Montréal* demonstrates, Dollier was deeply sympathetic to the founders of Montreal and aware of the tensions between Montreal and Quebec. In a letter to the Ursulines of Tours written in late 1671, Marie de l'Incarnation commented that "the Gentleman of Saint Sulpice who are in charge at Montreal want only the Filles séculières who are free to go out, to move about, to seek out and help their neighbour."[36] "Filles séculieres," (secular women), was, of course, the designation by which the Congregation would long be known, as distinguished from *religieuses*, or nuns, members of a cloistered order or congregation.

If Bishop Laval still expected the eventual installation of the Ursulines at Montreal and their absorption of the Congregation, this did not prevent him from giving the Congregation an important mark of his approval. He was in Montreal in May 1669 to discuss, among other things, the building of the parish church. On this visit he gave Marguerite Bourgeoys and her companions permission to teach throughout his diocese, which at that time comprised the whole of New France.[37] While it was still some time before the Congregation would establish permanent missions outside Montreal, this permission opened up that possibility and authorized the existence of the *missions ambulantes*. Whether or not the bishop was open to new forms of religious life for women, he was very much aware of the necessity of religious instruction in the small settlements developing in his far-flung diocese, a need that could not be met by cloistered nuns. Whatever might happen in the future, the conditions of the moment demanded the presence of the Filles séculières.

So with the certainty of strong civil support and some amount, at least, of ecclesiastical approval, Marguerite Bourgeoys got ready to undertake another journey to France. Her primary purpose was to obtain the letters patent that would give the Congregation legal existence, but she also went to seek new recruits for her community. The population of Montreal had more than doubled in the second half of the 1660s, and now, with Bishop Laval's permission, the whole of New France was open to the work of the Congregation. One of her first acts in preparation for her departure was to draw up a list of the possessions of the Congregation and to obtain a notarized document stating that these were the result of the labour of the women currently working with her in her mission of education and of alms that had been given to support that work. The list was verified by the bursar of the seminary and included the stable school, the Charly house, the farm at Pointe-Sainte-Charles, and sixty acres of woodland on the mountain.[38] This document could be used in France to demonstrate that the Congregation was self-supporting, but its main purpose was to protect the organization in the event of Marguerite's death and any resulting claim made on her estate. Her encounters with sickness and death on previous voyages must have made Marguerite all too conscious of the possibility that she might not survive this one.

The thought of her departure must have caused a considerable amount of trepidation among her companions. As they remembered the plague-ridden ship on which they had made their own voyage to New France,[39] they too must have been conscious of the perils of the journey and the possibility that they would never see her again. Two more decades were to pass before the Congregation was to show itself ready to accept another superior than Marguerite Bourgeoys. Her companions had been upset when she removed a few hundred yards from the main house to live with the filles de roi in 1663. How would the group sustain an absence which they knew would last at least a year and, in the event, lasted two? Since Catherine Crolo was now living at the farm, only Marie Raisin and Anne Hiou were left with the women boarders and pupils at the main house in Montreal. However, in spite of all the difficulties and worries, they accepted the risk of this journey, leaving its outcome in the hands of God. During Marguerite's absence, Marie Raisin fulfilled the role of superior. It was she, then, who supervised the continued building of the new house, whose interior was still unfinished.

Marguerite saw to one thing more before her departure: she took steps to protect the site of the chapel of pilgrimage she was still determined to build. Remembering the disappearance of all the building materials collected for that purpose during her previous absence in France, she may have feared she would return to find the site itself given over to another use. She says she erected a "small framework" on the site before her departure, and Marie Morin writes of "a little wooden building." The site was even at this time a place of pilgrimage for the devout, and Marguerite would not forget it during her absence.[40]

CHAPTER TWO

OBTAINING ROYAL APPROVAL
1670–1672

I found it necessary to take a second trip to France in 1670 ...
to seek sisters ... and at the same time to obtain a charter.[1]

Supplied with what she describes as "many testimonials from the Seminary as well as from Quebec and Montreal,"[2] Marguerite Bourgeoys set off for the home country in the summer of 1670. The documents she carried expressed the approval and support of the governor, the intendant, and the colonists of Montreal and of the bishop and the parish priest. Unlike that of the 1658 voyage, the date of Marguerite's departure from Montreal is not known. On her previous trip she did not leave Montreal until the end of September, but this time she was in Quebec possibly by mid-August.[3] From the outset of the journey, she encountered difficulties, but in meeting them she also found help she would have called providential. She took ill on the trip from Montreal to Quebec or was perhaps unwell even before she set out. Displaying her usual propensity for understatement, she describes herself as having become "slightly indisposed," but the "slight" illness kept her in the hospital for several days. She would not have found herself quite friendless at the Hôtel-Dieu in Quebec, for there she would have encountered several persons she already knew well: Edmée Chastel, the recruit of 1659 who had later changed her mind about the Congregation; Barbe de Boullogne, with whom she had worked to set up the Confraternity of the Holy Family in Montreal; and the hospital sisters the Abbé de Queylus had tried to install in Montreal and who had looked after the school during Marguerite's absence in 1658–59. Her stay at the hospital perhaps was a factor in the growth of the warm relationship that seems to have developed between the Congregation in Montreal and the hospital sisters in Quebec.

Like the date she left Montreal, that on which Marguerite Bourgeoys set sail for France is unknown. Jamet's biography places her departure in late October and her arrival in France at the beginning of December, but de Maisonneuve's letter supporting her application for letters patent, a document Jamet did not see, states that she arrived in Paris in October 1670.[4] Before embarkation, Marguerite sought a blessing on her voyage, both divine ("I went to Benediction of the Blessed Sacrament") and human ("and to the Bishop for his blessing"). She was to stand much in need of them in what was to prove a worrying and uncomfortable trip.

The first night aboard ship but before leaving port, Marguerite found that her box had not been loaded. This box contained her papers, her change of clothing, and her blanket for use during the voyage and was to have been put aboard by the servant of François de Salignac de La Mothe-Fénelon, a Sulpician priest also returning to France.[5] Night passed, and the next morning Abbé de Fénelon tried to pay someone to go back on shore and look for the missing box, but since the ship was about to sail, no one was ready to take the risk. Marguerite's description of her predicament implies that whatever financial arrangements she had made for the voyage were also affected by the misplacement of the box: "There I was, on board! I did not have ten cents; I was alone of my sex on board, but there were two priests. I made do with tow and a coil of rope." She concludes: "The trip lasted only thirty-one days."[6] The absence of other women aboard the ship meant that there was no one with whom she could share accommodation or from whom she might perhaps borrow a change of underwear. The latter problem she attempted to solve by fashioning a chemise out of a piece of canvas someone gave her to make a mattress. She did not change into this garment aboard ship, perhaps for lack of privacy or perhaps because she was saving it for her arrival in France, and it was lost at the time of disembarkation. Probably, despite all she lacked, Marguerite was just grateful that her services to the sick and dying do not seem to have been required on this journey as they had been on both her outward voyages from France.

A much greater source of worry than the loss of her meagre wardrobe was that of her papers, all those precious documents accumulated to support her application for letters patent. Before she left Quebec, however, she was able to send a message to Zacharie Dupuy, the town major of Montreal and a friend of the Congregation, who, she learned, was in the capital. She asked him to send the papers after her on the next ship and to return the box and the rest of its contents to Montreal. The belief she had expressed at the time of her first departure from France that "if this is God's will," there is no need for possessions must have been severely tested. This time she lacked even the little bundle with which she had first embarked for Canada. But God and Zacharie Dupuy repaid her confidence. The papers presumably did leave on the next ship that sailed from Quebec, for she certainly had them by the time she reached Paris. As for the box, a small calfskin box believed to be the article in question is still in possession of the Congrégation de Notre-Dame and is displayed in the Marguerite Bourgeoys Museum. The fact that the lock and handle were changed in the eighteenth century would indicate that it continued to do service long after its abortive journey of 1670.

Marguerite's port of entry in France was La Rochelle. When she got there, she wrote later, she borrowed 50 livres from Abbé de Fénelon. Of this she had to pay 45 livres and 10 sous for her coach fare to Paris – her precision here raises the possibility that she was using financial records still in her possession at the time of writing. She says, "I arrived in Paris without money, without clothes, without acquaintances." This statement is only partly true and is an unusual example of exaggeration on her part. (The purpose of the entire account of this journey in Marguerite's writings is quite clearly to emphasize the necessity of relying exclusively on God's help. It might even have been written at a moment when the sisters of the Congregation or those who exercised authority over the community were looking for more tangible forms of security.) Although Marguerite may have arrived in Paris without money or clothes, she was certainly not without acquaintances and even friends in the capital, as her own account goes on to show.

She reached Paris, she says, "very late" at night and went at once to the Sulpician seminary, where she was given the address of a woman living near by with whom she could spend the night. The hospitality included bed but apparently not breakfast, for when

Marguerite went next day to deliver a letter from Abbé Pérot, parish priest in Montreal, to his sisters, she was immensely grateful when they gave her a meal. This and other references to letters from Montreal indicates that she had received these and her other papers before she left La Rochelle for Paris. Now that daylight had arrived, she could return to Saint-Sulpice.

Of the events that followed, Marguerite writes:

I was on my way to Saint-Sulpice. I followed Our Lord as he was being carried to some people who were ill. We passed in front of the Church of the Premonstratensions, which I entered to pray and to go to confession ... I went to the Seminary to deliver some letters and to inquire where I could find M. de Maisonneuve. While I was waiting at the door, I heard a priest say: "I have been told to give 100 livres to a woman I don't know." And when I heard him mention the name, I said: "It's mine!" M. Pérot the younger confirmed that this was so. At once I followed this gentleman who lived on the rue Princesse. He gave me 100 livres. I gave him a receipt in duplicate.[7]

This passage in Marguerite's memoirs displays to perfection those characteristics whose combination might appear paradoxical. Here speaks at once the mystic and the capable businesswoman. She is suddenly the recipient of what might appear almost miraculous divine bounty, and she writes a receipt – in duplicate!

With her immediate financial embarrassment relieved, at least for the moment, Marguerite set off at last to look for Paul de Chome-dey de Maisonneuve, whom she had not seen for five years. The words that follow suggest that she perhaps had a little difficulty finding him in what was for her an unfamiliar part of the city: "I managed to find M. de Maisonneuve who was living on the Fosse de Saint-Victor, near the Fathers of Christian Doctrine." Her day had been so filled that night was again falling by the time she got there. Her description suggests that this was one of those moments that remained forever vivid in her memory: "When I knocked at the door, he came down (for he lived on the second and third floors with Louis Frin), and opened the door to me with great joy."

A little more is known of de Maisonneuve's life after his return to France than of the years before his arrival in Canada, but not a great deal. He remained in Paris rather than return to his ancestral home in Champagne. It has been suggested that he did so because he did not want to get involved with the family disputes that had already led to the murder of his sister and her husband and, indeed, that such a desire might have been a factor in his decision to go to New France in the first place.[8] But there could have been other reasons for his remaining in the city. When he first returned, he quite likely retained the hope of going back to Montreal, of which he remained the nominal governor, at least in the eyes of the Sulpicians, until the appointment of François-Marie Perrot in 1669. Even after any expectation of returning to Montreal had disappeared, Paris, especially the Sulpician seminary, remained the place to get news of the little settlement. De Maisonneuve's will, drawn up on the eve of his death, is evidence that until his death Montreal remained first in his memory and affections. Marguerite Bourgeoys's description of their meeting portrays him as eager to offer hospitality to visitors from Montreal. She says that just a few days before her arrival he had caused a small room to be prepared whose furnishings included what she called a "cabane à la facon du Canada," a bed enclosed with shutters, to receive persons who would come from Montreal.[9] Marie Morin mentions an account given her by a prominent Montrealer who had visited Paris and was much impressed by the fact that the former governor did not stand on ceremony but went out himself to buy them a bottle of wine.[10]

Both these descriptions indicate the very modest circumstances in which the former governor of Montreal was living. In his biography of Marguerite Bourgeoys, Jamet used the inventory made at the time of de Maisonnneuve's death to suggest what she would have seen when she entered his lodgings: old and shabby furniture, a large chest covered with black leather, six little chairs, badly upholstered, a table infested with woodworm, a few tapestries. De Maisonneuve's study was furnished with a writing desk and a bookcase containing close to forty books, among them the works of St François de Sales, that most humane of seventeenth-century religious writers, and a history of Rome, England, Flanders, and France in three volumes. The inventory also mentions a terra cotta statue of Virgin and Child "façon marbre." Jamet pictures the two looking at his belongings and remembering the years when Marguerite had looked after his household in the fort of Montreal.[11]

Certainly, Marguerite Bourgeoys would have had a great deal to recount to an old friend who must have been even more eager for news of the little settlement over whose beginnings he had presided. Their exchange would have been of the type that is only possible where there is confidence, a certainty of being understood, and a shared past. No doubt, things were said that could never be included in more official reports. Perhaps the two were even able to share some of the old laughter.

De Maisonneuve now gave his attention to helping Marguerite achieve the primary purpose for which she had come to France, the obtaining of letters patent for the Congregation. And right at the beginning, he was able to offer quite unexpected financial assistance. Marguerite's description of events in her account of her arrival in Paris is somewhat confusing, perhaps because of the fragmentary nature of what remains of her writings. She begins her account of her arrival in Paris with the statement: "I do not remember how many years ago I loaned a young boy 120 livres at the request of M. de Galinier. M. de Maisonneuve also loaned him 12 livres. This young man gave me a promissory note which I sent to M. Blondel to have paid to us. M. Blondel died and I was told that the note had been lost. I did not think any more about it."[12] After describing her arrival at de Maisonneuve's lodgings, she continues: "Several days later when he was showing me something in his study, he put his hand on a shelf and picked up the promissory note from this young man. I repaid the 50 livres I had borrowed at La Rochelle, M ... – I do not know his name – wrote the letters patent and would not take a fee. I looked for the young man to have him acknowledge his note. I found his mother who was a widow and who told me that her son ..."[13] The rest of this passage has never been found, perhaps a casualty of the practice of distributing portions of Marguerite's writings as relics or of one of the fires at the Congregation; it was already missing when Montgolfier wrote *La vie de la vénérable soeur Marguerite Bourgeois* in the last quarter of the eighteenth century.

Recovery of the debt does not look very promising at the point at which the passage breaks off, but the larger context suggests that this was an example of the way in which Marguerite found herself provided for, despite arriving in Paris without money, clothes, or acquaintances. Montgolfier says that the young man presented himself to her one day and put the money owed into her hands after following her in the street without knowing who she was. Faillon expands the passage to say that Montgolfier was reporting an oral tradition. Marguerite herself is supposed to have said that as she was walking one day along a street in Paris, she heard a gentleman running after her who asked, when he caught up with her, whether she knew a woman from Canada called Marguerite Bourgeoys. When she identified herself, he tried to give her a sum of money which she absolutely refused to take, not knowing the reason for such generosity. However, she was reassured when she learned that it was the repayment of the sum she had loaned him in Ville-Marie.[14]

There is no direct information about how Marguerite spent the following weeks. While she enjoyed de Maisonneuve's hospitality, she would, according to her custom, have prayed in the nearby church of Saint-Étienne-du-Mont. There she would have seen a remarkable series of stained glass windows of which the masterpiece is a representation of the mystic winepress. The interpretation differs from that with which she was familiar in the cathedral at Troyes and is much more elaborate. But as she looked at it, she could continue to reflect on her vision of the role of the Christian educator: to gather up the drops of the blood of Christ that are being lost through the ignorance of the people.[15] Perhaps she had hoped to complete her business in time to return to Canada that summer, but then as always, bureaucracy moved slowly.

Finally, in May 1671, more than six months after Marguerite's arrival in France, King Louis XIV signed the letters patent that for the first time gave official legal recognition to the Congrégation de Notre-Dame de Montréal. Fictionalized treatments of the life of Marguerite Bourgeoys, especially plays, almost always contain a scene that places Marguerite at the royal court in search of the letters patent. The striking contrast between the ostentation and imposing display of the Sun King's entourage and the modest, self-effacing Marguerite is almost too powerful to resist. The reality was probably much less dramatic, for Marguerite's business was with Colbert, the king's minister, rather than with the king himself, and the way had already been cleared for her dealings with him.

Talon's memoir on Canada directed to Colbert and dated 10 November 1670 contains the following passage:

I must not forget to make it known that M. the Abbé de Queylus applies himself strongly to the reform of his clergy, to enlarge the Montreal Colony and to supply subjects for the missions who conduct themselves worthily and usefully for the King by the discoveries they make. He extends his zeal further by the care he intends to take to remove the children of Indians who fall into captivity in the hands of the Iroquois to have them raised, the boys in his seminary, and the girls by persons of the same sex who form at Montreal a kind of congregation to teach young people reading and writing and handicrafts.[16]

Colbert himself wrote in the margin beside this paragraph, "Il faut s'employer à cet établissement" (We must look after this establishment).

Abbé de Queylus might in the past have caused difficulties for Marguerite Bourgeoys, but there can be no doubt that at this time he was held in such high approval at the court that association with him and with the Sulpicians could only be a benefit. The Sulpicians with their superior, Alexandre de Bretonvilliers, would have been helpful in the obtaining of the letters patent at every step of the way, even finding someone to do clerical work for free, as we have already seen. The man who wrote the letters patent – an important service when such documents had still to be handwritten – and whose name Marguerite could not remember has been identified by Faillon as M. de Sérancourt. Faillon says that he did the same thing for the seminary six years later, asking only prayers in payment for his labours.[17] In Colbert, Marguerite would have encountered another native of Champagne and even one with whom her family had a remote connection, for Édouard Colbert, a distant relative of the minister, had been godfather to her brother Édouard in 1628.[18]

The secular interests of the civil authorities are apparent both in the documents offered in support of the application for the letters patent and in the wording of the letters patent themselves. It was no secret to those who advised Marguerite at this time that to officials who seem more interested in the "useful" explorations made by missionaries than in their spiritual endeavours, the material success of the Congregation was of paramount importance. This is apparent even in the letter of support supplied by de Maisonneuve. It is worth quoting that document at length both to illustrate this point and because, signed on the afternoon of 22 November 1670, it is the earliest known biographical note about Marguerite Bourgeoys.

The notarized document is phrased in legal terms and almost without punctuation, according to the custom. In it de Maisonneuve begins by identifying himself as the former governor of the island of Montreal in New France and then briefly describes the circumstances of the recruitment of 1653. He continues:

Marguerite Bourgeois, a native of the city of Troyes in Champagne, dwelling there on the rue du Chaudron then aged thirty-three, wishing to contribute all she could to the establishment of the faith in the said region of New France and particularly to the instruction of the young children of the said country went to join the said sieur de Maisonneuve at Nantes in Brittany, the place of assembly of the said reinforcement and to embark on the same ship for New France as the said sieur de Maisonneuve which she did, performing every possible service of charity for those who were aboard ... the said Bourgeois having arrived on the Island of Montreal employed herself with all possible zeal not only in the instruction of the young but also in all the works of charity and piety to be met on all kinds of occasion for the public good in consideration of which and to give her the means of continuing in the same works, he gave her various land concessions which she had cleared at her own expense and had a farm established and supplied the necessary cattle and also at her own expense had two buildings erected to shelter the women near the port and the Saint-Joseph hospital of Villemarie on the said Island of Montreal ... to enlarge the said establishment the said Bourgeois made a trip to France in 1658 where she gained three women associates with whom she returned to the said country to continue the same functions which she has done with zeal and charity until the present year when it was judged proper for the good of the said country that the said Bourgeois go to France to increase the number of women in her community and to procure letters patent for her latest establishment ... the said Bourgeois having arrived in this city in October, showed him the certificates she had from the Bishop of Petrée, from Monsieur de Courcelles, lieutenant-general of His Majesty in the said country and of Monsieur Talon, Intendant of His Majesty in the same country with the results of the assembly of the settlers of the said Island of Montreal and the certificate of the parish priest of the same Montreal.[19]

The letters patent themselves were signed and dated at Dunquerque in Flanders, for the king was on a tour inspecting the readiness of his military for the war with Holland that would break out before Marguerite's return to Canada. The document echoes much of the wording to be found in de Maisonneuve's testimony, with some additions and clarifications. It states that Marguerite Bourgeoys is established on the island of Montreal with several other women who live with her in community and exercise the function of schoolmistress, "freely teaching the young girls the crafts that will make them capable of earning their living." With the help of

Providence, they have worked so sucessfully that "neither the petitioner nor her associates have cost the country anything, having
put up at their expense, two buildings suitable to their purposes,
had several land concessions cleared, built a farm provided with
everything necessary." The petitioner, her associates, and those who
will succeed them are promised the king's support to spread and
become strong wherever it is considered suitable for the glory of
God and the good of the country. The letters patent conclude:

We have approved, confirmed, authorized, approve, confirm and autho-
rize by the present letters, signed by our hand, the establishment of the ...
Congrégation de Notre-Dame on ... the island of Montreal in New France,
to instruct young girls in piety, to render them capable of the practice and
exercise of Christian virtue and morality, in keeping with their state in life;
under the jurisdiction of the ordinary, without their being disturbed, under
any pretext whatsoever.
    Given at Dunqerque, in the month of May, in the year of grace sixteen
hundred and seventy-one, the twenty-eighth of our reign. Louis[20]

    The Congrégation de Notre-Dame de Montréal was now a legal
entity, and Marguerite Bourgeoys had attained the main objective
of her journey. However, she was still not ready to return to Montreal. There was more business to do before she could seek passage
back to Canada. On 20 June 1671 she registered the letters patent
in the Parlement de Paris. (Faillon says that Colbert wanted this
done in Paris before it was done in Quebec "so that they would not
encounter any obstacle in the latter court.")[21] On 26 June she signed
a document making de Maisonneuve responsible for the business
affairs of the Congregation in France, "having authority and power
in this city of Paris and everywhere else where there is need in all
the affairs of the said Congrégation and community of women."
He was to continue to exercise this function until his death. De
Maisonneuve then went to Troyes, where he delegated some of his
powers to Canon Charles Le Bey, with whom he appears to have
stayed. In a document notarized and signed on 16 July, Le Bey was
given authority in the diocese of Troyes to accept for the Congregation all "donations, legacies and anything else which had or might
be given in favour of the Congregation."[22]
    At some time in the next months, Marguerite herself went to
Troyes. While there, she would have made some contact with the

families and friends of the women in the Congregation in Montreal, both to give them news and to be able to carry back word of them to Canada. Also, she could now turn her attention to the other reason for her voyage, the motive that seemed to her even more pressing than her legal business. She had come to seek out more women ready to dedicate themselves to the education of the children of New France in a community of uncloistered women. Previously, in her quest for new members for the Congregation, Marguerite had counted on finding them in the city of her birth. It was there that she had found three of the four women who had accompanied her back to Montreal in 1659. Once again she was to be successful in Troyes, though this time she was to draw her new recruits not from the extern congregation to which she had once belonged but from her own family.

Perhaps as a result of the commercial decline of Troyes in the seventeenth century, as well as of the low average life expectancy of the time, Marguerite would not have found many members of her immediate family still living in their native city. Of her twelve siblings, six were certainly dead before she left for Canada the first time: the unnamed stillborn child buried in 1617; Jeanne, Thomas, and Nicolas, who predeceased their mother who had died 1638; and Anne, who died suddenly in January 1643. Marie, the sister closest to Marguerite in age, died sometime between June 1655 and March 1659. Claude, the eldest in the family, had been living in Sens since before his mother's death. Sirette, the next born, had removed to Sens with her husband, a merchant, printer, bookseller, and binder, before 1642. Whether either was still living in 1671 is not known, but Claude had produced at least six children, and Sirette, fifteen. Jérôme, Marguerite's second oldest brother, was a surgeon practising his profession at Évreux by 1645 and later in the nearby village of Bailleul. Again, no trace of him has yet been found after the birth of a child about 1656. Édouard, born in 1628, might have remained in Troyes; it was he who chose to receive the materials and professional tools of his father when the property was divided at the time of Abraham Bourgeoys's death in 1651. Of the two youngest of her siblings to whom Marguerite had deeded her share of the family property in 1659, Pierre was quite certainly still living. He had followed his older brother to Évreux, where he became organist at the cathedral church, a position he still held at the time of his death on 28 March 1689. Of Marguerite's youngest sister, Madeleine, nothing is yet known after 31 August 1663, when she bought her brother Pierre's share of the family patrimony.[23]

There did remain in Troyes, however, three nieces of Marguerite Bourgeoys, the daughters of her sister Marie and Orson Sémilliard, her husband. These were Marguerite, baptized 29 November 1652, just before her aunt's first departure for Canada; Louise, baptized 24 February 1654; and Catherine, baptized 2 June 1655.[24] The eldest might possibly have remembered her aunt from the voyage of 1658–59. Did Marguerite stay with the family at this time, or did she, as on her previous visit, stay with the Congrégation de Notre-Dame of Troyes? (The departure of de Maisonneuve from Canada must have meant the end of that community's dream of an establishment in Montreal, but Louise de Chomedey was still there to welcome Marguerite.) Whatever the circumstances of Marguerite Bourgeoys's contact with her late sister's family, she must have presented them with a vision of Canada that aroused their enthusiasm. The impact was powerful: all three of her nieces decided to accompany her to Montreal.

Marguerite Sommillard (that is the form of their name consistently used by the three sisters in Canada) seems to have intended from the time of her departure from Troyes to become a member of the Congrégation de Notre-Dame of Montreal. She was, at nineteen, almost the age her aunt had been at the time of her "conversion" in 1640 and her decision to give herself to God. Louise, the middle sister, seventeen years old in 1671, appears to have left for New France with the specific intention of marrying. Catherine, the youngest, was just sixteen. Marguerite Bourgeoys seems to say that Catherine too left for Canada with the intention of marrying.[25] If that is true, she changed her mind after her arrival, for like her eldest sister, she became a member of the Congregation. But initially at least, only one new member of the Congregation was recruited from Troyes. Why these three young women decided to set out together for the New World is not known. Their father was still living, as is attested by Louise's marriage contract signed in Montreal in the summer of 1674. Perhaps they were motivated by the spirit of adventure once characteristic of the citizens of Champagne and so conspicuous in their aunt. Marguerite's encouragement of her own nieces to make the journey is a measure of the confidence in the future emerging among the people of New France.

Besides Marguerite Sommillard, Marguerite signed contracts with five other young women. Presumably these contracts would have resembled that signed by Edmée Chastel in 1659, in which she pledged herself to live in community and to teach the children of the French settlers and the Native people. Elisabeth de la Bertache, whom Marguerite gives first when she lists the names of this new group, came from Dijon and was thirty-eight years old in 1672. Although she was to serve briefly as bursar and as assistant superior, most of her long life – she lived until 1710 – was devoted to teaching in the school. Geneviève du Rosoy, about twenty-nine in 1672, Madeleine Constantin, twenty-six, and Perrette Laurent de Beaune, nineteen, all came from Paris. Claude Durant's place of origin is unknown. In fact, there is almost no information about her in the records of the Congregation, although she lived until she reached the age of eighty in 1723.[26]

Bishop Laval was also in France at this time, having arrived in Paris in the autumn of 1671 to see about the establishment of his diocese. Until this time he was bishop *in partibus* of Petraea and vicar apostolic in New France, as Quebec was not yet a diocese. Before leaving for the coast with her new companions, Marguerite presented them to the bishop and asked for his blessing: "Bishop Laval ... accepted them and received them in a ceremony in the chapel of the Seminary of the Foreign Missions where he was living."[27] At last, the group was ready to leave for Canada.

The surviving writings of Marguerite Bourgeoys tell us nothing else about the events of 1672. The only source of details about her return journey with her companions is Montgolfier's account in his *Vie de la vénérable soeur Marguerite Bourgeois*, written in the last quarter of the eighteenth century and therefore about one hundred years after the events described. Much of what he says is based on oral tradition. However, the memory can play tricks even on the best intentioned, and the situation is complicated here by the expectation that Marguerite would conform to accepted ideas of saintliness. Her humour and irony were not always recognized by those who recounted her words. Another difficulty faced by Montgolfier was that he was not always aware of the conditions that had prevailed in Montreal a century before. At the same time, his description of this return journey of 1672 contains some details that are so precise that it is difficult not to be convinced he was working from a written source which has since disappeared. Sometimes his very misconceptions tend to confirm the general fidelity of the account.[28]

According to Montgolfier, Marguerite was now accompanied by about eleven women, six for the Congregation and the rest to find husbands in Montreal. They left Paris just after Easter, which in 1672 fell on 17 April, Marguerite's fifty-second birthday. The first stage of their journey, like the last, was by river boat, though a greater contrast between the dirty and crowded Seine that carried them away from Paris and the wide stretches of the St Lawrence which would bear them to Montreal would be hard to imagine. Their destination was not Nantes or La Rochelle, Marguerite's ports of departure on previous trips, but the more northerly port of Le Havre, which had taken on increasing importance as the headquarters of the Compagnie des Indes occidentales. One event Montgolfier placed in Paris before their departure seems, in fact, to have taken place as they wended their way to the coast, but the documents connected with it serve to give general support to his itinerary and timetable. This was the visit to the Baron de Fancamp.

As they travelled through Normandy, close to their route, near Vernon, lay the priory of Notre-Dame de Saulseuse, where Pierre Chevrier, Baron de Fancamp, lived in retirement. It was now fourteen years since the death of Jérôme Le Royer de La Dauversière and almost a decade since the dissolution of the Société de Notre-Dame de Montréal, but some, at least, of the former members continued to take an interest in the settlement they had founded. The official acts that mention the seigneurs of Montreal between 1640 and 1663 placed Pierre Chevrier's name ahead of that of Jérôme Le Royer, an indication of his superior social position. Le Royer's closest friend and collaborator, Chevrier had contributed about a quarter of the funds used for the original expedition to found Ville-Marie on the island of Montreal. He continued to contribute generously to the welfare of the settlement and may even have considered coming to live in Montreal himself. Because his two sisters became nuns and his three brothers predeceased him without issue, the whole of a considerable family fortune was eventually his to dispose of as he pleased. (He had himself been ordained priest sometime between 1654 and 1659.) In the spring of 1672 he was sixty-four years old and living in retirement in the priory of Notre-Dame de Saulseuse, in what is now the diocese of Évreux.

Marguerite Bourgeoys does not specify where she saw the Baron de Fancamp, and none of the documents connected with her visit indicate where they were signed. Although subsequent biographers accepted Montgolfier's statement that their meeting took place in Paris, more recent research by Guy Oury indicates that it was, rather, at the priory in Normandy when she was on her way to the coast.[29] In the course of that meeting the baron presented Marguerite with a gift that remains a tangible witness to his continued regard for Montreal. This was a wooden statuette of Virgin and Child carved from the oak of Montaigu in Belgium. It has survived fire and theft and can still be seen in the chapel of Notre-Dame-de-Bon-Secours in Old Montreal.

Among the early sources there are diverging stories about how the baron came to present Marguerite with the statuette. According to the *Histoire de la Congrégation*, he offered to pay the cost of her return journey to Canada, but she asked him instead for a gift for the pilgrimage chapel she still intended to build in Montreal in honour of Our Lady. The baron scoured Paris for a suitable statue but could find none. Then into his hands came the miraculous statuette.[30] Certainly, there had been some contact between Marguerite Bourgeoys and the baron before he made his presentation, for the act of donation of the statue signed on 30 April 1672 shows that he had been aware of her plans for the chapel in Montreal at least two weeks earlier. That act and the testimony of the original donors supply the history of the little statue.

The baron certified that the statuette had been given to him by Denys and Louis LePrestre, who were, like him, former members of the Société de Notre-Dame de Montréal. The brothers testified that they wished to promote devotion to the Virgin Mary in Montreal and for this purpose were offering a statue that came from their own domestic chapel. They believed, on the testimony of their mother, who had died at over eighty years of age, that the statuette had already been venerated for almost a century. The image was placed in the hands of the Baron de Fancamp on the evening of Good Friday, 15 April 1672. During the night he felt the onslaught of symptoms of a serious illness of which there was an epidemic at the time. He prayed before the little image of the Virgin and Child, asking to be cured and pledging that he would do all he could to promote the building of the chapel in Montreal, beginning with the promise of thirty pistoles for the work. Immediately he began to feel better without the use of any medication. When he placed the statue in the hands of Marguerite Bourgeoys on 30 April, he also gave her a signed attestation of what he believed to have been his own miraculous cure.[31]

Did Marguerite make any other visits as she passed through Normandy? A slight detour from her route would have taken her to Évreux, where two of her brothers had taken up residence. Jérôme Bourgeoys, just two years her senior, might well have still been living. On her previous return to France, she had signed over her share of the family inheritance to her youngest sister and brother, Madeleine and Pierre. Pierre was certainly living in Évreux at this time, and like Marguerite, he was interested in the education of the poor. He was a member of a group called the Communauté des enfants du Saint-Esprit, a benevolent association consisting of a priest, who acted as teacher and chaplain, and a few educators. The purpose of this community was the reception into *la maison de l'Hermitage* of twelve poor children to be fed, lodged, and educated.[32] Did brother and sister meet at this time? Marguerite's writings are silent on this point, as they are on almost everything else about her family and her relations with its members, and in this case, no legal documents have yet been discovered to serve as clues.

Problems arose for Marguerite and her group of women when they reached Rouen. They were delayed there for a month because the ship on which they were to sail was not yet outfitted. The protracted and unexpected stay in that city severely taxed their financial resources. Montgolfier relates an anecdote connected with this event. He says that the woman charged with the common purse, whom he identifies as Madeleine Senécal, approached Marguerite Bourgeoys to say, "Sister, we have enough for this week but nothing for next week. What are we going to do?" To this Marguerite is supposed to have replied "coldly" that "you are mistrusting Providence." "Well, while we're waiting," teased the other, "we have to eat." Dom Jamet was deeply distrustful of Montgolfier's account of this incident, finding such apparent harshness uncharacteristic of Marguerite. Perhaps, though, this is one of the occasions where the tone and spirit in which the remarks were made has been lost in the retelling. Marguerite Bourgeoys had, after all, been popular among her young friends for her lightheartedness and wit, and her family had thought she was teasing when she announced her intention of leaving for Canada. Later she was able to laugh and joke with de

Maisonneuve and Abbé Souart in Montreal's early and "terrible" days. The spirit of the young woman's reply in this exchange indicates that she knew she was being teased.

Marguerite must have sent a message to Paris about the delay because help arrived in the person of Louis Frin, de Maisonneuve's servant, a sign that the former governor was fulfilling his function of looking after the business affairs of the Congregation in France. Frin brought the promise of an allowance of 200 livres for each of the women and a daily allowance of 11 sols, 6 derniers, for their food until their arrival in Quebec.[33] Faillon believed this money was supplied by Colbert, who was taking an interest in the success of the Congregation. The group may also have added another woman to their number at this time. Though there is no mention of the event in Montgolfier's *Vie*, the history of the Congregation states that Catherine Boni, certainly a member of the Congregation by 1676, was a native of Rouen who joined the group during their sojourn in that city.[34]

The women returned to the river for the last stage of their journey before embarkation for Canada and then spent some two weeks at Le Havre watching the final preparations for departure. They also made a pilgrimage to the nearby Marian shrine of Notre-Dame-des-Neiges. Finally, the weather was judged propitious for sailing, and the ship put out to sea with a total of forty-five passengers, among them Abbé François Le Febvre, a Sulpician priest also on his way to Montreal. According to Montgolfier, the departure took place on 2 July, feast of the Visitation of Mary to her cousin Elizabeth, and the arrival at Quebec on 14 August, eve of the feast of the Assumption of Mary. On this voyage, there was no outbreak of disease aboard ship. Certainly, if the dates supplied by Montgolfier are correct,[35] they must have encountered exceptionally favourable weather. Louis de Buade de Frontenac, who was coming to replace Courcelle as governor of New France, sailed from La Rochelle on 18 June 1672 and did not arrive in Quebec until early autumn.

During Marguerite's two-year absence, an era had come to an end in Quebec: Madame de La Peltrie had died on 16 November 1671 and Marie de l'Incarnation on 30 April 1672. A sour note was sounded for Marguerite when a "foolish person" (the narrator's epithet, not Marguerite's) approached her with the information "that the Montreal community was in decadence and that the house was about to fail." To this she is supposed to have replied, "Blessed be God! But He who brings about its fall can raise it up again."[36] Whatever she made of this report, she must have been eager to get back to Montreal and be reunited with her small community.

Marguerite's return to Montreal was a major event. Montgolfier says that she found the sisters in extreme poverty and again relates an anecdote which, like the earlier one about the shortage of resources in Rouen, should probably be read with Marguerite's sense of humour in mind. He says that she asked newly arrived Geneviève du Rosoy to prepare a meal for the group, a task that posed something of a challenge since there seemed to be only a little bread and a small piece of fat in the house. Again there are a few lines of dialogue: "What do you want me to prepare? I don't see anything in the house," says Geneviève. "Why do you mistrust Providence?" replies Marguerite.[37] The situation is saved by the arrival of the neighbours with gifts of food to provide supper for all the new arrivals. With fifteen years of experience of life in Montreal behind her Marguerite must have known the usual response of the settlers when anyone returned with news from the home country or even just from Quebec.

As for the material situation of the Congregation, Dollier de Casson, who was actually in Montreal at that moment and whose *Histoire* was begun at the time of Marguerite's return,[38] gives a different picture: "What I marvel at ... is the way in which these women, lacking in resources, are so unselfish that they are ready to give instruction free, and to do other things in the same way, and yet by the blessing that God gives to their work, without being a burden to anyone, they have acquired several houses and land of value on the Island of Montreal."

Marguerite would not have been called upon only to relay news; after two years, there also would have been much for her to hear. Some of it was distressing: Dominique Galinier, one of the first Sulpicians to come to Montreal in 1657, had died suddenly in the seminary garden the previous autumn; Jeanne Mance's health was in steady decline. But much of the news was positive and filled with promise for the future. The foundation stones for a parish church had been laid on 30 June 1672, the last of them by Jeanne Mance. The genial and capable François Dollier de Casson, with his great energy, his zest for life, and his leadership abilities, was now superior of the Sulpicians in Montreal. With Bénigne Basset, notary and surveyor, he had begun to lay out Montreal's first streets: Saint-Joseph, Saint-Paul, Saint-Charles, Saint-François, du Calvaire, Saint-Lambert, Saint-Gabriel, and Notre-Dame. Most of these streets can still be seen in Old Montreal today. Armed with their charter and enriched in talents and numbers, Marguerite Bourgeoys and her Congregation were ready to play their part in the building of this new Montreal. And they were ready to look beyond Montreal as other settlements began to grow along the St Lawrence.

CHAPTER THREE

WHEREVER CHARITY OR
NEED REQUIRED
1672–1679

The Blessed Virgin was not cloistered, but wherever she was, she preserved
an interior solitude. She never refused to go wherever charity or need
required her assistance ... We will go into whatever places the Bishop
judges suitable, to instruct girls and to maintain schools.[1]

Marguerite Bourgeoys had now been in Montreal for almost twenty
years. In the next decade her Congregation was to enter a period
of transformation. Geographically, it would expand its horizons,
establishing its first permanent residences in settlements outside
Ville-Marie itself. At the same time, its membership would become
younger and more varied. The six new members who accompanied Marguerite on her return from France in 1672 were the last
large European recruitment. In a very few years, the Congregation
would begin to admit women born in North America. By the end of
the 1670s the shape that the future Congregation was to take had
already begun to become visible.

The arrival of the recruitment of 1672 more than doubled the
size of the Congregation. Whatever qualms Marguerite felt about
the building of the new house – and a decade later she was to demonstrate that these had never left her – her enlarged community and
household were immensely relieved to move into roomier and more
convenient quarters. The new building is believed to have stretched
from the stable school of 1658 to the former Charly house of 1662
at a distance of some two hundred feet from the St Lawrence. With
the onset of winter, the experience of being housed in a single building must have made its advantages felt very quickly. As soon as

the community was more adequately housed, Marguerite herself at last felt free to advance the project that she had been planning since the second year after her arrival in Montreal. After so many difficulties and delays, she was to bring about the realization of a dream that only her patience and determination had kept alive: the building of the chapel of pilgrimage dedicated to Our Lady. The importance that the construction of this chapel continued to have for Marguerite Bourgeoys is a reminder of the context in which all her other activities must be seen. However much her efforts were directed toward helping the settlers earn their daily bread, she took seriously the words spoken by Christ at the time of his temptation in the desert: "Man does not live on bread alone." In the midst of the struggles of their daily life, the chapel and the act of pilgrimage that would take them there were to speak to Montrealers of a larger reality.

Marie Morin reports that Marguerite had work resumed on the chapel "as soon as she got back from her journey."[2] The wooden statuette given by the Baron de Fancamp spent its first winter in Montreal in the house of the Congregation. On 8 June 1673, on the octave day of the feast of Corpus Christi, the statuette was ceremonially installed in the little wooden oratory Marguerite had built before her departure for France in 1670. That summer, however, her choice of the original site for the chapel was called into question. Bishop Laval was of course still in France. In a letter dated 24 August 1673, Jean Dudouyt, his vicar general, expressed approval of the plan to encourage devotion to Mary in Montreal by the building of a nearby chapel of pilgrimage. However, he had consulted Claude Pijart, the Jesuit missionary with whom Marguerite Bourgeoys had begun the chapel, and learned that the site was a very short distance from the settlement. Dudouyt questioned whether it would not be better to build the chapel somewhat farther away, but he left the final decision to the authorities in Montreal. By this time, Montrealers no longer lived in the kind of acute danger that had surrounded them when the chapel was first begun, and it would indeed have been possible for them to visit a chapel outside the immediate shadow of the settlement without risking their lives. Whether or not serious consideration was given to the choice of another site in Montreal is not known. All the contemporary records state that the chapel was constructed on the site chosen by Marguerite Bourgeoys nearly two decades earlier, a high spot on the banks of the St Lawrence with a view along the river in both directions, a site that had apparently also been attractive to Native groups in earlier times.[3]

In a letter to Marguerite Bourgeoys dated 4 November 1674, Henri de Bernières, who by that time had replaced Dudouyt as vicar general, approved the choice of the Assumption of Mary as the titular feast of the chapel. A ritual procession went out after vespers on 29 June 1675 to plant a cross at the chosen site and begin preparations for building. Next day Abbé Gabriel Souart was accompanied by another procession to lay the first stone of the chapel in the name of the Baron de Fancamp.[4] The building of the chapel was financed by the Congrégation de Notre-Dame and by the funds given by the Baron de Fancamp and invested by Marguerite Bourgeoys. On at least one occasion, the Congregation was called upon to offer more than financial or moral support, as is illustrated in the only surviving anecdote about the actual construction of the chapel. Marguerite Bourgeoys wrote this account of an experience of her niece Marguerite Sommillard and a surly workman:

When the masons were building the steps at the door, we had a hired man who was not willing to go and help the masons. At that time, Sister Sommillard had an abscess in the head from which she suffered so much that she was unable to bend over; she was even obliged to kneel when she wanted to sweep her room. Nevertheless she went to work immediately and helped the masons for two or three hours with all the strength of a man and without even thinking of her condition. It should be noted that from that moment she felt no more pain in her head for a whole year.

Marguerite adds, "Many marvels were accomplished by the prayers that were said in that chapel."[5] The suspension of her usual caution with regard to "signs and wonders" gives some indication of Marguerite's love for her little chapel. The Congregation would not have a private chapel for many years yet, and after its completion in 1678, Notre-Dame-de-Bon-Secours became like a conventual chapel for the sisters in that they went to sing high mass there on the feast of the Visitation, the patronal feast of the community. Marguerite says that there they always renewed their promises made to God.[6] The Sulpicians also supported the chapel. Dollier de Casson gave the chapel the stipends for all the masses offered there during the first three years after its opening. Marguerite Bourgeoys's comment that these numbered more than a thousand, "although there were few priests and few people in Montreal," implies that there must have been a celebration almost daily.[7]

Of course, much else was happening in Montreal, in the Congregation, and in the life of Marguerite Bourgeoys during these years. As had been true from the time of her arrival in Ville-Marie, she was closely involved in the life around her, with its round of births, marriages, and deaths. It was the last of these three that touched her twice in the summer of 1673. One death was that of one of Montreal's most distinguished citizens, the consummation of a life long in accomplishment and experience; the other was that of a child who would probably be forgotten now if it had not been for the manner of her dying. The earlier death was that of Jeanne Mance, co-founder of Montreal and founder and administrator of the Hôtel-Dieu, whose ship had arrived in Quebec in 1641, even before that carrying de Maisonneuve. The other was a five-year-old child named Catherine André.

Jeanne Mance's biographer Marie-Claire Daveluy pictures the period between the departure of de Maisonneuve in the autumn of 1665 and her death in June 1673 as a time of darkness in the life of this woman to whom Montreal owed so much. "How sad," she writes, "never to be able to rejoice with a light heart at the present prosperity of Montreal and of New France! All had become calm, filled with all the pleasant tasks that peace makes possible."[8] The sadness of those years had two causes. Jeanne was now in her sixties and suffering from physical problems that caused her considerable pain and sometimes kept her in bed for months at a time. Worse still was the moral suffering that resulted from "the persistent blame" of Bishop Laval "touching the unhappy question of the 22,000 *livres* she had once laid out for the common good of Ville-Marie." This was the money originally intended for the hospital that she had put at the disposal of de Maisonneuve to raise the "great recruitment" which had saved Montreal from extinction or abandonment in 1653.

Jeanne Mance's ill health did not prevent her from continuing to administer the hospital or from taking an interest in happenings in Montreal. From the time of his arrival, she seems to have got on well with Dollier de Casson, as is first evident in the concern she showed in sending supplies to Fort Saint-Anne in 1666. Her friendship with the abbé gave her an exceptional opportunity: it provided a chance to transmit to posterity an account of the origins and early history of Montreal from her point of view. When Dollier decided to write the history of Montreal for the benefit of his confreres in France, she was able to confide to him her memories of the past. Jeanne Mance was described by Marie Morin as an eloquent woman. In the face of a present in which de Maisonneuve was gone and she found herself exposed to misunderstanding and even calumny, she might have found some comfort in knowing her own version of events was recorded for the future. In 1669 she saw the arrival from France of the nuns who prepared the sisters of the Hôtel-Dieu for their first pronouncement of solemn or perpetual vows. She was still sought after as a godmother, though at a baptism that took place on 17 January that year she had to send eight-year-old Cécile Closse to stand in for her, because she was unable to leave her bed.[9]

Her failing strength and her desire to make sure everything would be in order at her passing led Jeanne Mance to draw up her last will and testament on 3 June 1669. She left all of which she died possessed to be divided equally between the hospital sisters and the poor of the hospital and named Bishop Laval her executor. The document stipulated that immediately after her death her apartment was to be sealed and the bishop was to take possession of all the papers relating to her personal affairs and those of the hospital. Daveluy sees in her naming of Laval as executor Jeanne Mance's recognition of the bishop's "rigorous probity." No doubt this is true. But more important, as Daveluy also points out, was protection of the hospital and the transition of administration after her death. There might have been another consideration: Jeanne Mance would have been only human if she also wanted to leave the bishop a last demonstration of her own integrity, of her own "rigorous probity."

Later in 1669 Jeanne Mance regained some strength, but Marguerite Bourgeoys must have wondered when she left for France in 1670 whether she would ever again see the woman with whom she had shared the harrowing events of Montreal's early years. In February 1672, given the absence of Bishop Laval in France without any return in sight, Jeanne added a codicil to her will naming Gabriel Souart, former parish priest of Montreal, executor in his stead. In June 1672, however, she somehow found the strength and determination to take part in the ceremonies that accompanied the laying of the cornerstone of the parish church. Perhaps when Marguerite Bourgeoys returned from France later that summer,

Jeanne Mance was one of the neighbours who sent over food for the first evening meal at the Congregation. There certainly must have been a meeting between the two women to enable Marguerite to give Jeanne the news from France and perhaps to bring messages from de Maisonneuve and others among Jeanne's friends and contacts there.

Jeanne Mance made her last recorded public appearance on 19 September 1672, when she became a godmother for the forty-first time in Canada and the last. By May 1673 she was permanently bedridden, and Daveluy pictures Marguerite Bourgeoys, Sister Catherine Macé, and Jeanne Groissard, an old friend, as keeping watch beside her in turn during her last days. On 27 May she was able to discuss with Abbé Souart the arrangements to be made immediately after her death and to dictate further codicils to her will.[10] Among the new bequests was 100 livres for use in the construction of the parish church now underway and 100 livres for a tabernacle in that church for the reservation of the Blessed Sacrament. Daveluy wondered whether, as she made these bequests, Jeanne's mind went back to that May morning in 1642 when she had prepared the altar for Ville-Marie's first mass. Jeanne Mance also left the sum of 200 livres to "Sister Marguerite Bourgeois and her Community in recognition of the good Services she and Her other Sisters have given her begging Them all to pray God for her and to offer her to Our Lord." Angélique de Sailly, a twelve-year-old godchild for whom Jeanne was caring during her mother's absence in France (the father had died in 1668), was confided "into the hands of Sister Marguerite Bourgeois ... requesting Her to take Care of her" until the mother's return, expected within the year. Jeanne Mance died at ten o'clock on the night of Sunday, 18 June 1673, and tradition has placed Marguerite Bourgeoys at her side to close her eyes for the last time. She was sixty-six years old.

Just over a month later, on Wednesday, 19 July, at about seven in the evening, a distraught woman arrived at the door of the Congregation asking for Marguerite Bourgeoys. Her name was Françoise Nadereau; Marguerite had known her for some time. Françoise, who would at this time have been about twenty-nine years old, was not unacquainted with violence and grief. In September 1658 she had married Michel Louvard, *dit* Desjardins, a member of the recruitment with whom Marguerite herself had arrived in Montreal in 1653. He was a miller whose land grant bordered on the southern edge of property acquired by Marguerite Bourgeoys.[11] However, on 23 June 1662 he was struck down and killed on the steps of his own house. The burial record states that he was believed to have been killed by members of the Wolf tribe, who were very numerous in the area at the time. There do not appear to have been any children from this union. In May the following year the widow married Michel André, *dit* Saint-Michel. Their first child died at the age of about eighteen months, but there were four other children by the summer of 1673. These ranged in age from one to seven years. It was about the second of these, Catherine, aged five and a half, that Françoise had come: the child had perished, her mother said, in a terrible accident.

The story and its aftermath unfold gradually in the judicial documents of the time. Catherine had died by strangulation, and her mother told Marguerite Bourgeoys that the accident had come about because she had put the child in a cupboard in a barn or stable to control her disobedience. The door did not fit tightly, and the child had accidentally strangled as she tried to squeeze under the door. Marguerite suggested that they first inform the parish priest and religious authorities, and she went with the grieving mother to support her on this mission. When they were told that the civil judicial authorities must also be informed, Marguerite Bourgeoys again accompanied Françoise. As they returned, however, the mother made a confession to Marguerite: "I didn't tell you the Truth. I have to tell you. I put the child in prison in a barrel in a barn at some distance from the house and I put a plank over the barrel with a sack of grain on top and trying to get out she was caught between the plank and the edge of the barrel."[12]

The mother's original tampering with the facts of the case were no doubt due to panic and fear lest she be accused of harming the child deliberately or through negligence. Such terror was scarcely surprising: torture was permitted in the questioning of suspected criminals, and the penalties for serious, and sometimes not so serious, crimes could be truly horrific. However, the changes in her story could make her open to the very suspicions she feared, and the authorities began to ask whether, "through a fit of anger or some secret hatred," she had brought about the death of her child. Marguerite Bourgeoys stood by Françoise Nadereau in this ordeal, and through her testimony and that of the neighbours, she managed to convince the authorities that Catherine's death had indeed been an accident.

The personality of the little girl whose life had come to such an untimely end emerges clearly from the court documents. She was lively, adventurous, and funny and often completely unmanageable – "incorrigible" is the word used – but much loved by both her mother and her father. (Since the father never appears in the court proceedings, it is to be presumed that he was away.) The mother, with two children younger than Catherine and all the tasks of a pioneer household to attend to, had adopted the habit of putting her "in prison" in the barrel when she was especially difficult. This had become a kind of game with Catherine, pleased to demonstrate to the neighbour children how she could escape from the barrel and even, at times, get into the barrel herself. According to the testimony of one neighbour, when Catherine was placed in the barrel the day before the accident, she called out to the neighbour's son to come and get her out of prison or she would get out herself, at which she climbed out and went to pick strawberries.

On the morning of the fatal day, according to the eleven-year-old son of the neighbour, Catherine was in the barrel for having thrown water and ashes on her baby brother, but she managed to climb out within half an hour in spite of the weights on top. In the afternoon she was again disobedient and again back in the barrel. When she did not appear for supper, her mother went to get her, only to discover that this time Catherine had not been successful in escaping from her prison. Caught between the metal rim of the barrel and the weighted plank, she had been able neither to breath nor to call out. Her mother laid her body on the straw and tried to breath into her mouth and ears, "weeping and lamenting and saying My God what am I going to do. I'd much rather be dead." She had sought the help of the neighbours, but it was too late. It was then that that she had come to Marguerite Bourgeoys. The testimony they heard satisfied the authorities that the death of the child had not been deliberate, and the incident, at least in its juridical aspect, was brought to a close. This story throws some light on the relationship between Marguerite Bourgeoys and the ordinary colonists of Montreal. A woman who did not know where to turn was able to confide in her, to tell her the truth, and to find in her not just a sympathetic listener but a counsellor and advocate.

At the end of 1673 the land holdings of the Congrégation de Notre-Dame were considerably increased. On 12 November, Zacharie Dupuy and his wife, Jeanne Groissard, made a gift of all their property, with the exception of a town house, to the "Filles de la Congrégation." They were childless and declared themselves "desirous of withdrawing from the cares of the world and offering themselves to God." In return, the Congregation agreed to care for them both for as long as they lived. Dupuy had succeeded Lambert Closse as town major or assistant to the governor in 1662 and had become acting governor on the departure of de Maisonneuve in 1665. In 1671 he was granted a fief of 320 acres at the Saint-Louis rapids, to which he gave the name Verdun, the area of France from which he had come. Another land grant in 1672 gave him a series of islands in front of the Verdun fief, including Île aux Hérons. He apparently also had holdings in the Bon-Pasteur fief on Île Jésus. Dupuy was buried from the house of the Congregation on 1 July 1676. His wife returned to France, where Marguerite Bourgeoys agreed to pay her a pension of 100 livres a year.

One of the happier and more hopeful events of these years was the marriage of Marguerite's niece Louise Sommillard to François Fortin in the summer of 1674. Louise had taken almost two years to find or to choose a husband and was now twenty years old. Her bridegroom, identified in the marriage contract as a settler from Brittany, was about nine years her senior. Her sisters, Marguerite and Catherine, and Marguerite Bourgeoys, her "Maternal aunt Superior of the women of the Congregation established at Montreal," were present both at the signing of the marriage contract on 8 July (in the "Maison Neufve," the "new house" of the Congregation) and at the wedding the next day.[13] Louise's first child, a daughter named Marie-Catherine, was baptized on 24 March 1675. The godmother was Louise's sister Catherine. The fact that Catherine is identified in the baptismal register as a *fille de soi*, a term denoting her independent single status, would indicate that she had not yet made the decision to enter the Congregation. As other children followed in the Sommillard-Fortin family, Marguerite Bourgeoys was able to see descendants of her own family growing up in the New World.[14]

Although Montreal was free from Iroquois attack during these years, it was certainly not free of conflict. As *filles de paroisse*, Marguerite Bourgeoys and her companions would have been present, with the rest of the population of Montreal, at a high mass on Easter Sunday 1674, when some contentious issues found truly dramatic expression. Dollier de Casson was in the hospital extremely ill. He had suffered severe hypothermia in a fall through the ice on the St Lawrence and, as seems often to have been the case in these times, subsequent medical treatment had aggravated rather than improved his condition. The celebrant of the mass was Abbé Pérot, the parish priest, and the homelist that same Abbé de Fénelon who had sailed from Quebec with Marguerite in 1670. As the sermon progressed, some of his remarks on the duties of Christians who occupy positions of authority could be interpreted as an attack on Frontenac, the governor of New France. Among those present at the mass was René-Robert Cavelier de La Salle, a supporter and ally of Frontenac. The description of his position during mass – "at the back, near the door" – suggests that his presence was not due to any great religious fervour. During the sermon, he rose from his place and proceeded to disrupt the mass with a dumb show. It is not difficult to imagine what must have been the main topic of conversation at all Montreal dinner tables that day. Dollier de Casson's recovery can scarcely have been helped by the fact that Jean Cavelier de La Salle, René-Robert's Sulpician brother, rushed to his bedside immediately after the mass to tell him what had taken place. The other Sulpicians were appalled by these happenings and alarmed about their possible consequences.[15]

Fénelon's sermon was, in fact, a response to the activities of Frontenac in the fur trade. As governor, Frontenac was reponsible for the military affairs of New France, while the intendant supervised civil matters. However, Jean Talon had left for France immediately after Frontenac's arrival, and no deputy had been named, so that Frontenac had tended to assume the authority of the intendant as well as that of governor. He had also been quick to see the possibilities in the western fur trade. In 1673 he had a trading post constructed on Lake Ontario at the mouth of the Cataracoui (Cataraqui) River, where Kingston stands today. He did this without informing Colbert, who was more interested in the consolidation of the colony along the St Lawrence than in western expansion. His action brought him into conflict with the more prosperous elements of the population, the merchants of New France, who thought he was cutting off part of their trade. It also caused considerable problems for the ordinary settlers of Montreal, who were forced to spend much of the summer of 1673 on a corvée constructing the Cataracoui fort or carrying supplies to it. His activities in the fur trade also brought Frontenac into conflict with the governor of Montreal, François-Marie Perrot, who had set up his own illegal trading post on the island west of Montreal, which still bears his name. When Perrot attempted to stir up and unite the resistance, Frontenac had him arrested, and Abbé de Fénelon had come to Perrot's assistance by circulating a petition in his defence. This was the background to the Easter sermon. Afterward, the situation continued to worsen, until finally it had to be settled by the king himself.

Such was the state of things to which Bishop Laval returned in the autumn of 1675 after an absence of four years. His departure for France in the autumn of 1671 had something in common with that of de Maisonneuve in 1651. At that time, de Maisonneuve had decided that he must either find a significant number of new recruits or abandon the plan for the missionary colony in Montreal; Bishop Laval had left resolved that unless Quebec become an episcopal see, he would never again return to New France. At the time of Laval's consecration in 1658, the archbishop of Rouen still claimed jurisdiction over New France; Laval became bishop of Petraea *in partibus* and vicar general of New France. Although Louis XIV had assured him of his appointment to the proposed see of Quebec and asked the pope to create such a see in 1662, the project suffered an unexpected setback when a diplomatic incident in August of that same year resulted in severely strained relations between Louis and Rome.[16] The king then demanded that the new see be attached to that of Rouen.

In Rome the Congregation for the Propagation of the Faith moved in 1662 from agreeing that the moment had come to establish the see, through a promise to study the question, to an apparent ignoring of the matter altogether. Meanwhile, Bishop Laval wrote letters describing the difficulties of his position. Because there was no ordinary in New France, that is, a bishop whose jurisdiction was not deputed to him but was his ex officio, the Compagnie des Indes occidentales was preparing to send priests, set up parishes, and appoint priests to them. In addition, the colonists were contesting Laval's right to institute and collect tithes. When Rome resumed its study of the creation of the diocese in 1666, the king demanded that its establishment be carried out in accordance with the privileges of the Gallic church. In June 1668, Rome sent a model of a proposed bull to be examined in Paris. This was studied and sent back, but the question of the attachment of the diocese of Quebec to the archdiocese of Rouen remained. The next year brought an ironic twist: Bishop Laval wrote to Rome expressing his willingness to accept the attachment to Rouen, while at the same time Louis and Colbert decided to abandon the condition.

All now appeared to be proceeding smoothly toward the creation of the diocese, but one more hurdle remained. Despite his descent from one of the oldest and noblest families in France, François de Montmorency de Laval had no personal fortune, and the establishment of a bishopric was expensive. He wrote to Rome asking that the bulls be sent free and then went to Paris in 1671 to advance the cause. Bishop Laval did not succeed in obtaining his bulls gratis, but Rome did agree to reduce the cost. Even so, the matter took time, and the bulls were not sent until October 1674. In September the following year, the bishop returned to a Quebec that was now the seat of an episcopal see. Many changes had taken place during his absence, including the advent of a governor who saw the trading of liquor to the Natives as an economic necessity for the expansion of the fur trade. The bishop would need all his newly invested authority for the struggles about to take place. His first efforts on his return were devoted to the official establishment of his administration. But as soon as navigation opened the following spring, he set off to visit the local churches of his vast diocese and once more acquaint himself with conditions at first hand. By May 1676 his tour brought him to Montreal, where, in early June, he made his official visit to the Congregation.

The *Histoire de la Congrégation* suggests that Catherine Boni and Marguerite's niece Catherine Sommillard were formally received into the Congregation as candidates at this time. Apparently the bishop was impressed with what he saw of the resources and work of the small community and remembered it as he visited other settlements and villages. In August, after his return to Quebec, he issued the first canonical approbation of the Congrégation de Notre-Dame de Montréal. The document refers to the permission Laval had granted to the Congregation on 20 May 1669, but this new authorization had behind it the power now vested in him as bishop of Quebec.

The bishop writes of what he has observed of "Our dear daughter Marguerite Bourgeois and the women who have joined her and live in community on the Island of Montreal."[17] He describes them as having been "employed for several years, without payment, as schoolmistresses, raising the little girls in the fear of God and the practice of the Christian virtues, teaching them to read and write and other things of which they are capable." As in the statements prepared in support of Marguerite's application for the letters patent and the letters patent themselves, the bishop stresses that, while teaching gratuitously, the Congregation is self-supporting: "developed enough and can subsist from the farms and revenues they possess and from the work of their hands without being a burden on anyone." The members of the Congregation "offer themselves to fulfill the functions of schoolmistresses on the Island of Montreal as well as other places that will be arranged for this purpose and can provide for a schoolmistress, where we and our successors will judge necessary for the good of the church." To give the group strength and stability, the bishop is pleased "to approve and confirm it allowing them to continue the said functions of schoolmistresses living in community as *filles seculières de la Congrégation de Notre-Dame.*"

Other statements in the document make clear what motivates the bishop in giving approval to what was still a novel form of consecrated life for women:

After giving mature consideration to everything and knowing that one of the greatest goods we can obtain for our church, and the most effective means of conserving and increasing piety in Christian families is the instruction and good education of children; considering also the blessing that Our Lord has given the said Bourgeois and her companions in the said functions in the elementary schools where we have employed them and wishing to favour their zeal and contribute with all our power to their pious designs we have approved and approve the establishment by the said Bourgeois of the women who have joined her and will be admitted in the future, allowing them to live in community as *filles Seculières de la Congrégation de N.D.* observing the rules we will later present to them and to continue their service as schoolmistresses as much on the Island of Montreal as the other places to which we and our successors find opportune to send them.

He concludes with the insistence that he is not approving a form of "religious life," that is, cloistered life, either now or in the future, "which would be against our intentions and the end we have proposed, to support by this means the instruction of children in the country parishes." Whatever Bishop Laval's reservations might have been about *filles séculières,* they were overcome by his awareness of the needs of his vast New World diocese and the effectiveness of the Congregation in meeting them. The bishop's approval meant that although the members of the Congregation could not make solemn or public vows, they could live in community, they could teach, the group could increase its numbers, and they could move out to new places in a vast diocese that stretched from Hudson Bay to the Gulf of Mexico.

Before 1676 the only permanent residences of the sisters of the Congregation were the house in the area now known as Old Montreal and the farm at Pointe-Saint-Charles. In that year they established their first permanent missions beyond that boundary. The first new mission, the term usually employed to designate any place the sisters went to work outside the mother house, was established at a location invested with a particular significance for Marguerite Bourgeoys. This was the Native village that came to be known as the Mountain Mission, located near the site where de Maisonneuve and the first settlers had erected the cross on 6 January 1643 in thanksgiving for their deliverance from a threatened flood. There, soon after her arrival in 1653, Marguerite herself had found the banner sent by the Congrégation de Notre-Dame of Troyes and felt confirmed in her own vocation to Montreal.[18]

At the request of some of the Iroquois of Lake Ontario, the Sulpicians had established a mission at Kenté (now Trenton) as early as 1667 and from then on had gone out to work among Native tribes at a variety of places. Like other missionaries, they had come to the conclusion that travelling missions bore little lasting fruit and that it would be better to establish a permanent mission where the Natives could be taught to lead sedentary lives in the European style. The Jesuits established such a mission at La Prairie de la Magdelaine near Montreal in 1670. The site chosen for the establishment of the Sulpician mission on the island of Montreal was a piece of land that had been set aside for the cutting of firewood and around which some Huron families were already living. Part of it had been in a land grant made to Marguerite Bourgeoys by de Maisonneuve, which she had later exchanged with the Hôtel-Dieu and the Sulpicians for land in Old Montreal.

The site of the Mountain Mission can still be easily identified in modern Montreal by the continued presence of two stone towers in the grounds of the Grand Séminaire on Sherbrooke Street West near Atwater Avenue. However, those towers date from later in the seventeenth century; in 1776, when the first two members of the Congregation – according to Congregation tradition, Anne Meyrand and Catherine Boni – went there to teach the little Native girls, conditions were much more primitive. According to the *Histoire de la Congrégation,* "They were very poorly lodged at first; their shelter made of bark like those of the Indians was as poor and rustic as could be. They had a fire in the middle and the smoke escaped through a hole made in the roof that they were careful to cover with a piece of bark when the weather was bad."[19] The following year numbers at the mission were augmented when the mission at Kenté was closed and its population moved to Montreal. A Sulpician priest, Guillaume Bailly, also took up residence there.

The decision to locate the new mission at some little distance from the town was prompted, of course, by the desire to remove its inhabitants as much as possible from the evils of the brandy trade. The practice of trading brandy to the Native population was now the major source of conflict between religious and civil authority. In their attempts to influence legislation, the missionaries and the Native chiefs argued that the brandy trade had a degrading and demoralizing effect on aboriginal society. Moreover, rendering them drunk made the Natives much easier to cheat in bargaining for their furs. But the merchants and the civil authorities with whom they were associated argued that the trade was an economic necessity for New France, given that the English and the Dutch both engaged in it. The struggle was a bitter one, and the Récollets were supposedly returned to New France by Talon in order to serve as instruments of the secular government and to undermine Bishop Laval and the Jesuits. An ordinance of November 1668 permitted the sale of liquor to Natives but forbade them to become drunk and imposed penalties on them if they did so, with part of the fine going to the one who reported them. Frontenac permitted all established colonists to sell liquor to the Natives in their own houses. It was forbidden to take liquor out into the woods for trade in the Native villages, but this regulation was difficult to enforce. The Mountain Mission would eventually have to be moved even farther from Ville-Marie.

At the beginning, however, there were high hopes for the new mission, and it became an important area of activity for Marguerite Bourgeoys and her community. Writing after the Seven Years War, Montgolfier says: "It was in consideration of the great good reverting to the state and to Religion, and in consideration of the expense assumed by Sister Bourgeois and her community for this kind of good work, that the King of France, in 1676, attributed to the community of Sisters, on the state of his domain in Canada, a pension of two or three thousand livres paid regularly from that time until 1756 when it was entirely suppressed on the occasion of the last war."[20] This pension was the result of visits to the mission in which colonial officials were favourably impressed by the work being done there. In 1683 Jacques Demeulle, who had replaced Talon as intendant, wrote of the Native girls at the mission: "Two sisters of the Congregation ... are teaching them religion, having them sing in church, teaching them to read, to write, to speak French and everything suitable for girls. If His Majesty would grant a little fund of five or six hundred livres for the Indian girls of the Mountain, they could be taught to make stockings, knitted or in French stitch. They are naturally very skilful."[21]

Montgolfier also draws attention to even more important non-material advantages that flowed to the Congregation from the Mountain Mission: the expansion of its membership to include Native women. He observes: "Sister Bourgeois never ceased to support several Indian girls at this mission to form them in virtue and make them able to inspire their companions. She also supported several among the boarders of Ville-Marie, of whom some (there were at least two) having entered the Congregation, made themselves very useful to the Mission."[22] The two women of whom Montgolfier is speaking were Marie-Thérèse Gannensagouas and Marie-Barbe Atontinon.

More is known about the background of Marie-Thérèse than of Marie-Barbe, and it is a fascinating story. Her grandfather was François Thoronhiongo, a Huron who had been baptized by Jean de Brébeuf. Although he later was enslaved by the Iroquois in the village of Tsonnonthouan, he persevered in the Christian religion. After Tracy's arrival and the establishment of peace with the Iroquois, he moved to the Native village where the Mountain Mission was to be established. He played an important role at the mission until his death in 1690 – reportedly at the age of one hundred – renowned for his devotion and his charity. With him came a married son with his family and a granddaughter, Gannensagouas. She was adopted by Courcelle, then governor of New France, before his departure for the home country in 1672 and given as her Christian name that of the queen, Marie-Thérèse. The child was entrusted to the care of Marguerite Bourgeoys and the Congregation. Although the *Histoire de la Congrégation* and François Vachon de Belmont picture Marie-Thérèse as being educated at the Mountain Mission,[23] both Montgolfier's statement and the dates involved would suggest that the governor's protégée was raised in the Congregation house in Ville-Marie. The 1,000 livres settled on her by the governor was intended as a dowry when she married. It had been invested for her by Marguerite Bourgeoys and tripled in value in the next decade, another example of Marguerite's business acumen. In 1679, however, Marie-Thérèse chose to enter the Congregation, rather than to marry, and she would eventually become a teacher at the Mountain Mission.

The same year, a second Native woman, Marie-Barbe Atontinon d'Onotais, also entered the community. According to the records of the Congregation, she was an Iroquois, born in 1656 in the village of Onnontagué, who came to the Mountain Mission in 1676 at the age of twenty. Three years later she was accepted as a candidate in the Congregation. Because of the destruction of so many of the Congregation documents from this period, nothing is known of her work in the community, though Montgolfier seems to imply that she too taught at the Mountain Mission.

The Mountain Mission was not the only new Congregation mission established in 1676; another was founded at Champlain. The *Histoire de la Congrégation* cites as evidence a document of that year signed by Marguerite Bourgeoys "for myself and for the other sisters of our Congregation who are at Champlain and elsewhere."[24] Marie Raisin was the teacher assigned to this first fixed mission off the island of Montreal. The proximity of Champlain to Trois-Rivières made it an extension of the travelling missions Marie Raisin had undertaken in the area since soon after her arrival in Canada in 1659. The identity of her companion at this time is unknown, and only Marie Raisin herself is mentioned in the 1681 census. The mission had to be given up in 1683 because the region was too poor to support it, but it would be re-established by 1697. Histories of the area emphasize the respect and affection with which Marie Raisin was regarded. Since they speak of the sorrow occasioned in the region by the news of her death in 1691, she perhaps continued some kind of contact with the area.

If Marguerite Bourgeoys could see life expanding in some areas, there were others where it was drawing in. The arrival of the ships from France in the spring of 1677 brought news that must have touched her deeply. The previous September, too late for the report to cross the Atlantic that year, Paul de Chomedey de Maisonneuve had died in Paris at the age of sixty-four. No doubt she found comfort in her faith that "life is changed not taken away." Still, Marguerite must have known the sadness that is part of the universal human experience as age removes those who have shared our past most closely and the world becomes a lonelier and emptier place. Of the trio from Champagne who played so central and vital a role in the origins of Montreal, now only she remained. At the time of his death, the former governor was still living in the little house rented from the Pères de la Doctrine chrétienne, where Marguerite had visited him. His servant, Louis Frin, was still in attendance.

De Maisonneuve's death had material consequences for the Congrégation de Notre-Dame. On 6 September 1675 he had officially invested Philippe de Turmenyes with the power of attorney given him by Marguerite Bourgeoys in 1671. This transfer of responsibility suggests that there was already a deterioration in the health of the former governor. Philippe de Turmenyes, who appears to have been de Maisonneuve's closest friend, was named in his will as executor of his estate. This will was signed at 9:30 on the evening before the former governor's death. The first and largest bequest was one of 2,000 livres to the "congregation Notre Dame de Montreal in New France of which Marguerite Bourgeois is superior." The will also includes legacies of 1,000 livres to the Hospitallers in Montreal and to the "Congregation de la Ville de Troyes," where his sister and his niece were religious. There is evidence that the former governor had never lost his love of music: a lute figures in the inventory made after his death, and a legacy of 200 livres went to Robert Caron, master lute-player. The documents describing the sealing of the effects and the taking of the inventory report the sudden appearance and objections of Marie Bouvot.

This married niece of Maisonneuve was dissatisfied with the provision made for her in the will and intent on upsetting it on the grounds of undue influence.[25] She and her sister, a nun at the Congrégation de Notre-Dame in Troyes, were both daughters of de Maisonneuve's sister Jacqueline. The incident suggests that not even two murders had dampened the enthusiasm of the family for litigation over inheritances. Either Marie Bouvot abandoned her attempt or it proved unsuccessful: Turmenyes remained executor and also continued to exercise the power of attorney for the Congrégation de Notre-Dame de Montréal in France.[26]

Meanwhile, in Montreal, through a decision made long ago, de Maisonneuve was making one other last gift to Ville-Marie, a bell for Notre-Dame-de-Bon-Secours chapel. Marguerite Bourgeoys recorded, "That bell which weighs a little less than 100 pounds was cast from a broken cannon which I obtained from M. de Maisonneuve. M. Souart paid for the casting."[27] The transformation of a cannon into a church bell, recalling the biblical imagery of beating swords into ploughshares and spears into pruning hooks, seems a fitting memorial for Montreal's first governor, who had tried so hard to obtain peace for the little colony he had founded.

The year 1678 saw the opening of yet another mission of the Congregation on the island of Montreal, this time at its easternmost tip. The settlement at Pointe-aux-Trembles had begun after the arrival of the Carignan-Salières regiment seemed to guarantee a little more safety and stability. At first, the Sulpicians came there to celebrate mass in the house of one of the colonists, but eventually a chapel was built which was blessed on 13 March 1678. Two sisters of the Congregation were sent to teach the children and took up residence in a borrowed house near the church.

If the Congregation was able to undertake these new missions, it was because its numbers were increasing, and this through local, not European, recruitment. Besides the two Native women already mentioned, Ursule and Marguerite Gariépy, two sisters born in Quebec, the elder in 1658 and the other in 1660, made their way to the Congregation in Montreal. As they had grown up in Château-Richer, where their family had taken up residence, the sisters must have come to know the community either as boarders in the school in Montreal or through the travelling missions. After them came the entrances into the Congregation of the first Montrealers, several of them with roots stretching back to the very founding of Ville-Marie.

The first Montrealer known to have entered the Congregation was Marie Barbier, youngest daughter of Gilbert Barbier, the carpenter who had arrived in Montreal in that first summer of 1642 and had helped Marguerite Bourgeoys re-erect the cross on the mountain shortly after her arrival in 1653. Marie later confided to Charles de Glandelet, her spiritual director, that her parents were not much in favour of her entry into the Congregation "because of lack of means." This statement indicates that Marguerite Bourgeoys had some difficulty in implementing her wish about dowries in her community.[28] For her, lack of dowry should never be an obstacle to the reception of a candidate into the Congregation: "I always held to the purpose which we had hoped to realize in Troyes – that there would be a refuge for those girls who had all the qualities but who could not become religious for lack of money."[29] In Marie Barbier's case, her parents agreed, on her entry into the community, to a dowry of 300 livres to be paid out of their estate at the time of their death. They were also to supply ten *minots* of wheat each year for the next four years.

Marie Barbier's contract was not, like earlier agreements made when women entered the Congregation, just to live in community and to teach. In wording that appears again in the contract of Françoise Le Moyne in 1680, Marie Barbier is described as wishing "to give and consecrate herself to the service of God and of the Blessed Virgin in the *congregation des filles de Nostre dame de Montreal*"; a 1684 document says that Marie "has consecrated herself to the service of God under the protection of the Blessed Virgin."[30] These documents reflect the promises that its members must have made in the Congregation at this time. The contracts made by some of the men who became *donnés*, or brothers of the Congregation, in the same period contain some similar language – they give themselves to the service of God and the Blessed Virgin – but the word "consecrate" does not appear in these formulas.[31] Marie Barbier later confided to her spiritual director that her brother Nicolas helped to persuade her parents to allow her entry into the Congregation. It has sometimes been assumed that he offered financial help, but this does not appear so in the documents. Her greatest difficulty might have been objections from her mother, who less than twenty years before had prevented Marie's older sister, Adrienne, from becoming the first Canadian to enter the Hospitallers in Montreal.[32]

There is another sign in these documents that the Congregation was taking on some of the more formal aspects of a religious community. Remarks made by Marie Barbier to Charles de Glandelet, as well as Françoise Le Moyne's reception contract, make it clear that by this time candidates to the Congregation went through some kind of clothing ceremony when they entered their period of probation in the community and hence that the sisters were wearing a habit. When this practice began is not known, nor are there any detailed descriptions of the habit from this period. The earliest visible illustration of it is the Le Ber portrait of Marguerite Bourgeoys, done at the time of her death in 1700.

There are two statements about the dress of the sisters in the writings of Marguerite Bourgeoys, and both are intended as inspirational texts. Comparing the dress of the sisters with that of the Blessed Virgin, Marguerite writes:

Her dress was a long white robe, worn simply; she wore a belt, and on her head, a veil. Her robe signifies to us her purity; her belt, the care she took to let nothing escape her in performing her duty of charity, the veil [her concern] not to be seen by the world except through necessity. The sisters have a long black dress to remind them that they come into the world darkened by original sin; a woolen belt to remind them to subdue their passions; a woolen headdress as a sign that they have left all that could please them in the world.[33]

However, in another place, Marguerite observes:

It seems to me that ... it is a great weakness on our part to wish to be singled out by the people of the world because of particular clothing or some visible mark. When we left the world, we ought to have left its ideas and its concerns behind us and we ought to have no solicitude for the exterior. Let us be known by our works, by the sound education of children, by the good instructions we give them, by the edification of our neighbour, by Christian modesty and detachment from all things, by our love for God's word and by virtue. It is not by their dress that men are known, but by their works.[34]

The editor of *The Writings of Marguerite Bourgeoys* was troubled by the apparent contradiction between these two passages, but perhaps the contradiction is not so great as it seems at first glance. The first passage is a pious reflection, conventional for the time, on a habit that had become an established fact. In the second, Marguerite Bourgeoys voices a basic conviction from her heart. Behind the second statement lies her strong distrust of ostentatious piety and her insistence that the members of the Congregation seek no

honours or preferential treatment that would separate them from
the ordinary people. It is not a rejection of some kind of uniform
dress. In fact, as many inventories of the period show, the form
of dress that was the first habit of members of the Congregation
was so close to that worn by the women around them – minus
the jewellery, coloured ribbons, frills, and furbelows used by their
contemporaries on special occasions – that the sisters would have
stood out only by the absence of these ornaments. By the 1690s at
latest, they wore the plain silver cross that can be seen in the Le Ber
portrait of Marguerite Bourgeoys.[35] Otherwise, their dress was like
that of their neighbours, plain, serviceable, worn day in and day
out.[36] Marie Morin wrote in 1697, "They also have a habit that is
black on top and grey underneath [petticoats], that is very modest
and distinguishes them from the world."[37]

Like Marie Barbier, the next young woman to enter the Congregation after her also had a connection with the first days of the
Hospitallers in Montreal. Marie Denis, who came from Quebec,
where she had been educated by the Ursulines, was the younger
sister of Catherine Denis, the second Canadian to enter the Hospitallers of St Joseph in Montreal. Marie Denis was followed into
the Congrégation de Notre-Dame by Madeleine Bourbault, who
had been born in Charlesbourg, and then by another Montrealer,
Marie Charly, daughter of Marie Dumesnil, the very young prospective bride entrusted to the care of Marguerite Bourgeoys on her
first voyage to Canada. She was followed by Françoise Le Moyne,
daughter of Mathurine Godé, the youngest of the little group of
settlers who founded Montreal in 1642, and of Jacques Le Moyne,
member of what was becoming one of Montreal's most distinguished
families. Another candidate, Thérèse Rémy, born in France in 1661,
had been brought to Canada by her uncle, Pierre Rémy, a priest
of Saint-Sulpice and ecclesiastical superior of the Congregation at
this time. Finally came Catherine Charly, younger sister of Marie.
Marguerite Bourgeoys had known some of these women from earliest childhood and had prepared them for their first communion.
They chose to enter the Congregation, although she promised them
only "poverty and simplicity,"[38] because she communicated to them
something of her own inspiration: that to work for the Christian
education of women was an important way of ensuring that Christ
would not have died in vain; that they had a vital role to play in the
building of their church and their society.

There is evidence that life in the Congregation could be challenging for some of these young candidates. Marie Barbier told Glandelet several years later:

I do not understand how, being young and weak as I was, I could do all the work I had for five years running. I had two cows to care for from which I took milk and made butter; I led them out in the morning and went almost half a league away, being a laughing stock for those who had known me in the world as I walked through the town. Sometimes I carried the wheat to the mill on my back and brought the flour back the same way. I did the baking alone ... I taught school and I made three batches of bread a day during the summer, two or three times a week. The days I didn't bake I sifted. I got up two or three hours before the Community to have a batch ready before eight o'clock that is the time of the pupils' mass.[39]

Some of these first Canadian sisters would die young, but others would ensure the survival of the Congregation after the death of the founder and carry it almost into the middle of the new century.

The list of women entering the Congregation and the order of their entrance in drawn from the census of 1681. "Rank" in the Congrégation de Notre-Dame and the assignment of a community number has always depended on the date of religious profession and, within a group making profession together, by chronological age. That appears to have been a guiding principle in the compiling of the census list. Jamet pointed out that this list includes only the first known Canadian entries and that, like the Hospitallers, the Congregation might have had earlier candidates who did not stay. This interpretation is born out by at least some evidence. In a notarial document of 1676 concerning a dispute about some calves, Marie Touchard is described as a "fille de la Congrégation."[40] On 5 February 1679, however, she married Jean Caillou-Baron. Since he had become a *donné* of the Congregation the previous year, it appears that an attachment had developed between the two while he worked for the Congregation. They seem to have maintained good relations with the Congregation, of which their daughter, Marie-Gabrielle, later became a member.[41] Although departure from the Congregation was much easier at this time than it would become at the end of the century, this may have been an isolated incident. All of the sisters listed in the census of 1681 remained in the Congregation.[42]

Yet, despite all the signs around her of expansion and new life, of growth and of hope, all was not well with Marguerite Bourgeoys herself. This was so much the case that she decided to embark on another trip to France. The voyage was not, as far as is known, attended by any of the dangers and mishaps of some of the earlier trips. There was no plague and no lost luggage, no sick to care for or children's bodies to bury at sea. But it seems to have been the most disheartening of all the voyages undertaken by Marguerite Bourgeoys, and it ended in apparent failure. It points forward to the period of immense moral suffering she was to endure at the end of the next decade.

CHAPTER FOUR

THE LAST VOYAGE TO FRANCE
1679–1680

*In 1680, Madame Perrot needed to go to France. With the consent of
the sisters, I offered to go with her. But it was my mental anguish
which made me undertake this voyage more than the pretext I used –
the Rules and Bishop Laval who was then in Paris.*[1]

Changing conditions now made it advisable, some would even have
said urgent, for Marguerite Bourgeoys and her companions to elaborate and obtain ecclesiastical approval of a rule of life. The members of the Congregation were bound to the community by civil
contract and, it would seem from references in the writings of Marguerite Bourgeoys and from the discussions that were to take place
with Bishop Saint-Vallier in the 1690s, by "promises" made when
they were formally received into the Congregation. If any of them
made private vows, as Marguerite Bourgeoys had done in 1643,
the content of these would have been determined between the sister
and her spiritual director. They appear to have followed the rule
prepared by Antoine Gendret for the little experimental community
that Marguerite Bourgeoys and two companions had attempted to
establish in Troyes in the 1640s, modified and developed to suit
conditions in Montreal. Not all of this rule of life would yet have
found its way into writing. Certain beliefs and practices would have
developed according to custom and been transmitted simply in the
process of living them. Now, however, given the geographical expansion of the Congregation and the entry of young Canadians,
certain questions became pressing. How could unity be achieved
and maintained when some of its members would be living at some

distance from the rest of the community? How should the new entrants into the Congregation be formed?

Montgolfier says that for the early Congregation, Marguerite was herself "the living rule and a model of the most sublime perfection."[2] But the force of Marguerite's personality and the rule drawn up by Father Gendret in Troyes nearly forty years earlier were no longer enough in a growing and spreading community. Marguerite saw the Virgin Mary, Christ's mother, as the most perfect model of Christian discipleship and repeatedly emphasized that "the love of God and neighbour includes all the law,"[3] but not all the entrants to the Congregation had the same spiritual gifts as the founder or her rare ability to infuse practical day-to-day affairs with spiritual insight. In addition, even if the young Canadian women now entering the Congregation were ready to face the insecurity accepted by Marguerite and her first companions, their families wanted to see them more firmly established. A more formal structure and clearer approbation of their way of life was becoming increasingly necessary. Yet, as she makes clear, the rule was not Marguerite's first concern on her last voyage to France in 1679–80.

Although on this visit to her homeland, Marguerite did indeed seek advice about a rule for the Congregation, she indicates in both references to the event and in her writings that, for her, consultation about the rule was not the main purpose of her trip. Besides the statement quoted at the beginning of this chapter, she also wrote: "In 1680, I returned to France on the pretext of our Rules but it was because of my great suffering at seeing that everything was not as I would have wished."[4] What were the nature and cause of the mental suffering to which she alludes here? Her characteristic reluctance to elaborate on her feelings means that they can only be conjectured from knowledge of the general situation, from statements elsewhere in her writings, and from later developments in the Congregation.

In 1680 Montreal was no longer the fragile settlement in constant peril to which she had come in 1653. But while no longer under daily threat from the Iroquois, the island was governed by a man who exploited the settlers, harassed those who challenged him, and conducted his own clandestine operations in the fur trade from the island at the juncture of the St Lawrence and Ottawa Rivers, where he could intercept the fur-laden canoes of the Natives before they reached Montreal. François-Marie Perrot had obtained from the Sulpicians his appointment as governor of Montreal through the influence of Jean Talon, whose niece he had married. He then also obtained a royal appointment and used it to ignore or defy their seigneurial authority. The moral tone of the settlement had deteriorated too. It must have been a sad day for Marguerite Bourgeoys when, in late August 1679, she and Elisabeth de la Bertache, the sister in charge of the boarding school, were called upon to testify at the trial of a man accused of the sexual molestation of his young daughters. This man was not a new arrival but a member of the great recruitment with whom Marguerite herself had arrived in 1653, a man who had served as a member of the militia of Our Lady in the days of de Maisonneuve.[5]

But Marguerite had more immediate sources of doubt and anxiety. She was living through the beginning stages of the process through which all new communities must pass if they are to endure. This is the process of institutionalization, when the insights of the founders take on a form more accessible to entrants not capable of the same degree of heroism. In the case of the Congregation, the situation was complicated by the fact that, like a few other groups in France, it was so radically different from the traditional communities of women already in existence. All of these were enclosed or cloistered, even those that taught or cared for the sick. Marguerite Bourgeoys was deeply committed to the same values as the cloistered communities: she rejected the search for wealth and for worldly honours and recognition; she believed that life should be permeated with a spirit of prayer. But she believed that these values could be lived in the midst of the world at the service of the larger Christian community. Marguerite's first companions were French women like herself. When they committed themselves to the Congregation, they made a radical break with their families and their past. As Canadians entered the community, this was no longer the case. Even when they left Montreal to go on mission, the country could never be as strange to them as it had been to the women who came from France. And if they remained in Montreal, they would be living, in some cases quite literally, next door to their families. Marguerite expected the members of her Congregation to be involved in the life of the society around them but also to be detached from it. Being so could become more difficult for new members bound to that society by ties of blood and family interest.

It is abundantly clear in Marguerite's writings that the virtue of poverty was extremely important to her. The way in which that virtue should be practised in the Congregation seems to have been one of the principal sources of conflict and misunderstanding between Marguerite and the sisters and had made its first appearance in her reluctance to build the large house that replaced the stable school. Perhaps, in a sense, this conflict reflected one within Marguerite herself. Passages in her writings show that she certainly knew and appreciated the arguments that could be made against the ideal she was attempting to practise and to hold up to her community. Concerning mortification, she writes: "Experience teaches me that we very easily return to the comforts of the body, that nature comes to terms with them sometimes after a few small scruples which are over in a moment, especially when we feel obliged to do so by some soothing words ... our poor nature never says 'Enough' ... For it is easy for us to consider whatever pleases us as necessary."[6] Elsewhere, in developing the contrast between divine and human prudence, she recognizes how easy it is to justify the acquisition of material goods and advantages as necessary to the well-being of the members of the community and the success of its work: "Human prudence says that we must serve God but that He is quite willing to have us put something aside for old age and illness; He wishes us to have what we need. Our health is better when we are well fed; we pray better when we are comfortable; to sleep on a hard bed can cause infirmity; to suffer contempt often does much harm and it gives others too much freedom to commit sin."[7]

Marguerite Bourgeoys believed that poverty is primarily and above all an attitude of mind and heart, a detachment from material things. However, she also believed that in the Congregation this spiritual attitude would have real material consequences, that the sisters should live in great simplicity making use of the goods of this world only as they were necessary for their life and work. For her, poverty was the consequence and evidence of an absolute trust in God, of the conviction that "in their need God does not fail those who are faithful to Him."[8] She was convinced that only through the activity of God could the work of the Congregation be effective and fruitful and that this activity was directly related to a detachment from material possessions. Her writings contain a passage in which she compares the Congregation to the college of the

Apostles, though only "as I would compare a snowflake which falls in the shape of a star and melts at the least warmth, to a star in the firmament." She continues: "The apostles went without a purse or second tunic. The sisters of the Congregation go to teach without any assurance of their livelihood and with as little clothing as they can manage. The apostles trusted in God who fed them when they had no food. The sisters of the Congregation leave the concern for all their needs to the Blessed Virgin and they will never lack what is necessary." The Apostles, she says, were "common men who were held in little esteem by the world," but they "were sent in the name of Our Lord and they worked wonders."[9]

For Marguerite Bourgeoys, the practice of poverty was essential to the following of Christ, whom she recognized in the poor among whom she lived. To share their conditions was a necessary consequence of leading a completely Christian life. An aspect of Congregation life that was to cause her immense distress after her resignation as superior was the failure of the community to share a common bread with their servants, a practice that had a sacramental significance for her: "For a long time now, we have been baking bread like that which is sold in the bakeries; we have brown bread for the servants and white bread for the community. Formerly, all the bread was the same."[10]

Had Marguerite Bourgeoys not been such a capable woman, had her Congregation not attracted other capable and hard-working women, problems about the practice of poverty would never have arisen. The sisters would have had no choice but to live in abject poverty. It is ironic that the very qualities that won the approval of the civil authorities and guaranteed the material survival of the Congregation also produced conditions that seemed to Marguerite a threat to the spiritual ideals with which she had begun. Obviously, she did not see a rule as the answer to the difficulties she faced. She knew that attitudes of mind and heart cannot be legislated. But if she saw the Congregation as falling short of the ideal that had taken form for her more than thirty years before, she felt responsible. As in the case of her decision to live with the filles du roi in 1663, she believed that she was failing to make the sisters understand.

There is some indication that Marguerite Bourgeoys believed that her own position of leadership in the community was being undermined at this time. In her published writings, it immediately follows the passage describing her difficulties with the sisters at the time of the arrival of the filles du roi and that describing the conflict about the building of the larger house. She writes:

About 1677 or 1678, we had to send a certain woman to a property to look after it, with another younger woman. Our [ecclesiastical] superior said: "I would not send the woman you are sending." I did not answer, but told the sisters I could not do anything else and I let it pass. The sisters wished to receive this woman as a sister, but that could not be, and I told the reason to the bishop and to M. Souart. This caused a great deal of trouble among the sisters and I believe that from that time on the sisters lost confidence in me and I lost the freedom to speak to them.[11]

This passage appears to describe the seeds of a situation that would reach a crisis in the 1690s. Certainly, it indicates that Marguerite Bourgeoys was beginning to question her effectiveness as superior and that the challenge to her authority came first from the sisters recruited in France, since the date, if it is accurate, is too early for the Canadians to have been responsible.

The fact that Marguerite describes herself as obtaining the permission of the sisters to make a trip to France at this time is another sign that life in the Congregation was becoming more formalized. Before her departure, someone had to be selected to act as superior during her absence or even, Montgolfier suggests, to replace her permanently. He places at this moment an event recorded in Glandelet's biography of Marguerite Bourgeoys. Glandelet writes, "Sister Bourgeoys also said that once when the Community was holding an election, they unanimously chose the Blessed Virgin for their first Superior, Establisher, Foundress and their true Mother." This event is cited in both biographies as evidence of the extent to which the sisters had absorbed Marguerite's idea that Mary was patroness, founder, and first superior of the Congregation.[12] This may well be a valid interpretation of what happened. But it is also evidence that no leader apart from Marguerite Bourgeoys had yet emerged in the Congregation. Nevertheless, a temporary superior had still to be chosen. The *Histoire de la Congrégation* reports that Geneviève du Rosoy was elected assistant (and therefore acting superior during Marguerite's absence), that Anne Hiou continued to be responsible for new entrants to the Congregation, that Elisabeth de la Bertache took over direction of the school, replacing Geneviève du Rosoy, and that Marguerite Sommillard became bursar.[13] If this account is accurate, then the governing structure of the Congregation had already taken the form that was to persist for many years to come.

Montgolfier also says that it was at this time that Marguerite composed a prayer to the Blessed Virgin which is quoted by Glandelet immediately after he describes the election of Mary as superior. After addressing Mary by the titles mentioned above, the prayer makes two requests. For this life, it asks for "the lights and graces of the Holy Spirit that we may work for the enlightenment of the young women and the school children who have been entrusted to us in virtue of our profession." And it ends with the plea that all the women then in the Congregation, all who would one day become members, and all who would help them advance in the spiritual life might be numbered among the elect.[14]

The date of Marguerite's departure from Montreal on the first stage of her journey is not known, but it was sometime after she signed the document admitting Marie Barbier into her period of probation in the Congregation on 11 August 1679. She may have been forced to spend some considerable time in the capital waiting for passage. Certainly, she was still there in November, as two of her letters illustrate.

The first of these is dated 5 November and was written to Abbé Rémy, ecclesiastical superior of the Congregation in Montreal. After dealing with various small business matters and errands entrusted to her, she says: "I thank God for the good care that the Bishop takes of our little community and for the persons He inspires in regard to our rule."[15] It was probably this sentence that led Montgolfier to the erroneous supposition that Marguerite saw Bishop Laval in Quebec before her departure and that the bishop with whom she was to have difficulty in France was Laval's successor. Since the bishop was already in Paris at this time, Marguerite's statement implies that he had encouraged a favourable attitude toward the Congregation among the officials with whom she had to deal in preparation for her departure. For, as on her previous voyage, Marguerite carried with her to France testimonials from a variety of colonial officials, and the letter describes some of the difficulties she had encountered in soliciting those she obtained in Quebec, where the usual pettiness and pitfalls of colonial politics were apparent. When she showed Frontenac the testimonial she had received from the procurator general, it made him "very angry. He said the procurator general could not issue testimonials in these matters." Father Claude

Dablon, superior of the Jesuits in New France, wanted to help but told her he feared a letter from him would be more likely to harm than to help her, an indication of the current attitudes toward the Jesuits at court.

Marguerite's reference to showing Count Frontenac testimonials she had already received is a clue as to why the testimonials she was given are so remarkably similar in content and wording. Their likeness springs not just from an awareness on the part of the writers of what would impress the authorities in France but also from the fact that one could use the other as a model. Like the documents she obtained to support her application for letters patent, the new documents stress that the Congregation is self-supporting and that its members offer instruction gratis and are a burden to no one. They educate their pupils not only in Christian doctrine but in reading, writing, and arithmetic and also in various kinds of handiwork that will enable them to earn their living. There are also some new elements. Jacques Duchesneau had noted in 1678 that "they are expanding in both the French and the Indian settlements." There is mention of the boarding school and particular praise of the work at the Mountain Mission. References to the good use made of funds already allocated by the king suggest the hope of obtaining further financial support for the work of the Congregation.

The conclusion of this letter again illustrates the uncertainty of departure dates, from the Canadian side of the Atlantic as well as from France. Marguerite writes, "I went to the ship this morning with Madame Perrot to put her chests and her clothing on board, believing that we would have to set sail tomorrow. But now it will not be until Tuesday. It can well be postponed again, so that I cannot tell you the day." It was fortunate that she felt able to add, "It will be when God wills it," for she was still in Quebec on 11 November, as another letter to Abbé Rémy shows.[16] The arrival in France, then, must have taken place very late in the year. It is perhaps a measure of Marguerite's adaptability that her companion on this trip was Madeleine Laguide Meynier, niece of Jean Talon and wife of the rather shady governor of Montreal, certainly a contrast with Jeanne Mance, her companion on the voyage of 1658. The two parted company at La Rochelle, where Marguerite's first act was to seek help for what she has described as the real motive for her journey: her spiritual distress. As always, her statement is terse and reveals no details about the nature of either the distress from which she was suffering or the advice she was given: "I spoke with a Capuchin who restored my peace of mind very quickly."[17]

Was it the memory of the comfort she had found in a Capuchin church at Nantes in 1653 that led her once more to this Franciscan community? Again, she has left us no clue. Marguerite would have known the Capuchins in Troyes, for from 1610 they were established in the Croncels district within the boundaries of her native parish of Saint-Jean-au-Marché.[18] Unless she is giving a date ("we arrived in Montreal on the feast of St Michael"), the saints mentioned by Marguerite in her surviving writings are those associated with the life of Jesus in the New Testament or in apocryphal writings about Mary. There is one exception and that is Francis of Assisi. Writing of the hardships a member of the Congregation must be ready to endure, she asks rhetorically, "Is Saint Francis reproached for having his friars go barefoot?"[19] Obviously, she felt a considerable affinity with the spirit of simplicity and poverty characteristic of the Capuchin community. In early seventeenth-century France, its churches had become favoured places of prayer for many of the devout, attracted by their cleanliness and by the use of flowers on the altar as well as by the simplicity of their chants and services. Contact with the Capuchin friars could only help confirm Marguerite in her own convictions about evangelical poverty. When she finally did resign as superior of the Congregation in the last decade of the century, she spoke of having made and often repeated a promise to God "not to give up the office in which He had placed me for all the pain that I could suffer."[20] Perhaps the support and encouragement she received from this unnamed Capuchin helped her make such a promise. Perhaps, on the contrary, it made her resolve to resign and hold elections after her return to Montreal. She gives us no hint.

Having found some solace in her spiritual difficulties, Marguerite Bourgeoys felt free to turn her attention and efforts to the business matters she had to conclude in France. Her first problem was to get to Paris, since, as on previous voyages, she had very little money, the economy of Montreal at this time not being based on money. She records: "I was advised to take the coach because of the [kind of] people who travelled with the cart drivers." The coach fare was beyond her means, but, as on other journeys, she encountered generosity she would again have described as the providential care of God. A group of men from New France, which included the Jesuit missionary Jacques Frémin and two other priests, offered her a place in a coach they had hired at a lower rate. "Through their kindness," she says, "I had sleeping accommodations for very little." But she was concerned not to trespass too far on their hospitality. Though the group wanted her to share their food, she declined: "Each day, I took with me whatever I had left over from my supper and I did not get out of the coach except to sleep." The group had to get up very early on these dark winter mornings in order for each of the priests to celebrate mass before they continued their journey. Marguerite was now almost sixty years old and no longer had the resilience she displayed on earlier trips. It is scarcely surprising that by the time they reached Paris, she was, she says, "somewhat ill."[21] Yet once again she describes herself as finding friends and kindness.

On her arrival in the capital, Marguerite went first to the house of Mademoiselle de Bellevue, the cousin of Jeanne Mance with whom she had stayed before her departure for Canada in 1653. Philippe de Turmenyes, de Maisonneuve's friend and executor, had been confirmed as agent for the temporal affairs of the Congregation in France in September 1677 after the news of de Maisonneuve's death had reached Montreal. When he learned that Marguerite Bourgeoys was in Paris, he sent a servant and a sedan chair to fetch her. "He had a room prepared and treated me as though I were his sister," says Marguerite. "I stayed there until my health was restored."[22] Later she went to stay with a new religious community called the Filles de la Croix, just off the rue Saint-Antoine. This was a good place to regain her strength: although it lay in the heart of the city, the complex occupied by the community consisted of several buildings with gardens and inner courts. Marguerite was certainly out and about by 1 February 1680, for on that day she deposited a business document with a Paris notary.[23] One of her first acts after her recovery was to call upon Bishop Laval, but his reaction to her presence in Paris came as a great shock and a source of unanticipated difficulties: "I went to pay my respects to Bishop Laval who told me I had done wrong in making the journey for the sake of the Rule and that he did not find it the right time for me to bring back women [for the Congregation]."[24]

It was unfortunate but perhaps not surprising that Marguerite Bourgeoys found her bishop so discouraging, for she had approached him at a very bad moment. Laval had left Quebec in the second week of November 1678. (One of his last acts before his departure had concerned the Congregation: he signed the act attaching the chapel of Notre-Dame-de-Bon-Secours to the parish of Notre-Dame in Montreal.) The circumstances that led him to make the journey to France were scarcely happy ones; nor had events since his arrival given him much cause for rejoicing. He was finding himself on the losing side in disputes he believed put the entire future of the church in New France at stake.

Just before Bishop Laval's return to his diocese in 1675, the king had reorganized the Conseil souverain at Quebec. The governor, the bishop, and the intendant were members ex-officio, with the intendant acting as president. In addition, there were to be seven other councillors appointed for life by the king. These measures were intended to prevent future conflicts like those Frontenac had caused by his flagrant abuse of power during his first three years in New France. They were not to be completely successful.

The bishop had also found, on that return, that Talon had brought the Récollets into his diocese, purportedly to undermine the influence of the bishop and the Jesuits. On the two main issues dividing the religious and secular authorities, the trade in spirits and the creation of parishes and the tithe, the Récollets supported the positions of the secular authorities. They have even been accused of going so far as to spread rumours in France that the real reason for the Jesuits' opposition to the brandy trade was their desire to keep their own monopoly on it. Bishop Laval had sent Abbé Jean Dudouyt to defend the Canadian church at court. The bishop had obtained an opinion from the theologians at the Sorbonne making the giving or trading of liquor with a Native in sufficient quantities to make him drunk a reserved sin, one for which only the bishop could give absolution. His opponents turned to the theologians at the University of Toulouse and obtained a contrary opinion: the bishop of Quebec could not legally make the sale of spirits a mortal sin, much less a reserved sin. In an attempt to settle the dispute, the king ordered Frontenac to convoke twenty of the leading inhabitants of Canada to give an opinion on the trade in spirits. Since most of the twenty were engaged in commerce, the outcome was predictable: at a meeting held on 28 October 1678, the majority of them declared themselves in favour of complete freedom for the liquor trade. One notable exception among the five settlers who opposed the majority opinion was Jacques Le Ber of Montreal, reputedly the richest man in New France, whose children were later to have important connections with the Congrégation de Notre-Dame.

It was at that point that, despite his failing health, Bishop Laval decided to go to France himself to try to put the case to the king. There he found that even his best efforts were able to accomplish little: the final result was a very unsatisfactory compromise. On 24 May 1679 the king published an ordinance forbidding the trading of liquor outside the French settlements. This meant that the traders could not legally carry liquor out to the Native villages. In return, Laval promised to bring the question of reserved sin in accordance with the ordinance. This was certainly not the decision that the bishop had hoped and striven for in his twenty years in New France. However, all too aware that politics is the art of the possible, he had to accept it as the most that could be achieved.

Nor was the bishop to encounter any more success on the other issue close to his heart. In 1663 Bishop Laval had obtained royal approval for setting up the seminary of Quebec. While this institution would undertake the education and training of young priests, it was also to be something much more. Through the seminary, Bishop Laval intended to inaugurate a system suited to the needs of New France that he believed would eliminate the many evils attached to the manner of holding ecclesiastical benefices in the Old World. The seminary was to be a community of secular priests who could be sent out as they were needed to serve as parish priests or to fulfill other functions and who could also be recalled. Tithes would be paid to the seminary, not to individual parishes, and the seminary would provide for the needs of its priests "in sickness and in health." Members of the seminary were to pool all their wealth and property.

All this too was called into question in the winter of 1678–79, criticized, and violently attacked. The bishop was accused of opposing the creation of parishes. In fact, until he became the ordinary in 1675, he had not had the power to do so, and afterwards he was limited by the lack of means in most areas to set up parishes of reasonable size able to provide for a parish priest. However, despite all the bishop's protestations, in May 1679 the king signed an edict that provided that in the diocese of Quebec the tithes would go to the priest of a fixed parish, in which he would be established permanently.

This decision, like that relating to the liquor trade, was heartbreaking for the bishop. Indeed, his acceptance of these defeats, his effort to carry on and still do all within his powers for the well-being of the church in New France despite betrayal and failure, is one more indication of the inaccuracy, not to say injustice, of the common image of Bishop Laval as always quarrelsome and intransigent in his dealings with the secular authorities.[25] But it was a sad and discouraged man whom Marguerite Bourgeoys went to call on in early 1680. Given these circumstances, it is perhaps not surprising that when he saw her, he was not prepared to add a non-traditional congregation in Ville-Marie to his other problems with the court.

When Marguerite wrote of her interview with Bishop Laval, she added, "After having spoken to the bishop, I went to find Madame de Miramion to ask her to help me in this matter."[26] This comment raises the possibility that, despite the discouraging nature of his reception, the bishop did relent sufficiently to offer her at least some help. Such a response would be quite in keeping with some of his previous dealings with the religious communities of New France, when an apparently harsh rejection was quickly followed by a sudden relenting on the part of the bishop. After initially threatening to send them home, for example, he had not only permitted the establishment of the Hospitallers of St Joseph in Montreal but had even sent them their first Canadian postulant. It is also possible that the Sulpicians or even the Filles de la Croix suggested this meeting with someone whose opinion might perhaps carry weight with Laval. Madame de Miramion was one of the founders of a community called the Filles de Sainte-Geneviève or, more popularly, the "Miramionnes" and was highly respected in French ecclesiastical circles. Contact with both the Filles de la Croix and the Filles de Sainte-Géneviève was very important to Marguerite Bourgeoys in the fulfillment of her announced purpose for this visit to France, for both of these recently established uncloistered communities of women had been successful in obtaining canonical approbation for their way of life.

It was most likely the Sulpicians who introduced Marguerite Bourgeoys to the Filles de la Croix, with whom she lived during this stay in Paris. Her writings indicate that the Sulpician seminary was usually one of the first places she visited on her arrival in Paris, and Jean-Jacques Olier and other Sulpicians had been closely associated with the Filles de la Croix at the time of their establishment in Paris. When Marguerite visited them, their house was located just off the rue Saint-Antoine, part of the main transversal of Paris parallel to the Seine, which prolonged the rue de Rivoli to the Bastille.

The district was already known to Marguerite Bourgeoys, for the Jesuit house where she had gone to seek advice before leaving for Canada the first time was situated nearby. If, during her stay, she attended services at the nearby Jesuit church of Saint-Louis, King Louis XIV's favourite place of worship, she could have seen many of Paris's wealthy and fashionable assembled.

Marguerite Bourgeoys's contacts with the Filles de la Croix and the Filles de Sainte-Geneviève in Paris in 1680 is a reminder that, unique though it was in many ways, her congregation was deeply rooted in the church of her native France. The establishing of the Ursulines and the Hospitallers in Quebec, the founding of the Hôtel-Dieu in Montreal, the funding of the Montreal recruitment of 1653 that brought Marguerite Bourgeoys to Canada – all these had been largely the work of the devout women who played so large a role in the Catholic revival in seventeenth-century France. Aware of the activities they had supported in the New World, Marguerite now had the opportunity, after a twenty-seven-year absence, to learn what had been taking place in the home country.

Of the two French communities, it was especially the Filles de la Croix that seem to have impressed Marguerite Bourgeoys most. Certainly, in their aims and in their way of life, the members of the two groups had much in common. The Congrégation des Filles de la Croix was the first uncloistered community of women to obtain letters patent, but it did so only after a painful struggle in the course of which the community was in many ways transformed. Because of the difficulties encountered in the founding years of this community, its early history has been recorded in some detail. The events themselves were very different from those that marked the beginnings of Marguerite's congregation. However, descriptions of the attempt by this community to educate women and the content of the religious instruction given can also cast light not otherwise available upon the work of the Congrégation de Notre-Dame de Montréal.

The Congrégation des Filles de la Croix came into being in the small town of Roye, in the diocese of Amiens in Picardy in the mid-1620s as a response to repeated "scandalous behaviour" (a later period would use the term "sexual abuse") on the part of a male teacher in the local school, which admitted girls as well as boys. The vicar general of the diocese, Christophe Bellot, decided that in order to prevent similar incidents in the future, the girls should have their own school, in which they would be taught by women. At first he encountered difficulty in his search for suitable schoolmistresses, but one of the local parish priests, Pierre Guérin, suggested to him certain candidates from among the young women of whom he was the spiritual director. Four of these were chosen: Françoise Vallet, Marie Samier, and Charlotte and Anne de Lancy. The women were between twenty and thirty years of age and connected to one another by family ties. A meeting of the leading citizens of the town was held, an assembly whose membership included women and representatives of the parents, and the group of schoolmistresses was approved. A house was found for them and they moved in on 4 August 1625. They lived according to a rule drawn up for them by Bellot and Guérin, the former concerned with the material and the latter with the spiritual aspect of their life.

In the models invoked to describe the spirit of the Filles de la Croix, in the work they took on, in the means by which they supported that work, and in the costume they adopted, there are many similarities with Marguerite Bourgeoys's congregation in Montreal. She had referred to New Testament models for religious women in the church: the Blessed Virgin Mary and Martha and Mary, the sisters of Lazarus. Under the direction of Father Gendret, she had come to see Mary, the mother of Jesus, as the model for uncloistered women, and Martha and Mary as models for cloistered women. The Filles de la Croix saw themselves as combining the roles of Martha and Mary, action and contemplation. Like the sisters of the Congregation, they gave religious instruction to the daughters of the people and taught them reading, writing, and manual skills. The four women who were at the origin of the Filles de la Croix did not come from wealthy families. They could not endow their group with large dowries but had to be self-supporting. They earned their living by doing sewing and laundry and were a burden to no one. Like the women in the early Congregation, they found they could do this only by prolonging their work well into the night. The costume they adopted "in order not to be noticeable," although not identical in all details, calls up the earliest illustrations of the costume worn by Marguerite Bourgeoys and her companions: a black dress, a neckerchief pointed in front, and a small wooden cross at the breast. To this they added a bonnet fastened with three ribbons, one of them stamped with a cross, and a rosary at the waist.[27]

The details of Antoine Gendret's rule used by Marguerite Bourgeoys and the early Congregation are unknown; nor have surviving documents given us any idea of the exact daily timetable they

observed. It is suggestive, then, to look at the rule of the Filles de la
Croix, as the two communities probably had some common characteristics, although the fact that the Congregation in Montreal always
shared its house with other women and children would have made
some aspects of this rule impossible for its members. Each day there
were two half-hours of meditation, one in the morning and one in
the evening, as well as two examens and two periods of spiritual
reading. The sisters attended mass daily and received communion,
in accordance with the customs of the time, on Sundays, feast days,
and those Thursdays that did not precede or follow feast days. They
went to confession on Saturdays and on the eve of feast days. They
attended all services in the parish. Each morning they opened the
school after an hour of work in silence. The first act of the day
was to take the children to mass. On their return to the school,
they conducted classes from nine to eleven in the morning. There
was reading during the midday meal and then a writing lesson until
two in the afternoon. The periods of school work began and ended
with vocal prayers in which the children shared. After supper the
teachers had a half-hour of recreation followed by two hours of
work. Then came the prayers and devotions of the evening and the
period of complete quiet known as "grand silence." On Sundays,
after the morning services of the parish, the sisters welcomed into
their house the older girls and women of the parish for religious
instruction and conversation.[28]

Very early in its history, the congregation of Filles de la Croix
found itself in trouble. The existence of so innovative a group of
women could not go unchallenged for long, and the first attacks
on it came from two quarters. The disgraced former schoolmaster
and his supporters started a series of obscenely vicious rumours
about the teachers and their school. More serious, the provost of
Roye, who had not been part of the consultation process for the
setting up of the school, declared its existence illegal and an affront
to the royal authority. Vicar General Bellot was almost frightened
into scuttling the whole project. However, there was a reconciliation, and the result was a document signed by the deans, canons,
and chapter of the church of Saint-Florent de Roye and the royal
provosts and aldermen of the town on 27 July 1627. It permitted
the four women to act as schoolmistresses to persons of their own
sex. It also allowed them to charge five cents a person a month for
lessons in religion, reading, and writing, while fees for an appren-

ticeship in sewing were to be determined by mutual agreement between the persons concerned. The document gives some insight into the content of the religious instruction given at the time: the pupils were to learn to recite the Lord's Prayer, the Apostles' Creed, the Ten Commandments, and the laws of the church "according to their ability."[29] Presumably, then, much of the time of religious instruction would be given to the interpretation, explanation, and memorizing of those texts.

Opposition to the group was still far from vanquished. Pierre Guérin and two other priests connected with it were accused of the heresy of illuminism. This heresy, their enemies argued, was being spread by schoolmistresses who had the temerity to preach and even to offer spiritual direction, a function reserved to the clergy. The controversy splitting the town became so violent that the Filles de la Croix sent two of their number to present their case to the faculty of theology at the Sorbonne. The memorandum they presented there is a remarkable document.[30] It summarizes the content of the religious instruction given by "a certain number of women living together in great harmony, peace and tranquillity." With simplicity and even naïveté, it describes their pedagogical methodology and attempts to answer the accusations being brought against them, incidentally presenting some insight into the lives of the women they were endeavouring to teach.

To demonstrate the orthodoxy of the group, the memorandum gives a much fuller account of their teaching than the approbation cited above. To the prayers mentioned there, it adds the Hail Mary and the rosary and makes it explicit that these and the catechism are to be explained, that the students are to learn the "sense of the articles." Among the articles given particular mention is the Trinity and the end for which humanity was created, as well as the sacraments, the theological virtues, and the duties of Christian justice. The women and girls are to be taught to live as true and not just nominal Christians, practising the spiritual and corporal works of mercy. All this, they stress, is to be in perfect conformity with the official teachings of the Roman Catholic Church.

The defence mounted in the memorandum makes it apparent that it is the teaching of women rather than of little girls that is chiefly under attack, for it is mainly the work of the sisters with adult women that the document attempts to explain and justify. The sisters explain that because they are poor, they must earn their bread by the work of their hands. That is why, they say, they have many women going in and out of their house, women who are often very ignorant, poor servants from the town and from the surrounding countryside. They go on to describe their manner of gently trying to interest these women in religious instruction without embarrassing them and of giving this instruction simply and informally. One of the accusations against their work can probably be seen behind the insistence in the memorandum that the women the sisters teach are always instructed about the importance of obedience to their superiors. The sisters go on to describe their manner of dealing with the more well-to-do and worldly women who come to the house on business: "We approach them in speaking of what they like best" and then lead them gently and without their noticing it to a discussion of the vanity of earthly pleasures in the face of eternity.

In the last paragraphs of the memorandum, the Filles de la Croix answer the charge that they have been assuming the prerogatives of the clergy in a passage that vividly conveys the problems of some of the women they encounter:

Sometimes it happens to poor servants who can never get out of the house without one or two children to care for, that their mistresses send them to the preaching or the catechism lesson with these children. They, knowing that it only creates a disturbance and that preachers ordinarily say it is better not to come, ask themselves where to go so as not to waste the time so rarely given them. Knowing that there is always one of the ... sisters keeping the house, [they] go there instead of going walking, thinking they are more likely to learn something there than elsewhere. This sister, who is occupied in saying the Office of the Blessed Virgin or the rosary or doing spiritual reading, asks the poor servant if she couldn't come back at another time. She says no and that if she left she would just have to walk about the streets with the children. So it seems to the other that charity urges her to leave her meditation to accede to the request and the need of the poor servant, teaching her what she needs to know in the little time she has. Other poor women, suffering from scruples, not always able to speak to their confessors as they would like, and yet sufficiently informed on the necessary points, come to clear up and find light on a thousand trifles that trouble their minds and having found light, they remain peaceful and tranquil of soul. See, if you please, if that is outside the duty of such persons, who beg you to kindly tell them whether they should cease or continue, for they do not wish or believe that in all this they seek anything else than the greater glory of God and the greater good of souls.

The memorandum was favourably received by the seventeen doctors of the Sorbonne. In a document signed on 26 November 1630, they testified that they had found in it nothing that was not "good, useful, worthy to be received, approved and authorized by the pastors and magistrates of the places where the women mentioned live." However, Pierre Guérin and Claude Bucquet, two priests who had been most active in the establishment of the Filles de la Croix, were not so fortunate.

The two men were denounced as heretics, and Cardinal Richelieu ordered their arrest and trial. Imprisoned in Paris, they might well have been found guilty if the trial had not included an interrogation directed by Vincent de Paul. After questions from the royal commissioners, the two accused were put into his hands, and he proclaimed them innocent of the charges brought against them and so able to return to their functions. It was through this incident that the Filles de la Croix came to the attention not only of Vincent de Paul but also of other influential figures in the capital who were soon to transform their future.

Despite all the differences, the many similarites between the Filles de la Croix and the Congregation in Montreal are obvious: both were concerned with the education of the ordinary people; both attempted to reach women who were already beyond school age; both supported their work and earned their living by the work of their hands. Marguerite Bourgeoys directed her community, "When the sisters are traveling and it is necessary to sleep away from home, they ought to choose the homes of the poor where they ought to give very good example and always give some informal instruction."[31] This prescription recalls the attempt of the earlier group to seek every opportunity to give familiar and informal instruction to the women with whom they came in contact in the course of their work.

Important differences cannot be ignored, however. The defences of the Filles de la Croix cited above are almost exclusively concerned with religious instruction; the teaching of reading, writing, and suitable handicrafts are mentioned only in passing. In the documents supporting the Congrégation de Notre-Dame already mentioned, the role of the community in giving poor people the skills needed to earn a living is a major theme. Nor can this difference be completely attributed to the fact that the documents defending the Filles de la Croix were directed to the religious authorities, while those supporting the Congregation were addressed to the secular powers. In the Congregation, this emphasis on the teaching of the poor was part of its heritage from Pierre Fourier, who had been drawn toward the work of education through a concern for the immense poverty he found in his parish. A comparison of the beginnings of the two communities also suggests that even with all its dangers and hardships, Montreal had the advantage of being far away from the enmities and jealousies of the old country; that those very dangers and hardships did not encourage rivals.

The approbation of 1630 was only a step along the way for the Filles de la Croix, and their history then took an unexpected turn. One of their number who had gone to Paris to present the memorandum to the Sorbonne was Marie Samier, the second member of the original four. She now remained in the capital on community business and thus came to the attention of various influential persons, the most important of whom was Marie L'Huillier, Madame de Villeneuve. Marie L'Huillier, born into the legal nobility in 1597, had been married at the age of fifteen to Claude Marcel, seigneur de Villeneuve and king's counsellor, and had borne him two daughters before he died in 1621 leaving her a well-to-do widow. Acquainted with both François de Sales and Vincent de Paul, she became one of that very large group of upper-class women in seventeenth-century France who exercised a strong influence over some of the most prominent male religious leaders of the time, while themselves founding and endowing new communities as well as French branches of old communities.[32] Madame de Villeneuve was responsible for the establishment of the Visitation sisters at Paris with her sister Hélène-Angelique, who became a member of the community. As a founder or endower, she had the privilege of living in the convent with her two daughters. When the Filles de la Croix came to her attention, she had just been set free from further family responsibility by the marriage of her second daughter.

Madame de Villeneuve had already developed a strong interest in the education of the poor. The establishment of schools in Paris was made very difficult by the number and complexity of religious and civil regulations and the power of the various groups of teachers, especially the writing teachers. She turned, then, to opening schools in the country, employing teachers from Paris, but she had found this approach unsatisfactory. Increasingly, she saw the need of a community both to get the necessary authorization for teaching and to give the work stability, a community whose members would retain the freedom to go out. The appearance in her life of the Filles de la Croix seemed to be an act of Providence, for they appeared ready-made for her purposes. When her request to the community that several other members of the group be sent to Paris was refused, she turned to Pierre Guérin. He sent her Charlotte de Lancy, whom he considered the most intelligent and devout member of the new association. The others still refused to come to Paris and Marie Samier entered the Visitation community, but Charlotte de Lancy and Madame de Villeneuve made plans for a new society whose members would be bound by promises and would work together for the salvation of souls in a regular community. In 1636 the Filles de la Croix were forced out of Roye by a Spanish invasion during the Thirty Years War. With the help of Madame de Villeneuve, they found refuge at Brie-Compte-Robert on the outskirts of Paris. There they were so successful at setting up their work that when the Spanish withdrew in 1639, Roye and Brie both vied for them. Madame de Villeneuve decided that they would remain at Brie but that she would be able to withdraw members and send them elsewhere.

With the intention of forming her own community out of the Filles de la Croix, Madame de Villeneuve now drew up a rule for them. It was based on the rule designed by François de Sales for the Sisters of the Visitation at the time that they had still intended to remain uncloistered. In April 1640 she obtained from François Gondi, archbishop of Paris, approval for the establishment of "a community of women, unmarried and widows, who would be neither nuns nor seculars, but have the virtue of the one and the honest freedom of the other to work for the sanctification of the neighbour as well as their own progress in perfection."[33] They were to devote themselves to the education of their sex and to join vows to the secular state. That same year Madame de Villeneuve chose the nucleus of her community from among the Filles de la Croix at Brie. Among their number were the remaining three of the original group that had begun the community at Roye in 1625. In 1641 she established them in a house at Vaugirard, just outside Paris, and in

August of that year she pronounced the vows of chastity and obedience. (Poverty was to come later after she had finished making financial arrangements for the community.) When she called on her companions to pronounce vows also, however, it caused a rift in the already existing community of Filles de la Croix. Among those who refused to make vows was Françoise Vallet. The original group at Roye had not used the term "superior" but had designated the one who fulfilled that role as the *première*, or first, and that person was Françoise Vallet. At Vaugirard she was the superior of the group. Rather then take vows, she left the group and returned to Roye. From that time on, the group directed by Madame de Villeneuve at Vaugirard and later at Paris was separate from the Filles de la Croix at Roye and Brie, although they shared the same name, something that caused difficulties when Madame de Villeneuve's group obtained letters patent.[34]

That event happened in 1642, with the help of the Duchesse d'Aiguillon, Richelieu's niece, but the letters patent were not registered with the Parlement de Paris until September 1646. The long delay was occasioned by an inquiry into the means by which the community would be supported and the financial difficulties associated with their acquisition in 1643 of large quarters, part of a former royal residence on a street off the rue Saint-Antoine near the Visitation convent. The following year this became their *seminaire*, or seed ground, the place where the members of the community would be formed and where they would teach externs and conduct a boarding school, train teachers, receive retreatants, and even accept as boarders certain secular women who wished to live a simple and recollected life without, however, becoming part of the community. It was also a place from which the sisters could go out to teach in the various parishes. There they would remain and continue their work until they were driven out at the Revolution.[35] That was the house to which Marguerite Bourgeoys came in 1680, thirty years after the death of Madame de Villeneuve.

How much of this history Marguerite learned during the time she enjoyed the community hospitality is not known, nor how it affected her perception of the role of wealthy patrons or the dangers of division in a community. What she heard would no doubt have been presented from the point of view of the Paris foundation, rather than that of those who chose not to follow Madame de Villeneuve, but Marguerite Bourgeoys could perhaps read between the lines. The role played by Madame de Villeneuve in the story of the Filles de la Croix throws light on the significance of Marie Morin's statement that Marguerite's accomplishments were all the more remarkable in that she was a woman "without birth or goods, animated by the love of God and zeal for his glory."[36]

The other person Marguerite Bourgeoys mentions having consulted about the rule was Madame de Miramion in a statement which implies that she was carrying with her some written version of the Congregation rule. She says that Madame de Miramion "asked permission from M. de Rodes, her superior, and then from Bishop Laval, to delete from and to add to our Rules whatever she found appropriate. But she could not offend the bishop."[37] The woman of whom Marguerite writes was born Marie Bonneau de Rubelle in November 1629. She was a younger member of that circle of devout women to which Madame de Villeneuve also belonged, and their histories have many similarities. Both were born into the legal nobility, both entered into arranged marriages at a very young age, and both were widowed early. Jean-Jacques de Beauharnais de Miramion died in November 1645, less than seven months after the wedding; his wife gave birth to a daughter the following March. Unlike Madame de Villeneuve, she is supposed to have loved her young husband and been much grieved by his death. However, she resisted all attempts to arrange a second marriage for her and repelled the advances of a count who abducted her and had her carried off to his castle. Eventually her family accepted her decision to remain unmarried, and she was able to devote herself to a variety of good works, visiting hospitals and prisons as one of Vincent de Paul's Dames de Charité, setting up an orphanage, and working with delinquent girls. The marriage of her daughter in 1660 gave her even greater freedom for her works of charity, and like Madame de Villeneuve, she took over a community founded earlier, though she did so in very different circumstances from those in which Madame de Villeneuve had taken over the Filles de la Croix.

Madame de Miramion's community, the Filles de Sainte-Geneviève, had been founded in 1636 in the parish of Saint-Nicolas-de-Chardonnet in Paris. There Adrien Bourdoise, one of the leaders in the attempt to reform the French clergy and to use the parish as a means of offering Christian education to the laity, had set up a model seminary for the training of young priests. When a Mademoiselle Blosset was forced by ill health to give up the idea of religious life in the abbey of Montmartre and came to live in the parish, Bourdoise became her spiritual director. Under his influence, she founded a community to educate little girls and to take care of the parish church. Mademoiselle Blosset died in 1642, but the three or four women in the community continued the work. They asked Bourdoise for a rule in 1650 and obtained letters patent in 1661. By that time Bourdoise was dead, and the community, numbering about ten, in severe financial straits. Their director was now Hippolyte Feret, the parish priest. He was also the ecclesiastical superior of a similar group located nearby, the Communauté de la Sainte-Famille, whose patron was Madame de Miramion. At that time she was planning to become a member of the Communauté de la Sainte-Famille and ready to follow Feret's suggestion of uniting the two groups. The resulting community used the name and official status of the Filles de Sainte-Geneviève but depended on the financial support of Madame de Miramion. The two groups moved into a house on the Quai de Tournelles, and that is where Marguerite Bourgeoys would have visited them.

Madame de Miramion and her community were highly respected, and she was called on several times to mediate in problems that arose in other small communities. Marguerite's comment quoted above makes it clear that Madame de Miramion did make some suggestions about the Congregation rule, but in the discussions about their rule that would take place in the 1690s, the sisters of the Congregation refer to the example of the Filles de la Croix, rather than the Miramionnes, as the other community was popularly known.

No evidence has been discovered to prove that Marguerite visited Troyes in the course of this sojourn in France, and it has been generally assumed that she did not do so, given the fact that Bishop Laval had forbidden her to take back any recruits for the Congregation. However, on 13 November 1680, some three months after her return to Montreal, Marguerite Bourgeoys was a witness at the signing of the marriage contract of Pierre Chantreux (or Chantereaux), the parish verger, to Marie Cordier, whose place of origin is given as Troyes in the province of Champagne. The parish record of the wedding describes the bride as "newly arrived from France."[38] Since Marie Cordier's parents had been married in Marguerite's native parish of Saint-Jean-au-Marché in 1652, they may well have been known to her before her original departure for Montreal.[39] Certainly, these records raise the possibility that Marguerite had some contact with and may even have paid a last visit to her native city. A letter written by the superior of the Congrégation de Notre-Dame of Troyes after Marguerite's death says that she had always stayed in contact with that community.

Pierre Bourgeoys, Marguerite's younger brother, was still alive in Évreux, but her route home from La Rochelle would not have taken her near that town. Although she could not bring new members for the Congregation, Marguerite did not start the return journey alone. As on previous voyages, she had been given the care of several women recruited as prospective wives for the settlers.[40] She was also given a more problematic charge, of whom she writes:

But at this time, Father Charles had spoken to me about Sister Chauson whom he described as a woman of unusual virtue and I accepted his opinion. I thought I would bring her out like the other girls to get married. I told him she would have to take off her hospital dress, her wooden shoes and her cornette. He agreed. But instead of a simple dress, she bought a silk dress with all the accessories and told me that Father Charles had approved it. M... gave me passage money for which I accounted to him. But at La Rochelle when I saw that she continued to add to her finery, I advised her confessor of this. He could not remedy it any more than I could.[41]

What happened to this young woman is unknown. Her name does not appear in the Montreal area in the census of 1683; nor is there any indication that she married in Montreal or was ever in either of the women's communities there, although a "soeur Chozon" was involved in a dispute over the leasing of a house in October 1687.[42] One other person who quite certainly accompanied Marguerite back to Montreal was an old acquaintance. She writes, "I had a letter from the sisters asking me to engage Brother Louis ... He accompanied us as far as Montreal."[43] This was Louis Frin, who had been Paul de Chomedey de Maisonneuve's servant when she visited him in 1671–72, who had remained with his master until the end, and who now left for Montreal as a *donné*, or servant of the Congregation.

It was most likely on this voyage that an incident occurred which Montgolfier says was described in a section of Marguerite's writings that has since disappeared. War had been declared between England

and France, and for the fifth time the English were in possession of Acadia. The ship on which Marguerite and her fellow passengers had left La Rochelle was unarmed, and the sudden appearance on the horizon of four heavily armed enemy ships struck panic among the French crew. They begged Marguerite Bourgeoys and her companions to pray. The women, however, were too overcome with terror to do any such thing, convinced, as they were, that capture was certain. Instead they lamented and demanded of Marguerite what was to become of them. To this she is reported to have replied: "If we are taken we will go to England or Holland, where we will find God as we find Him everywhere else."[44] Her words had a calming effect, and a priest prepared to say mass, for it was a Sunday. After about two hours, the enemy ships were lost to sight, and the company sang a Te Deum. The captain was so grateful to Marguerite for the role she had played in calming the hysteria that he invited her to take her meals at his table. She declined, but when he sent her food anyway, she was able to pass it on to other passengers in need.[45] The rest of the voyage appears to have passed without incident.

The *Histoire de la Congrégation* and Marguerite Bourgeoys's biographers suggest that she saw this last return to France as a failure. Obviously, she was taken aback by Bishop Laval's attitude and disappointed that she could not bring back new sisters to help with the growing work of the Congregation. There are also other factors to be taken into consideration. Marguerite had now entered the seventh decade of her life and was no longer in good health. This journey to the homeland lacked the hope and excitement of her two earlier trips and was also much lonelier. She did not have the consolation of meeting old friends, such as de Maisonneuve. In fact, their absence from the places she had last seen them must have made their deaths more real. At the same time, she accomplished her primary purpose: she found the spiritual direction and the peace for which she had come. Although it does not appear that much progress had been made on the question of the rule, her stay had given her the opportunity to study and discuss problems with two communities similar to her own.

This last visit to the homeland had two other consequences of which Marguerite Bourgeoys would have been unaware at the time but which were very important to the future of the Congregation. The first was that because she did not bring back from France any recruits for the Congregation, it became much more likely that her first successor as superior of the Congregation would be a Canadian. The other was that this sojourn in Paris made it possible for Louis Tronson to get to know her and develop for her what Faillon calls "a singular esteem," to which his letters would soon bear "remarkable witness."[46] Abbé Tronson had become superior of Saint-Sulpice in July 1678 and would remain so until his death in February 1700, a few weeks after that of Marguerite Bourgeoys. His support during the last decade of her life was to be crucial to Marguerite's own well-being and to the survival of the Congrégation de Notre-Dame.

CHAPTER FIVE

BACK TO THE STABLE
1680–1684

*In 1683, the house burned down. In order to rebuild, we drew up a
document in which we promised God that we would ask to rebuild only
in order to be more faithful than we had been in the past. And we all
signed it. As for me I was happy rather than sad about the fire
because of the reason for which the house had been built.*[1]

Again, neither the date of Marguerite's departure from La Rochelle
in 1680 nor the date of her return to Montreal is known. However, she must have been back by 15 August, for on that day, the
feast of the Assumption of Mary, Marie Barbier made her promises
as a sister of the Congrégation de Notre-Dame. Nor is it known
how Marguerite was received by the sisters. When they saw that
she brought back neither new recruits to help with their work nor
reports of progress on the approval of a rule that would have given
the community greater stability, when they learned of her difficulties with Bishop Laval, did they perceive not only the trip but their
superior as a failure? Was this another factor in what she saw as
declining confidence in her leadership? None of the documentary
evidence that has survived from the period gives any certain answer
to these questions. As usual, however, once back in Montreal, Marguerite would have found little time for repining as the comunity
was faced with new demands for its services. The Congregation was
now entering a decade of significant expansion, for between 1680
and 1689 six new missions would be established and the work of
the community spread from the Montreal to the Quebec area and
even perhaps as far as Port-Royal in Acadia.

The first of the new missions established was at Lachine in 1680, immediately after Marguerite's return from France. Lachine had acquired the name it keeps to this day as a joke. The area, which lay near the rapids west of the original settlement on the island of Montreal, was originally called the Côte Saint-Sulpice. It had been conferred on René-Robert Cavelier de La Salle in 1667 in the hope that a settlement there would serve as a western outpost for Montreal. However, at the beginning of 1669, keeping only his house to use as a base for fur trading, he ceded back part of his seigneury and sold the rest to finance his explorations in search of a water route to the Southern Sea, and thereby a route to China.[2] When he returned that autumn from a fruitless expedition, Côte Saint-Sulpice was derisively given the name La Chine, or "little China."

The development of religious and educational services to the colonists who settled in the area followed a pattern similar to that already seen at Pointe-aux-Trembles. The Sulpician missionaries celebrated mass in the house of a colonist until a chapel was built. In his pastoral visit of 1676, Bishop Laval erected Lachine into a parish to which the Sulpician Pierre Rémy was appointed at the end of 1680. A presbytery had been constructed but had never been occupied, for the previous pastors had always lived at the nearby mission of Gentilly. Abbé Rémy had this building improved as a residence and school for the sisters of the Congregation. He wrote: "By this means ... the settlers hope to have a school for their daughters that could never be better conducted than by the sisters of the Congregation, as much for the good education they give with blessing wherever they are established as for the other spiritual assistance they give for the adornment of the altars and decoration of the churches." He added that another advantage for the parish was that the sisters of the Congregation did not ask for anything from anybody, neither from individuals nor from the wardens, supporting themselves by their own work and the help afforded them by Providence.[3]

Marguerite Bourgeoys is described as having founded this mission, although this would mean that it was established with her consent, rather than that she actually lived and taught there. She would certainly have visited Lachine before agreeing to send sisters to the outpost and would have continued to visit the sisters sent on mission there. According to the *Histoire de la Congrégation*, the first of these was her youngest niece, Catherine Sommillard. With this mission added to that at Pointe-aux-Trembles, the Congregation was now established at both the eastern and western outposts of the island of Montreal, dangerous positions as events at the end of the decade were to prove.

The following spring and summer an ailing Bishop Laval undertook a last tour of his immense diocese. He left Quebec at the end of May, moving from settlement to settlement to celebrate the sacrament of Confirmation, and arrived in Montreal on 19 June. After a few days spent with the Jesuits at Laprairie, he returned to Ville-Marie to celebrate a pontifical high mass on the feast of Saints Peter and Paul. He remained in Montreal until 9 or 10 July, during which time he made his official visit to both the Hôtel-Dieu and the Congregation. He had, of course, already approved the establishment of the new mission at Lachine. Again, nothing is known of what passed between him and Marguerite Bourgeoys at this time, their first meeting since their unfortunate encounter in Paris, or of the impact of his visit on the Congregation.

In the late summer of 1681 the Congregation had a new experience: for the first time, it lost a member in death. It is a testimony to the health and strength of the first sisters that the community had been able to exist for twenty-two years without a death, given the mortality rate of the time. On 5 September, Madeleine Constantin, one of the women who had accompanied Marguerite from France in 1672, was buried in the still unfinished parish church. The burial record, signed by Marguerite Bourgeoys and Geneviève du Rosoy, gives neither her age nor the cause of death, but the *Histoire de la Congégation* says that she was a Parisian thirty-five years of age at this date.[4]

In 1681 a general census of New France was conducted under the auspices of Intendant Duchesneau. The population for the island of Montreal is given as 1,418; the town proper had 140 families, 547 individuals. The census provides a record of membership in the Congrégation de Notre-Dame at that time. The community had nineteen members in Montreal ranging in age from Catherine Crolo, who was then sixty-three years old,[5] to Catherine Charly, aged just sixteen; eleven sisters were of French and eight of Canadian origin. Marie Raisin was at Champlain, and the names of the two Native sisters do not appear in the census. This was a young community: only Marguerite Bourgeoys and Catherine Crolo had reached their sixtieth birthday; three sisters were in their early forties, three in their thirties, six in their twenties, and five in their teens. Of the three whose names were absent, Marie Raisin was in her early forties, and if the dates of birth given in the *Histoire de la Congrégation* are accurate, Marie-Barbe Atontinon was in her twenties at this time and Marie-Thérèse Gannensagouas in her middle teens. There were three sets of biological sisters in the Congregation: Marguerite's nieces, the two Gariépys, and the two Charlys.

The census also gives information about the boarding school. The eight young girls there ranged in age from six to twelve years. The list of names demonstrates that the educational mission of the the Congregation was not now directed only toward the "little people" of the colony. Though most of the children taught would still have been those who frequented the day school and those who were prepared for first communion in the parishes, the boarders of 1681 were drawn from another class. Their fathers included a lawyer and judge, a ship's captain, an army officer, the seigneur of Varennes, a Lachine merchant, and a member of the lesser nobility.[6]

At this time, the Congregation had 150 arpents of land under cultivation, twenty-two horned cattle, five horses, and twenty sheep. The number of horses owned by the Congregation was unusually large for New France: the Quebec seminary had only two and the Montreal seminary three, as had the Quebec Ursulines. The Hospitallers in both places had none. Were the Congregation horses used for travel or perhaps lent or hired out to its neighbours at the Hôtel-Dieu and other farms? To work the land and care for the animals, the Congregation employed thirteen menservants, several of whom would have been *donnés*, or brothers.

Although these men were a significant asset to the community, they could sometimes cause problems. The first name on the list is that of Thomas Monier, who appears to have had a chequered relationship with the Congregation. On 23 October 1682 Marguerite Bourgeoys sent a letter by him to Dollier de Casson, who was in Quebec waiting for passage to France. In it she writes: "The bearer is Brother Thomas whom we have sent away and who is very much grieved at his dismissal. He believes he should return, but it would have to be very clearly the will of God and we are not asking for miracles."[7] There seems to have been a reconciliation, for in a will made on 14 July 1684,[8] Monier left half his property to the sisters of the Congregation. Subsequent wills signed on 28 August 1693[9] and 25 June 1699[10] greatly reduced the share of the Congregation in the estate but always retained a bequest to Notre-Dame-de-Bon-Secours chapel.

Twice in 1681 the Congregation was involved in legal proceedings involving its menservants. On 17 January of that year, toward the end of the afternoon, Marguerite Sommillard, then congregation bursar, sent the servant Barthélémy Lemaistre from the house in Montreal to Catherine Crolo at the farm at Pointe-Saint-Charles to tell her to have the horses moved because there was danger of flooding. On his way, he met Robert Cavelier, who warned him about the state of the ice, but he replied that he was light and so would be able to make it safely over without breaking through the surface. Lemaistre was never seen alive again. All sorts of inquiries were made, some by Marguerite Bourgeoys herself, who set out for Pointe-Saint-Charles at seven the next morning, daybreak at that time of year, accompanied by Françoise Le Moyne. People from as far away as Lachine were asked if they had seen the workman, but there was no report of a sighting. He was reported missing, and an inquest attempted to determine whether he might have disappeared voluntarily or even been murdered. He had been in trouble with the law in 1679 when he was employed by Antoine Primot,[11] but the sisters of the Congregation now gave him an excellent character. Accordingly, he was presumed drowned. This conclusion was confirmed in early April when his body was discovered and brought back to Montreal for burial.[12]

A problem of another kind arose in connection with Louis Fontaine, who made a gift of his person and goods to the Congregation on 13 February 1681. Marguerite Bourgeoys would have known Fontaine for a long time, for "le petit Louis," as he was called, had been a member of the great recruitment of 1653, with which she herself had come to Montreal. He died in the house of the Congregation a week after making his donation. It then turned out that he had previously made contracts giving his real estate to his godson, Louis Pichard, the son of another member of the great recruitment, who had died in 1658, and his movable assets to the parish with the provision that these two would pay his debts out of his estate. Marguerite Bourgeoys, with the consent of the sisters and the ecclesiastical superior, renounced a claim to any part of the estate, saying that Fontaine had been accepted as an act of charity. Indeed, it sounds as if a sick man without wife or children had looked for someone to care for him in his last days and also perhaps tried to ensure a better reception in the next world.

In waiving any claim to the estate, Marguerite was putting into practice one of her most basic beliefs about social relations, her response to the Sermon on the Mount in her own very litigious society: "God is not satisfied if we preserve the love we owe our neighbour, we must preserve our neighbour in the love he ought to have for us. We must give the cloak to him who wishes to have the tunic rather than take him to court ... When difficulties come along, there are always enough charitable people to bring about a reconciliation without going to court."[13] This event and others where acts of donation were changed or rescinded indicate that it would have been risky to place too much confidence in them until they were finalized by the deaths of the donors and the settlement of their estates.

September of 1681 brought another loss to the Congregation, and Marguerite found herself once more testifying at an inquest. Jean Brod, who worked at the farm at Pointe-Sainte-Charles, drowned at about sunset one evening when the canoe in which he was cross-ing the stretch of water in front of the concession capsized. His young companion survived by clinging to the overturned canoe. It was the custom at inquests to pose questions about the character of the deceased to ensure that the death had been the result of accident and not of foul play. Marguerite said that Brod had been a very peaceful man whom she had engaged at La Rochelle about a year before, that he was a willing worker with whom the community was very satisfied, and that he was well-behaved and not inclined to quarrel with anyone. Permission was then given for Christian burial.[14]

One fact that emerges quite clearly from the legal documents involving the Congregation in the early 1680s is that, despite some of the doubts she was to express a decade later, Marguerite Bour-geoys was still indisputably the leader in the community. It was she who had the last word: agreements entered into in her absence had to be confirmed by her on her return. It was she who walked out to Pointe-Saint-Charles early on a winter morning when a servant was missing. And it was she who could persuade her companions and the ecclesiastical superior to act with generosity in the question of acquiring material goods.

In 1682, news came that must have raised the morale of the inhabitants of Montreal. Frontenac was recalled to France, and the decision had been made to remove Perrot as governor of Montreal. There must have been hope that these changes would bring peace to the administration of the colony, an end to the various abusive practices of the two officials, and an improvement in the economy. For those interested in the moral welfare of the settlement, there was the promise that the fur-trading fairs held in Montreal each year would be the opportunities for the evangelization of the Native people anticipated by the founders, rather than the drunken orgies which they had become.

It may also have been in 1682 that, despite Bishop Laval's prohibition of 1680, several more French women were added to the Congregation; these were Anne Meyrand, Louise Richard, and Marguerite Tardy. The *Histoire de la Congrégation* supposed that because they were undoubtedly in the community by the 1680s, the first two must have been part of the recruitment of 1672. However, their names do not appear in the census of 1681, and Jamet is almost certainly right in suggesting that they were brought to Montreal by the Sulpician Étienne Guyotte when he returned from a four-year sojourn in France in 1682, and that Bishop Laval had permitted their entry into the Congregation.[15] If so, it was a means of circumventing the prohibition the bishop had imposed on Marguerite Bourgeoys in 1680. The addition of at least one of these women was not to prove an unmixed blessing for the community.

The year 1683 was a very difficult one for the Congregation, for it began in loss and culminated in a catastrophe that threatened to put an end to Marguerite's dream of a community of women who would emulate the uncloistered life of the Virgin Mary. First came the death of a second member of the community, this time of Marie Charly, one of the young and very promising Canadians. Marie stood in the relation almost of a granddaughter to Marguerite Bourgeoys. Her mother, Marie Dumesnil, had been the first *fille à marier* given at a very tender age into the care of Marguerite Bourgeoys on her own first voyage to New France. Marie Charly had entered the Congregation in 1679 after her younger sister, Catherine. She was buried on 25 April 1683, three months short of her twenty-first birthday. Even accustomed as they were at this time to the death of the young and convinced of the reality of eternal life, this death could not but have been a blow to a group struggling to meet the demands facing them and cut off from recruitment in France. Much worse was to follow.

Despite the loss of Marie Charly, the Congregation continued its expansion, opening yet another mission in 1683. Faillon says that in that year the community began a school at the Jesuit Native mission at Sault-Saint-Louis (now Kahnawake) citing as evidence a letter from the archives de la Marine. He adds that this school had a very short life and implies that the results were discouraging.[16] It was at the Sault-Saint-Louis mission that Kateri Tekakwitha, a young woman of Algonquin and Mohawk parentage, had passed her last days and died in 1680 at the age of twenty-four. Kateri, the first North American of aboriginal descent to be declared venerable, had practised her Christian religion in an exemplary way despite great persecution. In the summer of 1678 she had visited Montreal, where according to a contemporary source, "she saw religious sisters for the first time [and] was so enchanted by their piety and modesty that she inquired with great curiosity about the way these holy women lived and about the virtues they practised."[17] Over the centuries there has been much discussion as to the identity of the women who so impressed her. Her biographer Henri Béchard was convinced that the reference is to the sisters at the Hôtel-Dieu, but it is tempting to think she might also have been attracted by the sight of Marie-Thérèse Gannensagouas at the Congregation.

At the end of 1683 came the most serious physical disaster to befall the Congregation in the first century of its existence. On the night of 6–7 December 1683 a fire reduced to ruins the community's main house in Montreal. The outbreak of the fire was so violent that none of the contents of the building could be saved. These would have included not only furniture, clothing, and linens as well as books and school supplies, all of them scarce and expensive since they had to be imported from France, but also whatever food supplies had been stored for the winter season. All community documents and records were also destroyed. Worse still, two of the sisters were unable to escape and perished in the flames. These were Geneviève du Rosoy, at the time the assistant superior, and Marguerite Sommillard, the eldest niece of Marguerite Bourgeoys, who had been elected bursar in 1679. Some later historians of the event have suggested that they most likely died in the attempt to fulfill the responsibilities attached to their offices, ensuring that everyone else had left the building and perhaps trying to save goods or objects important to the Congregation.

The *Histoire de la Congrégation* states that at the time of the fire, Marguerite Bourgeoys had decided to resign as superior and that elections were to have been held the next day. The two sisters who died in the fire are supposed to have been the leading candidates to replace her. There is no mention of such a proposed election in the surviving writings of Marguerite Bourgeoys or in the biographies by Glandelet or Ransonet. The earliest source of this information is Montgolfier, who writes:

She had scarcely returned from France to Ville-Marie in 1684 [*sic*] than she renewed the appeals that she had made before her departure, that a new Superior be named in her place; and she was so insistent that they were ready to yield to her urgings. There had already been a meeting on this subject at which, however, they had been unable to reach any definite conclusion, the votes having been split between two candidates, excellent to tell the truth, but whom God had not chosen for this position. These were sisters Geneviève Rosoy, and Marguerite Soumillard: but when the formal election was on the point of taking place to choose one of these two as Superior, the great fire came ... and both perished in the flames; and the matter of the elections remained there for a long time.[18]

By virtue of their offices, the two women who died would already have stood directly in the line of succession to Marguerite Bourgeoys had anything happened to her. If Montgolfier's claims are correct and if she was contemplating resigning, the fire would have put a stop to any such intentions. There could have been no possibility of Marguerite's renouncing responsibility for the Congregation in these disastrous circumstances.

A little more than a decade later, in February 1695, the Montreal Hôtel-Dieu also burned during the night; Marie Morin has given a vivid account of the event and of its aftermath. Unfortunately, no such account of the Congregation fire exists, but it can be presumed that some of the details would have been similar: the difficulty of waking everyone in the middle of a winter night, the rush to get out of the burning building, the care to save the dependants – the sick in the case of the Hôtel-Dieu, the boarders in the case of the Congregation. Marguerite Bourgeoys has left us no word of her feelings that night, but they must have been at least somewhat like those expressed by Marie Morin, who was superior at the Hôtel-Dieu when it burned in similar circumstances: "You can ... judge in what frame of mind we all were, especially those who had greatest responsibility for the house such as the superior and the first officers, to see ourselves in a moment losing almost everything the Lord had given us, to be out on the cobbles stripped of everything ... Oh, how those moments were harrowing. You would have to have felt it to believe it."[19]

There would be no loss of life in the fire at the Hôtel-Dieu. In the case of the Congregation, the grim search for the bodies of the two women who had perished must have preceded the search of the ruins for anything that might be recovered. Because there is no record of the burial of either of the two women in the parish register, the author of the *Histoire de la Congrégation* concludes that the bodies were never recovered. In her notice on the life of Catherine Sommillard, she writes: "Who could describe all the tears shed by poor Sister Catherine near the smoking rubble that buried the object of her most legitimate affection? Who could measure her sighs and groans at the idea that nothing of her sister was left to her ... not an object that had belonged to her or that she had touched ... not a hair, not a bone ... nothing, nothing, that she could send to their family and friends across the sea to console them in such a terrible ordeal."[20]

Marguerite Bourgeoys's remarks about her feelings regarding the fire were written long after the event, during a particularly dark and trying period of her own life. She indicates in her writings that, at least in the last decade of her life, she believed that the material misfortunes which befell the community were related to moral failures on the part of the Congregation, especially failures in charity and in trust in God. For her, to seek security in material things was to reject the dependence on God that she saw as the only guarantee of the success of the work of the Congregation. She had undertaken the building of the house that now lay in ruins with an uneasy conscience, under pressure from her companions "without consulting God, nor I think, the [ecclesiastical] Superior, I said that we would build, and that with some difficulty from the sisters."[21] This is the context in which she makes the startling statement "As for me, I was happy [in French, *joyeuse*] rather than sad about the fire because of the reason for which the house had been built."

Although exaggerated statements such as this are not uncommon in the religious literature of the time, they are not characteristic of the usually sober Marguerite Bourgeoys and seem shocking and inhuman in view of the two deaths that had taken place. The statement just quoted has caused difficulty to her biographers. Neither Glandelet nor Faillon cites it. Ransonet writes: "The death of these two women was a very painful blow to Sister Marguerite Bourgeoys; but the burning of the house scarcely afflicted her at all."[22] Jamet sees the statement more as an anguished reflection of the problems Marguerite experienced in the last decade of her life than as a believable description of her attitude at the time.[23] And despite the sentiments she expressed in the 1690s, she turned at once to the project of rebuilding, and on a larger scale than before, in keeping with the ever-growing needs of the community.

In the immediate aftermath of the fire, the sisters of the Congregation went to stay with their neighbours at the Hôtel-Dieu. After a first day of receiving condolences and arranging funerals,[24] Marguerite Bourgeoys would not have had much leisure for grief. She must, instead, have had to give her whole attention to finding ways and means of ensuring the survival of the community and its work. The old stable school in which the Congregation had begun was still standing and perhaps some of the other outbuildings. In addition, there was the farm at Pointe-Saint-Charles and of course the community landholdings remained the same. One of Marguerite's first tasks was to draw up a list of these holdings and arrange to have her deeds and documents reconstituted. As early as 3 February 1684 she had appeared at the Séminaire de Montréal, to begin this process, and by the following 23 September the "grosse de tous les contrats" concerning the Congregation, detailing all the legal contracts previously deposited with the exception of those not under the jurisdiction of the seigneur of Montreal, was completed.[25] Jamet remarks that Marguerite must have obtained this summary rather than a separate copy of each individual contract to save on notarial costs, an indication of the penury resulting from the fire.

When the news of the destruction of the Congregation house reached Quebec, Bishop Laval wrote to Dollier de Casson on 12 January: "We are greatly moved by the fire that has happened to our good Sisters of the Congregation, but particularly at the loss of sisters Geneviève and Marguerite, consumed in the fire. They were fruit ripe for heaven, but also very necessary to that community. The judgments of men are very different from those of God; that is why we must adore the secrets of His Providence and accept them. I am writing a word in haste to the good sister Marguerite Bourgeoys."[26] The bishop's letter to Marguerite has not survived, but

Montgolfier says that the bishop believed the only course the Congregation could follow in these dire circumstances was to amalgamate with the Ursulines of Quebec. He sometimes confused Bishop Laval with his successor, Bishop Saint-Vallier, and it is quite possible that some of what he writes here belongs to later attempts by the second bishop of Quebec to unite the Congregation with the Ursulines. At the same time, it is very probable that in the desperate circumstances after the fire, Bishop Laval would have seen such a union as a desirable solution to the huge material loss suffered by the Congregation.

If, indeed, Bishop Laval put pressure on Marguerite Bourgeoys to accept the union of the Congregation with the Ursulines, a step that would in fact have destroyed the younger, groundbreaking, and more vulnerable community, he met with strong resistance. Whatever the doubts that plagued Marguerite in the later part of her life, there was one thing of which she always remained certain. She never failed in the conviction that she had been called by God to bring into being an uncloistered community of women who could move about freely, teaching the children of the "petit gens," the struggling working people among whom they lived, a community that the daughters of such people could join. Montgolfier's description of what happened is clearly based on some written source that has since disappeared, and whether it belongs to the aftermath of the fire or to events of the 1690s, it quite clearly presents Marguerite Bourgeoys's vision for her Congregation.

After mentioning previous attempts by the Ursulines to establish themselves at Montreal and the resistance to such attempts by the Sulpicians, Montgolfier writes:

Sister Bourgeois ... forcefully and respectfully represented to him [Laval] that the good she and her sisters offered themselves to do in the diocese was not compatible with the rules of another institute, and especially of a cloistered community; that this would entirely destroy the plans by which she felt herself inspired and which she believed came from God himself, because they had already been approved by legitimate superiors, and that the most Blessed Virgin, to whom she and all her Congregation were especially consecrated, had often given unequivocal signs that this establishment was very pleasing to her; that besides their general plan to teach young girls, they had a particular interest in the perfection and salvation of many Christian Virgins who, without the support of this institute would not find the means to give themselves completely to God. For, she said, there are to be found in all conditions of the world, girls commendable for their virtue and their talents but who, little favoured with worldly goods, and unable to pay a dowry strictly demanded everywhere else, were not able to make the vow of poverty, that her intention was to open the door of the Congregation to such people; and that she cared so little about riches that she would go and carry on her shoulders (it was her way of expressing it) a woman who could not even afford to clothe herself but had goodwill and a true vocation.[27]

If there was a struggle to resist the imposition of the cloister on her community at this time, Marguerite could have counted on the support of the secular authorities. Both governor and intendant were sending enthusiastic reports about the work of the Congregation to the ministry of the Marine in which they emphasized the advantage of the uncloistered status of the community.[28] Also, whatever Bishop Laval may have intended for the Congregation at this time, his main attention was elsewhere. After his last pastoral tour in 1681, he had fallen so ill that hope for his life had been almost abandoned. Although he recovered, his health remained such that he decided that his vast diocese was in need of a younger and more vigorous bishop. He stayed on to finish some aspects of his work and then, in the autumn of 1684, left for France to tender his resignation to the king, an act he performed in January 1685.

Ironically, the difficult material circumstances in which Marguerite Bourgeoys now found herself were the very ones in which her hope, her energy, her enthusiasm, and her confidence thrived. This was the woman who had left Troyes in 1653 with nothing but a few basic necessities in a little bundle and the belief that if she was called to Montreal, God would provide. This was the woman who had turned a dirty, cold, disused stable into a school and a cradle for her Congregation. She had inspired women to leave their native land and accept the challenge of educating the children of the New World, though she could offer them only bread and soup, hard work and danger. She had found that God provided when she was forced to make a voyage to France without even the meagre belongings she had prepared for the trip. She was always suspicious and even afraid of the effect that material prosperity might have on the Congregation because she saw the temptation to trust in material goods as a rejection of trust in God. Marguerite Bourgeoys truly believed that it is when one has nothing that God's help is most available and effective. To live a poor and humble life was, for her, to "wear the livery of the leader whom I follow." She stresses, "The more I follow Him without fear, the more will He protect me. The more I do His will, the more he will prove His love for me."[29]

So at the age of sixty-four, after the initial shock of the fire, which had left the Congregation nearly destitute, had abated somewhat, Marguerite Bourgeoys threw herself wholeheartedly into rebuilding. This was, in a sense, her second spring. Any inner doubts and difficulties that had been troubling her had to be set aside. It was perhaps of this experience that she was thinking when she said that the fire had made her happy rather than sad. Glandelet comments: "Her courage ... was undaunted; it remained firm and generous." And he adds, "It was not long before her confidence was rewarded. Divine Providence raised up charitable persons who provided the means to build an even larger, better, and more suitable house than the first."[30]

The new building was to shelter the Congregation until 1768, when it too would be consumed by fire.[31] The community had been acquiring other land adjacent to its original property, and the new house was located higher than the one it was to replace, on land lying north of rue Saint-Paul and immediately east of the property of the Hôtel-Dieu, a site the Congregation would not abandon until the beginning of the twentieth century.[32] According to the *Aveu et dénombrement* of 1731, the property, which ran along rue Saint-Jean-Baptiste from Saint-Paul to Notre-Dame, was 240 feet long on Notre-Dame and 397 feet deep along Saint-Jean-Baptiste.[33] In the centre of this lot arose the building that would house the day school and the boarding school and living quarters for the sisters and the aspirants to the community, as well as storage space and place for the permanent boarders, the adults who chose to spend the rest of their lives with the Congregation without becoming members of the community. Marie Morin would describe it as "large, spacious, and among the best built in the town."[34]

Les annales de l'Hôtel-Dieu de Québec contains a passage about the rebuilding of the Congregation house in 1684. In 1695 Bishop Saint-Vallier, Laval's successor, was urging the Quebec hospitallers to rebuild their house, which had become too small and was badly in need of repair. When they hesitated because of their lack of financial resources, "The bishop ... cited to us the example of Sister

Bourgeois, who had nothing in money but forty sols when she began her House, and who by her great confidence in God erected with the help of Providence one of the most beautiful Communities in Canada."[35] This is not the only record of Bishop Saint-Vallier's admiration for Marguerite Bourgeoys's success in rebuilding from nothing. After his first tour of his diocese, he reported on his visit to Montreal and to the sisters of the Congregation:

It is a marvel that they were able to survive after the accident that happened to them three or four years ago; their whole house was burned in one night; they saved neither their furniture, nor their clothes, only too happy to save their lives; still two of them perished in the flames. The courage of those who escaped sustained them in their extreme poverty; and although they were more than thirty in number, divine Providence provided for their pressing necessities. It seemed that this calamity served only to make them more virtuous and more helpful to their neighbour; for there is no good that they have not undertaken since then.[36]

Obviously, the Providence that preserved the Congregation had to act through human means. Glandelet, in the passage already quoted, mentions friends in France. Who these were is not known, and whatever aid they gave must have been many months in coming, for news of the event could not have reached France until the following summer. When Abbé Tronson heard of the fire, he expressed the hope that the court would provide some help, and it was reported to the minister of the Marine: "The sisters of the Congregation who do great good in the colony under the direction of Sister Bourgeoys were burned out last year and lost everything; they must re-establish, but they don't have a sol."[37] But the only record of a subsidy from the court is the usual 500 livres for their work at the Mountain Mission. One can only conclude that the credit rating of Marguerite Bourgeoys and her Congregation must have been very good and can guess at the hard work and sacrifice that enabled them to begin again in the stable in that long-ago spring.

CHAPTER SIX

THE DEMANDS OF A NEW BISHOP
1684–1689

The apostles went out to all parts of the world. The sisters of the
Congregation are ready to go anywhere they are sent in this country.[1]

While the Congregation was dealing with the crisis provoked by the
fire and with its aftermath, a new, or perhaps a very old, problem
was making itself felt in New France. The return to the stable was
not the only circumstance that must have reminded Marguerite's
first companions of the late 1650s and early 1660s. Since the arrival
of the Carignan-Salières regiment in 1665, Montreal had been free
of the constant fear of Iroquois attack, but that situation was changing. With the English established at Hudson Bay to the north and
controlling the Hudson River to the south, the French, under the
encouragement of Frontenac, had expanded west. As a result, they
came into direct conflict with Iroquois expansionism, and after the
Iroquois had subdued the Mohicans and the Andastes in 1676, they
turned on other French allies, such as the Illinois and the Miamis.
Ultimately, it was the French themselves they hoped to drive from
the St Lawrence valley. When the new governor, Joseph-Antoine
Le Febvre de La Barre, and the new intendant, Jacques Demeulle,
arrived in 1684, they found the colony in an increasingly dangerous
situation, but their urgent requests to the court for men and supplies
were as little heeded as had been those of their predecessors twenty-
five years before. Since Montreal was the point of departure for any

expeditions to negotiate or fight with the Iroquois, its inhabitants were all too well aware of their situation. At the Congregation, they would also have had access to more first-hand information. Charles Le Moyne, who was an important participant in all negotiations because of his expertise and his stature among the Iroquois, had a very close connection with the community: it now included two of his nieces, for Marguerite Le Moyne had joined her sister Françoise there.

In August 1685 yet another new governor arrived in Quebec. This was Jacques-René de Brisay, Marquis de Denonville, who has been described as "the first governor to have any care for the state of Canadian society and to attempt reforms."[2] A dawning awareness of the seriousness of the situation in New France and restoration of peace between France and Spain and the Holy Roman Empire enabled the king to send a man of superior qualities to Canada. His arrival with reinforcements brought new hope to the colony. During his four-year stay, he was to work with energy, intelligence, and integrity for the safety and the material and moral well-being of the colony.

The same ship that brought the new governor also brought Jean-Baptiste de La Croix de Chevrières de Saint-Vallier as successor to Bishop Laval. Because of tensions between the king and the pope, Abbé Saint-Vallier had not yet received the bulls that would enable him to be consecrated bishop and so had been designated vicar general. He too made an excellent impression on arrival. The bishopric of Quebec was not a position likely to tempt the worldly ambitious among the French clergy, and like Bishop Laval, who had personally chosen him as his successor, the new vicar general was an ascetic, devout, and dedicated man. He was also a strong and determined character with his own ideas and little interest in or tolerance for the ideas and advice of others; this characteristic would soon lead him into conflict with his predecessor and eventually with almost all the other religious authorities and institutions in his new diocese. Initially, however, it was his energy, his enthusiasm, his zeal, and his endurance that impressed his new diocesans. At the time of his arrival in Canada, Saint-Vallier was a few months short of his thirty-second birthday; he had been born on perhaps the very November day that Marguerite Bourgeoys first set foot on the island of Montreal. Beginning the next spring after his arrival, even before the disappearance of the ice, he set out to visit his vast diocese undeterred by hard labour, by cold or heat, by mosquitoes, or by lack of food or rest. His tour brought him, of course, to Montreal and to the houses of the Congregation, as well as to the parishes where the sisters had gone out to teach religion and prepare the young people for first communion, and he was impressed by what he saw.

In his 1688 report on the state of the church in New France, after expressing his admiration for the way in which the Congregation had recovered after the fire, Saint-Vallier commented:

Several schoolmistresses have gone out from this house to different parts of the colony where they teach catechism to the children and give very touching and useful talks to older women. Besides the elementary schools they conduct in their houses for the girls of Montreal, besides the French and Indian boarders they raise in great piety, they have established a house called "la Providence" that they run where they teach more than twenty older girls whom they train in all the work of their sex to enable them to earn their living in service.[3]

The tradition that La Providence was situated at the farm in Pointe-Sainte-Charles is very strong in the Congrégation de Notre-Dame, where this school is seen as an outgrowth of the work done by the community with the filles de roi. The *Histoire de la Congrégation* has this to say about it:

Besides the spiritual exercises of the extern congregation, [Marguerite Bourgeoys] also gave the young women of the region a new means of persevering in virtue; this was to teach them honest trades, which enabled them to live on the fruits of their labour. For this purpose, she established a workshop, called "La Providence," where the older girls were instructed and formed under her care. To do this, she supplied a house near Pointe Saint-Charles, and designated Sister Crolo to teach these girls to work. The day began and ended with a prayer; hymns were sung while they were working. There was catechism three times a week. Dinner was free for everyone and supper for the poorest.[4]

There are, however, many problems associated with the identification of the farm at Pointe-Saint-Charles with La Providence. Faillon observes:

Besides the spiritual exercises of the extern Congregation, Sister Bourgeoys also supplied the young women of the poorer class with a new means of persevering in virtue: this was to teach them honest trades that permitted them to live on the products of their labour. With this end, she established a workshop called "la Providence," where more than twenty older girls were instructed and trained by her care. For this use she supplied a house near that of the Congregation and appointed several sisters to teach these girls to work. The seminary undertook to support several of them and also supplied a certain amount of bread to feed them.[5]

Faillon's belief that the workshop was conducted in a house in Ville-Marie rather than in Pointe-Saint-Charles is based on a statement made by Sister Marie Morin. She writes that in the aftermath of the fire at the Hôtel-Dieu in 1695, the patients from the hospital were moved into a building which was "the old house of *la Providance* where Monsieur Guyotte, parish priest of Ville-Marie formerly maintained several poor women to have them instructed and taught to earn their living." She adds that these women were cared for by the "Congreganistes," the term usually used to designate the members of the Congrégation de Notre-Dame.[6] Clearly, the building to which she refers was within Ville-Marie. There are also certain puzzling references to the "filles de la Providence" in Tronson's letters during the crisis, which will be discussed in the next chapter.

Wherever it was located, the training of women beyond school age in the skills needed to support themselves in the society in which they lived was an important aspect of the work of the Congrégation de Notre-Dame in the seventeenth century and was to remain so across centuries of change. It was of paramount importance to Marguerite herself, as it had been to Pierre Fourier, whose ideas had reached her through the Congrégation de Notre-Dame of Troyes more than forty years earlier. Fourier's ideas had been confirmed by her own experience: it is essential that those who educate the poor give them the means by which they will be enabled to provide for themselves and for their families. Vicar General Saint-Vallier was not the only one impressed by the work done at La Providence, for in a dispatch to the ministry of the Marine, the intendant himself wrote: "I found at Ville-Marie on the island of Montreal an establishment of sisters of the Congregation under the direction of Sister Bourgeoys who do great good in the colony; and besides, an establishment of women of 'la Providence' who work together.

They could begin some kind of industry there, if you would be so good as to make them some kind of grant."[7]

The vicar general's enthusiasm for what he had seen of the work of Marguerite's community was to lead to the establishment of two missions of the Congregation in the Quebec area in the coming year, an indication that the rebuilding of the Montreal house did not absorb all the energy and resources of the community. The first of these was on Île d'Orléans, then known as Île Saint-Laurent, the place where, had Governor Charles Huault de Montmagny succeeded in overcoming de Maisonneuve's determination, Ville-Marie would have been founded in 1642. Marguerite sent two sisters there to open a school at the pressing invitation of François Lamy, pastor of the parish of Sainte-Famille on the island, an invitation that was supported by the vicar general. The elder, Anne Meyrand was twenty-six years old: French-born, she had been in the country only since 1682. Her companion was the Canadian Marie Barbier, just twenty-two years old. Marie Barbier was to take Charles de Glandelet as her spiritual director and over the years conducted a lengthy correspondance with him, a correspondence which he, in large part, preserved. The result is that more is known of her experiences than of any other Congregation sister of the seventeenth century except Marguerite Bourgeoys herself.[8] On the basis of his conversations with Marie Barbier, Glandelet gives a vivid description of the difficulties encountered in the establishment of this first mission of the Congregation in the Quebec area.

Marie Barbier's account of the events surrounding her departure for the new mission implies that a considerable amount of democracy and even personal independence existed in the early Congregation. From what she told Glandelet of her journey and early days at Sainte-Famille, there also emerges the portrait of a personality strikingly different from that of Marguerite Bourgeoys, whom she would succeed as superior of the Congregation. In 1685 Marie Barbier had been named to teach at the Mountain Mission. Her report on the deliberations leading to her appointment suggests that a discussion involving all the members of the Congregation preceded the sending of a sister on mission. She told Glandelet that a few days before she was to leave, Étienne Guyotte, then Montreal's parish priest, asked her who she thought should accompany Anne Meyrand to open the new mission on Île Saint-Laurent. She told him she thought she herself should be the one to go, and he teased her about her suggestion and then dropped the matter, telling her that the companion would be Madeleine Bourbault. Despite her insistence that she would be the one sent to the new mission, Marie Barbier was sent instead to the Mountain Mission.

When she arrived, she found that the sister already there had taken great pains to prepare for her presence and to make her feel welcome and comfortable. The hut where she was to sleep was neat and decorated with pictures of the Child Jesus, to whom Marie was known to have great devotion, and she was received with joy by her prospective companion. It is at this point in her narrative that the contrast between Marie Barbier and Marguerite Bourgeoys becomes pronounced. When Marguerite Bourgeoys wrote about her travels, she always expressed appreciation for all the consideration and kindness she received: in 1670 de Maisonneuve came down to the door to meet her and gave her the guest room he had prepared for visitors from Montreal; in 1680 de Turmenyes sent a chair for her and treated her as if she had been his own sister. Marie Barbier, however, was not at all pleased by her companion's efforts: "I looked all around, my heart outraged with sorrow, saying nothing except to God to whom I made this short prayer: 'My God, this is not the place you have destined me for, I am too well off here, do you want to lose me and make useless the blood you have shed for me. Oh, better to die than to be so at my ease!'"[9]

As it happened, Marie Barbier had to spend only one night in outrage at the Mountain Mission. The community in Montreal had been unable to reach consensus on who should accompany Anne Meyrand to Île d'Orléans, and a secret vote had to be taken to resolve the impasse. The choice fell on Marie Barbier – unanimously, she says – and Anne Meyrand was sent to the Mountain Mission to get her. When Marie broke the news of her impending departure to the other sister at the Mountain Mission, the latter urged her to refuse to go. Marie, however, decided to obey.

The November journey to Île d'Orléans was harrowing. Marguerite Bourgeoys had sailed the St Lawrence between Montreal and Quebec in November after her arrival in 1653, but she left no word of complaint about it. Marie Barbier, encouraged by her spiritual director, had much more to say, and when she alludes to the people she meets along the way, her tone lacks both the tolerance and the compassion that can be heard in the voice of Marguerite Bourgeoys:

I did not think of what we lacked in material goods; it was cold as winter and we only had one blanket for the two of us which was almost no good at all, very little linen, no material except what could cover us very lightly; for my part I had only an overdress and the rest to match. We thought we would freeze on the voyage we made about St Martin's day [11 November]. I was perfectly happy with what I was beginning to suffer. When we arrived in Quebec we did not lack humiliations. We were asked where our beds and equipment were: we were carrying only a little bundle; we were ridiculed and humiliated in every way. Some said we would die of hunger and that we had been sent to look for husbands, especially I who was young.

When the two sisters finally reached their destination, things were no better: "So we came to Île Saint-Laurent, I thought I would die the day I arrived. The cold had so laid hold of us we thought we were frozen. I would have been glad for myself [but] consoled my companion who was half-dead. We suffered greatly from the cold during that first winter."[10]

It is difficult to know why the two women were so ill-prepared for the journey. It is true that Marguerite expected the sisters to follow the example of the Apostles, who were bidden, "Take nothing for the journey, neither staff nor haversack, nor bread nor money, and let none of you take a spare tunic."[11] But she must have known that the climate of Canada in November is scarcely that of the Mediterranean world, and that if the sisters really did perish of cold or become ill on the journey, they would scarcely be able to function as schoolmistresses. In her instructions to the sisters about poverty and detachment, Marguerite stresses, above all, that they should be content with what they are given without complaint, but says that "each one is given everything she needs." While she condemns luxury, she does not seem to exact the degree of hardship and deprivation reflected in Marie Barbier's account. Marguerite Bourgeoys writes: "It is necessary ... and we owe it as much to our own perfection as to the edification of the people, that our dwellings, both the community house and the missions, be truly warm, clean and suitable, that our furniture be well arranged, our habits clean and modest, our food healthful and of good quality but all without embellishment, affectation or fastidiousness."[12] Did a sudden change in the weather, a drastic fall in temperature, take them by surprise? Marie Barbier was given to the practice of severe penances, in which she had to be restrained by her spiritual director, but her complaints seem to indicate that this was not another example.

At the age of twenty-two, Marie Barbier had possibly never before left the island of Montreal. Lacking the maturity, the sophistication, and the range of experience possessed by Marguerite Bourgeoys when she began her journey to the New World and very different from the older woman in temperament and outlook, lacking perhaps especially her sense of humour, Marie found other aspects of her situation very difficult indeed. The two sisters had no residence of their own but stayed with a widow, her numerous family, and her servants in a house at some little distance from the church. While Marguerite Bourgeoys mentions no difficulty in sharing close quarters aboard ship with an assorted group of other women, in living in the Montreal shed with the recovering members of the recruitment of 1653, in seeing her house as the house of the Blessed Virgin open to all women, Marie was in anguish in these close quarters: "Since I had never been out in the world, I found myself in hell, being obliged to be with men and women all the time, and to eat mixed in with them. We would most often come from church (which was about an eighth of a mile from the house where we were living) all wet and like icicles, without daring to warm ourselves and without the special protection of God we would have died of cold."[13]

One day, that very fate came very near to befalling Marie Barbier. Returning from mass on a day of severe cold and blowing snow and unable to see where she was going, she fell into a deep ditch filled with snow:

I could not ... get out and my companion was far ahead of me, I could do no more. The snow covered me more and more and I had no more strength. I begged the holy Child Jesus to help me if he wanted to prolong my life for his glory and [that I might do] penance for my crimes. I was completely sunk in the snow and only the top of my head was showing with my headdress. Its black colour made some of the people in the neighbourhood believe that one of their cattle had fallen into the ditch. They came running at once, and, having pulled me out, left me at the side of the ditch where I had a great deal of trouble getting back to the house.[14]

This anecdote suggests that not all the local inhabitants were grateful for the presence of the schoolmistresses in their midst, and it lends weight to the lament of both clergy and the new governor about the lack of civilized moral standards among some of the people in the colony. It might have been expected that Marie Barbier's privations would cut short her life, but this was not the case. Although stricken with breast cancer in her early thirties, she would survive what was perhaps the first cancer operation in Canada in 1700 and live until a little after her seventy-sixth birthday in 1739. Her companion, Anne Meyrand, however, was to die in 1691 at the age of only thirty-two.

Glandelet presents one other anecdote about that first winter on Île d'Orléans, a story that again illustrates how different Marie Barbier was from the practical and resourceful Marguerite Bourgeoys. One day the house in which the two sisters were boarding caught fire, and all the residents threw themselves into the attempt to put out the flames or save the contents of the house – all, that is, except Marie Barbier. She instead knelt in prayer before a wax statue of the Child Jesus. When Anne Meyrand and the widow who owned the house remonstrated with her, Marie reproached them for their lack of faith and assured them that the Holy Child would put out the fire. As the conflagration grew in intensity, she prepared to throw the image into the flames, but just at that moment the fire suddenly died down. Glandelet's account implies that this was the result of Marie Barbier's prayers.[15] Certainly, she was convinced that it was so.

Despite all these adventures, perhaps even because of them, the sisters gained considerable influence among the young people, particularly those who joined the association that they organized for the older girls. According to Glandelet, the young people of both sexes were growing up very wild and dissipated, an opinion shared by Governor Denonville. However, though the two missionaries had to endure "many contradictions and much mockery ... they little by little drew these souls to the love and practice of a Christian life in which they happily involved them by their gentle, strong, and persuasive ways, and especially by the instructions and conferences they gave them on Feast Days and Sundays, in assembling them in a house before the parish religious service to which they led them afterward, all together and walking two by two."[16] Glandelet goes on to say that several of these girls had since consecrated themselves to God in the Congregation. In fact, there were five women from the parish of Sainte-Famille among the sisters of the Congregation who pronounced the first public vows made by the community in

1698. These women would have ranged in age from nine to seventeen years when the first Congregation mission was established on Île d'Orléans.[17]

Marie Barbier spent only that first winter at Sainte-Famille (though she would return later). In the spring, Glandelet says, she was called to Quebec to open another new mission. Abbé Saint-Vallier wanted to see in Quebec an institution like La Providence, which he had so admired in Montreal the previous summer. The circumstances in which this first mission of the Congregation in the old capital was opened are very obscure indeed. How much were Marguerite Bourgeoys, the ecclesiastical superior, and the rest of the Congregation in Montreal consulted? Seventeenth-century sources tell us nothing beyond the statement in Glandelet.

Working from material supplied to him by the sisters of the Congregation in the second quarter of the eighteenth century, Ransonet attached to the event one of the most persistent traditional stories about Marguerite Bourgeoys, a story that obviously captured his interest and has continued to live in the popular imagination. He writes:

In 1686, being at Montreal, [Marguerite Bourgeoys] learned that the bishop of Quebec wanted her to come and carry out a project he had conceived in the episcopal city to give a Christian upbringing to poor girls. She left at once and made the greater part of the sixty leagues on foot, sometimes on ice where she dragged herself on her knees sometimes in water and sometimes in snow. The end of her journey was not the end of her labours. Arrived in Quebec she was fed on charity and what she was given was not enough to sustain her. However, she and she alone did whatever had to be done that was most rough and difficult, like carrying from the lower to the upper town the furniture and goods needed for a household. There was more, for after being employed in these labours the first four days of Holy Week, she passed the entire night of Thursday to Friday on her knees motionless before the Blessed Sacrament.[18]

How much of this account is true? While some elements of the story, like other statements in Ransonet's biography, seem to belong to the period of legend-making in the years following Marguerite's death, others correspond with some of the known facts. Saint-Vallier left Quebec for Acadia on 17 April, that year the Wednesday after Easter. If, then, Marguerite was to see him, she would indeed have had to make the journey to Quebec at a most difficult time of year, and if she wished to see him before his departure, Holy Week would have been the latest time for her arrival. Faillon and the *Histoire de la Congrégation* do not suppose that Marguerite herself went to Quebec at this time, but rather that the vicar general had discussed matters with her when he was in Montreal the previous year and continued to communicate by letter. Jamet, however, believed that this was the first of four trips Marguerite made to Quebec in connection with the establishment of missions there. He thought, however, that the trip was probably the outcome of discussions that had taken place the previous summer, that Marguerite did not reach Quebec until after the departure of Saint-Vallier, and that she had to remain several months in order to see him on his return in September. So far, no documentary evidence has been found to confirm her presence in either Quebec or Montreal that summer.

Certainly, the establishment in Quebec of a mission of the Congrégation de Notre-Dame de Montréal would have been a matter of some concern to Marguerite Bourgeoys. It appears from Glandelet's account that the removal of Marie Barbier from Île d'Orléans to Quebec was something neither the missionaries nor the community had anticipated when the two left Montreal. The new development left both Marie Barbier and Anne Meyrand alone at their respective posts. Perhaps, like several others who had come in contact with him both before and after his arrival in Canada, Marguerite Bourgeoys had taken something of the measure of the new vicar general and worried about the manner in which he was disposing of her sisters. Already the reports from Canada that were reaching Bishop Laval in Paris were sounding the alarm about his chosen successor. While they recognized Saint-Vallier's qualities of zeal, enthusiasm, austerity, and generosity, they were united in their recognition of the fact that he was a dangerous man to cross. Glandelet wrote of him that he "begins by using sweet words and acting in a flattering and gentle manner; but as soon as he is opposed he displays that indignation and those outbursts of anger which turn one's mind against him."[19]

In answer to some of the difficulties they had raised in their correspondence, the members of the Séminaire de Québec received the following perceptive analysis of Saint-Vallier's character from their confreres in Paris. Because the bishop was to play so large a role in what remained of Marguerite Bourgeoys's life, it is worth quoting in its entirety:

It would be impossible to foresee in detail the little difficulties that could arise between him and you, but it seems to us after thinking about it before God that the only means of settling them or at least of greatly alleviating them is to make every effort in the spirit of God to win his heart. He has such a lively and quick mind, as you have yourselves remarked, Gentlemen, in all your letters that one cannot hope to deflect him from anything he is set on by reasoning alone; he can be made to listen to reason for a moment, but an instant later he forgets it, his natural fire carries him away and plans of zeal take him back to his first feelings. It would be much better ... to go his way without resisting him at first then to gradually show him the drawbacks one finds, assuring him nevertheless that everything will be as he wishes, for we have found here that if there is any way of getting him to enter into any one else's sentiments it is that. Once he is convinced that he is liked and that one is accommodating toward him, he afterwards gets used to showing consideration toward those who have acted considerately toward him and you will have the consolation of seeing that with time he himself will relent on points on which he had been most adamant. It is more expedient even sometimes to put up with the unfortunate consequences of what he has too strongly demanded than to embitter his mind against us for although he tries, by virtue, to combat his ill-humour, it is to be feared that he remains habitually out of sorts with those who have annoyed him while when his heart is free, clear and open toward you, he will take anything you tell him much better.[20]

Given Saint-Vallier's prickly nature and the vulnerability of the Congregation, it is possible, even probable, that Marguerite Bourgeoys thought it necessary to go and deal with him in person. She might also have felt that the young, inexperienced, impractical, and unsophisticated Marie Barbier would need some help in setting up a new mission so far from Montreal. Above all, after thirty-three years in Canada, Marguerite must have been quite aware of the political pitfalls to be encountered in Quebec and the necessity of not antagonizing the religious communities already established there. It was one thing for the Congregation to accept invitations to work in villages where there were no other teachers; it was quite another to establish themselves in the capital. Traversing the shores of the St Lawrence when the thaw was underway and carrying furniture from the Lower to the Upper Town, if, indeed, she did these things, were minor chores in comparison with the diplomatic challenge facing her. If she spent the vigil of Good Friday before the Blessed Sacrament, her prayer might well have sought means to "maintain others in the charity they owe us."

There may also have been another problem to resolve with Abbé Saint-Vallier. His account of his journey to Acadia in the spring and summer of 1686 contains a passage that continues to puzzle the Congrégation de Notre-Dame. He wrote that when he arrived at Port-Royal (now Annapolis Royal in Nova Scotia), "I recognized with pleasure that a good Sister whom I had sent ahead of me from Quebec to that place had done a great deal of good there for the women and the girls; her house henceforth their general meeting place; she will teach them to read, to write and some of them to work; she can take boarders and among them some who will be able to replace her, and even to establish a little nursery of school Mistresses to spread in the area."[21]

The Congrégation de Notre-Dame has no written record and no trace of an oral memory of the establishment of a mission at Port-Royal. If, in fact, this is a reference to a member of the Congrégation de Notre-Dame of Montreal, who was the sister sent to Port-Royal? When did she arrive at and leave Quebec? Was she one of the sisters from France or one of the Canadians? What was the attitude of the Congregation toward this appointment? What happened to her and to her mission?

What *is* known is that Saint-Vallier was quite capable of sending sisters of the Congregation to Acadia without the consent of the community, for he did precisely that some thirty years later. In 1727 he sent Marguerite Roy, *dite* de la Conception, to Louisbourg alone and against the wishes of the Congregation. Eventually, and after Saint-Vallier's death, the Congregation sent other sisters to that stronghold, where they experienced both the sieges it was to undergo. The last of these sisters, all of them Canadian-born, were deported to France by the British authorities after the fall of Louisbourg in 1758. One of them died on the voyage, and the others died in France without ever being able to return to Canada.[22]

Whether she saw him before or after his tour of Acadia, Marguerite Bourgeoys must have come to some kind of understanding with Saint-Vallier. By the winter of 1686–87, Catherine Charly had joined Marie Barbier in Quebec, and the two were established

in a house with a courtyard and garden in the Upper Town of
Quebec. This had been bought for them by Abbé Saint-Vallier on
13 November, less than a week before his departure for France.[23]
Thérèse Rémy had replaced Marie Barbier on Île d'Orléans, so that
Anne Meyrand was no longer alone. The new Quebec establishment, called "la Providence de la Sainte-Famille," though inspired
by La Providence in Montreal, was in fact very different in character. Rather than a workshop for women beyond school age, it was
a boarding school devoted to giving elementary teaching, presumably to those too poor for the Ursuline boarding school nearby.
According to a set of rules drawn up by Saint-Vallier early in 1689,
the institution was to receive girls who were between eleven and
twelve years of age and who would make their first communion
within the year. For the most part, it was not anticipated that they
would remain at the institution longer than a year. Those whose
relatives could not provide their necessities were still expected to
contribute thirty livres "to avoid the difficulties that might arise if
goods must be bought for them, the house not being able to cover
the expense."[24] Besides religious instruction, the girls received other
forms of elementary instruction and training in the manual work
"proper to their sex."

It was at this time that Marie Barbier met Charles de Glandelet. He soon became her spiritual director and began to receive the
confidences and conduct the correspondence that form the basis of
the manuscript already cited. Abbé Glandelet had been in Canada
since 1675 and had been appointed canon of the cathedral and first
theologal to the chapter by Bishop Laval in 1684. He devoted several pages of his work to Marie's experiences at "la Providence de
la Sainte Famille," but what interests him most are the seemingly
miraculous cures and multiplication of food that accompanied her
prayers to the Child Jesus and her efforts to wean the girls away
from vanity in their dress.[25] Accordingly, he has little else to say
about the education given the girls. Implicit in his account, however, is the struggle to keep feeding the whole household, to find
enough "bread and meat and oil and vinegar," especially in the last
days before the arrival of the first ships from France each year, of
the panic when the attic in which the grain is stored is threatened
by flood; implicit also is the task not just of teaching and feeding
the girls but of caring for them in sickness, when even measles and
fever could be part of a deadly epidemic. Glandelet also believed

that Marie Barbier was able to win the confidence of the girls and that often they could confide to her problems that they were unable to confide to anyone else. Their presence in the capital also enabled the two sisters of the Congregation to establish their usual Sunday activities for the older girls.[26]

Marguerite Bourgeoys was again in Quebec in the early autumn of 1687 to transact business relating to the mission on Île d'Orléans. This time she would have been able to travel on the river as she usually did. In September she was at the signing of various contracts that gave the sisters a house near the church in which to live and to conduct a school. This was a gift of the parish priest, Father Lamy, who settled them on land originally provided for a presbytery.[27] But while the work on this mission was being put on a more secure foundation and conditions of life made easier for the sisters, the community in Montreal suffered a severe blow in the deaths of two of the Canadian sisters. Françoise Le Moyne, aged twenty-five, was buried on 26 September; two days later, Marie Denis, aged twenty-eight, followed her.[28] Whether the news of the deaths of the young women reached Marguerite at Quebec or awaited her on her return to Montreal, she was deeply affected by these losses, as her later writings would show. They were part of a gathering sadness as the decade went on. But as before, there was little time for indulgence in grief as still more demands were made on the Congregation.

When Abbé Saint-Vallier reached France on New Year's Day 1687, reports about the impressions he had made in Canada had preceded him. They were such as to cause Bishop Laval to ask his chosen successor to withdraw his candidacy as bishop. Much offended, Saint-Vallier refused, and since he had the support of the king, who feared yet more dissension in the church of New France, it was Bishop Laval who was forbidden to return there, although the old bishop's heart was set on returning to Quebec to die.

Despite the admiration he had expressed for the Congrégation de Notre-Dame, Saint-Vallier is said to have been favourable to a step that would have done immense, perhaps irreparable, damage to the young community. This was the establishment in Montreal of the Sisters of the Visitation, a cloistered teaching community in France.[29] Happily for members of the Congregation, they had an influential and no doubt tactful friend in Louis Tronson. When the Sulpician superior learned of the plan, he wrote to Dollier de Casson in Montreal:

I greatly fear that with the intention of doing too much good too quickly, one can spoil many things. I say this in regard to the establishment of the nuns of the Visitation de Sainte-Marie that is proposed for the island of Montreal; for I do not know but that this new community would do harm to that of the sisters of the Congregation who are already established there and who are doing good. This new establishment would certainly weaken that of Sister Bourgeoys. Also, far from being in favour of the plan, I am convinced that it is not to be thought of.

He adds, "Nothing must be done about it without consulting the former bishop of Quebec, and I am sure that you will find him in agreement."[30]

Tronson's remark implies that Bishop Laval looked on the Congregation with considerably more favour than has sometimes been supposed, as well as showing how different relations had become between Bishop Laval and the Sulpicians since the early days of conflict with Abbé de Queylus. In the same letter, Tronson pays the old bishop this tribute: "You know his devoutness, his disinterestedness, his prudence and his wisdom; he knows what the country is like, he knows better than anyone the state of his church." Later he adds: "Since I wrote the above, I have spoken with the bishop of Quebec and with M. de Saint-Vallier, and both agree that the matter must go no further. The disadvantages appear to me so great that I am astonished that it could have been considered." The Congregation depended on its own labours and the small fees, usually in kind, charged to the girls in its boarding school to support the free education offered to the children of the ordinary colonists. Once more, the danger that this work would be threatened by competition with one of the cloistered communities was eliminated, though the Quebec Ursulines would continue to hope for an establishment in Montreal until the end of the century.

Though there was still no settlement of the current dispute between the Gallican church and the papacy, the fact that Quebec was a mission bishopric, and a very poor one, enabled Saint-Vallier finally to obtain the bulls that permitted his consecration as bishop of Quebec.[31] The ceremony took place on 25 January 1688 in the church of Saint-Sulpice in Paris. The new bishop, motivated either by generosity or the fear that if he did not do so, he would find "all the colony terribly against him," immediately persuaded the king to allow Bishop Laval, henceforth known as "Monsieur l'ancien," to return to Canada.[32] Bishop Laval availed himself of the permission with such alacrity that he was back in Quebec by 3 June, while Bishop Saint-Vallier did not get there until 31 July. Given the differences of opinion, attitude, and personality between the two men, it was inevitable that the Canadian church would be plunged into another period of internal conflict.

Marguerite Bourgeoys herself went again to the capital in the summer of 1688. The reason for her journey, when travel on the river had again become dangerous, is not known. Jamet thinks it probable that she had come to see the new bishop, a meeting that had become imperative if he was already showing a tendency to dispose at will of members of her Congregation without either consulting the group or seeking the consent of the superior. She had already seen Bishop Laval, for he had gone to Montreal only a few days after his return to Quebec from France.[33] It would be interesting to know what conversation about the new bishop took place between Laval and Marguerite Bourgeoys or her Sulpician advisers. Her journey to Quebec would also have been prompted by her concern for the young sisters responsible for these new missions so far away from the centre of the Congregation and the support of the rest of the community.

The source that gives evidence of Marguerite's presence in Quebec also suggests that her worries were justified. According to Glandelet, Marie Barbier endured constant physical and mental suffering. Each year her pains would reach a climax around the feast of the Assumption of Mary, 15 August, the anniversary of her reception into the Congregation. In 1688 she became severely ill about six days before the feast. One night during the illness, she had, according to Glandelet, a dream or vision

that she has never been able to forget, of the inner state of certain persons of whom the evil conduct that has since become all too well recognized, has proved right what was revealed to the S[ister]. She was so tormented by it that, unable to bear any more she was forced to call the Sister who was with her [Catherine Charly]; she, in turn awakened Sister Bourgeoys, the superior, who was then in Quebec, staying with them and, both of them running to her bed she told them in extraordinary agitation that made her seem to them to be beside herself: "These people are being lost. Oh, but women like us who are exposed and could fall into the hands of such people must be watched over with great care."[34]

It is difficult to know how much Marie Barbier was affected, emotionally and psychologically, by an attempt to rape her at some date before her first communion. She was in a covered bed and repelled her attacker by holding the doors tightly closed and praying for extraordinary strength, a strength, she told Glandelet, was accorded in answer to that prayer. Mary Eileen Scott contrasted Marie Barbier's behaviour in this incident with that of Marguerite Bourgeoys when confronted with an importunate countryman in 1653[35] and saw it as another example of the difference between the two women. That is not completely fair: while Marguerite was a mature and confident woman at the time of the incident on the road to Nantes, Marie would just have been entering adolescence when the attempted assault took place, a much more vulnerable age.[36] What did Marguerite Bourgeoys make of Marie Barbier's dreams, she who was always so sober, so prudent, so careful about all claims to visionary experience? What could she say when Father Glandelet, Marie Barbier's spiritual director and a theologian, was obviously so favourably impressed by what he was told?

There were other problems to be faced. As on her visit to Quebec the previous year, bad news either reached Marguerite at Quebec or awaited her on her return to Montreal: Madeleine Bourbault, one of the first Canadian women to enter the Congregation, had died on 27 September 1688 at the age of twenty-six. Her death brought to at least seven the number of sisters who had died since 1681, more than half of them from among the young Canadian members of the community. Given the size of the Congregation at that time, this represented a loss of almost twenty per cent of the community.

It was not just the new missions that demanded Marguerite Bourgeoys's attention during these years. There were many developments also at the Mountain Mission in Montreal during the 1680s. The first Sulpician missionary to work there had been Guillaume Bailly, but his fear of the sorcery he believed was practised by the Natives had led Abbé Tronson to send François Vachon de Belmont to replace him in 1680. Although Vachon de Belmont was not ordained a priest until after his arrival in Canada, certain circumstances, apart from his qualities of mind and character, made his appointment especially suitable. He had already dealt with a situation involving witchcraft in the Faubourg Saint-Germain in Paris.[37] He also had access to family wealth made available to him by his mother. Because the Sulpicians were still suffering financially from the loss of the estate of Abbé Bretonvilliers, their late superior, it was important that the men sent to Canada be able to support themselves and the work of the association.[38]

Belmont was a highly cultivated man with a special love for music. Soon after his arrival, he built a chapel dedicated to Notre-Dame-des-Neiges and then a house for the priests. In succeeding years, he organized the placing of the huts of the village, established a cemetery, planted a vineyard, and even installed a fountain. The mission in many ways resembled the *reduciones* organized by the Jesuits in Latin America. At first it was protected by a wooden palissade and towers, but beginning about 1685, stone fortifications were built. Two of the four pepper-pot towers that formed the corners of the enclosure are still standing in front of the present Grand Séminaire in Montreal. The sisters of the Congregation taught in one of these and lived in the other.

The Mountain Mission attracted the attention of colonial officials because of the interest of the court in Frenchifying the Native peoples. The French were at first very optimistic about the ease with which the Natives would be Christianized and civilized in the French manner and would intermarry with the French to create a strong people adapted to the needs of New France. The missionaries, first the Récollets and then the Jesuits, soon discovered that there were immense, even insuperable, obstacles to this plan and even to question the identification of evangelizing and Frenchifying. However, the royal policy continued to be the Frenchification of the Natives through education and their intitiation into a sedentary way of life. One of the most basic obstacles sprang from the conflict between commmercial and evangelical motives: the fur trade was associated not just with the brandy trade but also with encouraging nomadism among the French allies. Another was the corrupting influence of many of the French colonists. Projects such as the Mountain Mission were intended to overcome these obstacles.

There is great approval, then, in a letter from Intendant Demeulle to the minister in Paris in November 1683. He writes:

A league from Montreal, the Gentlemen of the Seminary have an Indian mission at the Mountain that is very well designed and useful. There are several clerics who have a particular concern for it, their method of teaching the little Indians is very good. They have organized two classes: in one there are only boys, in the other, girls. They take care to teach the boys religion and to have them sing in the church in Latin, to read and write, to speak French and also to do woodwork. There are two sisters of the Congregation who have the same responsiblity for the second class and to teach them all that is suitable for girls.[39]

Demeulle continues his praise of the Congregation in an attempt to obtain more royal funding for their work:

You would not believe, My Lord, how much good these sisters of the Congregation do in Canada. They instruct all the young girls from all over to the greatest perfection. There are one or two for the settlements of Champlain and Batiscan, two at Sault de la Magdelaine that I just mentioned who teach the Indian girls to live in our manner: the rest are at Montreal, about eight or ten in number. If they could be dispersed in many settlements, they could do infinite good. This kind of life is to be held in high esteem and is more valuable than if they were cloistered. Their wisdom is exemplary and they can go everywhere and so teach all the girls who would [otherwise] have to live their whole lives in great ignorance.

Finally, he points out something learned from the experience of earlier missionaries:

Nothing is more useless than putting the Indian girls with the Ursulines because the austerities of which they make profession are in total disaccord with an Indian spirit and it is also true that as soon as they leave the Nuns' convent they go from one extreme to the other. If His Majesty would give a small grant of five or six hundred livres for the Indian girls of the Mountain of Montreal, they could be taught to make stockings. They are naturally very skilful and could be put in the way of earning something and using it to dress in the French fashion, to replace their blankets that leave their legs and almost half their bodies naked.

De Meulles ends with the suggestion that these French dresses could function as prizes do in the colleges of France, encouraging the girls to greater efforts in their studies.

   An unpleasant episode the next summer was perhaps a misguided and clumsy response to reports such as this. De Meulles wrote the following autumn that six women had been sent from France to teach the Native girls at the Mountain Mission to sew, knit, and make lace. He describes them as "six wretched servants" taken from the streets of La Rochelle whom "one would strongly wish would return to France they being of bad reputation."[40] Marguerite Bourgeoys and Abbé Souart came to see the new arrivals and were not favourably impressed: "They told me that they did not want to take them for fear they would corrupt the whole community and also the Indian girls whom the Sulpicians raise in great piety and devotion." The intendant says he was forced to dismiss them and adds that women are needed in New France, but that these should be prudent, mature, and skilled, while those just sent were young, vicious, and very ignorant. The incident serves as a reminder of something the missionaries saw as one of the main obstacles to the evangelization of the Native peoples. This was the presence of so many among the French colonists who were nominal Catholics but whose behaviour was far from the Christian ideal advanced by the missionaries.

The arrival of a group of prostitutes at the Mountain Mission was not, however, the only, or even the principal, problem Marguerite Bourgeoys faced in the attempt to evangelize the Native girls. She too appears to have questioned the wisdom and effectiveness of the policy of Frenchifying the Natives, though her objections seem to relate to taking them into boarding school rather than in working with the girls at the mission. No written expression of her doubts has been found, but there is indirect evidence of their existence in one of Abbé Tronson's letters to Abbé Belmont, who was, in any case, in complete agreement with the policy of the court.[41] It is not clear how Marguerite's doubts had reached the Sulpician superior, whether at second-hand or in a letter she had addressed to him, but she does seem to have had the support of Jacques Le Ber. In 1686 Tronson wrote: "The opinion of M. Le Ber would not be shared here and his proposal would not be approved at the court. For they want the Indian women to be Frenchified as well as the men. Now this can only be done by making them go to school and making them board. It seems to me that in not taking them so young, not keeping them so long, and not making them so regimented, we remedy the principal disadvantages, and Sister Bourgeoys will not be afraid any more if she listens to your reasons that seem to me very good."[42] In 1685 even Denonville, then governor, had added his voice to the chorus insisting that this policy could not work. However, as Tronson's letter shows, there was no deflecting the court.

In 1689 Bishop Saint-Vallier involved the Congregation in yet another of his projects, the creation of the Hôpital général at

Quebec. Institutions of this type had begun to come into existence in France in the middle of the seventeenth century. Among their founders were some of the same groups and organizations that participated in the foundation of Montreal.[43] The first *hôpital général* was established in Paris in 1656 as a response to an increase in the number of beggars caused by the Wars of Religion and the Fronde. The older institutions, the hospitals such as the Hôtel-Dieu in Quebec and that in Montreal, received the sick, who would either recover or die within a short time. The new institutions were destined for those needing long-term care. They soon housed orphan boys younger than fifteen and girls younger than thirteen, the aged, epileptics, the blind, the mentally ill, and those suffering from incurable diseases.

In the earlier part of the seventeenth century, such institutions had not been needed in Canada, given the small size and youthfulness of the population. However, in 1681 Bishop Laval, Governor Frontenac, and Intendant Duchesneau jointly petitioned the king for letters patent for such an *hôpital général* at Quebec, certifying that "for the past five or six years a large number of families overburdened with children have fallen into extreme poverty with many old men no longer able to earn their living and poor widows with many children who are all forced to take refuge in Quebec to live on the alms that they beg from door to door."[44] Because no funds were forthcoming either from the court or from any private donor in France, the response until 1688 was ordinances forbidding vagabondage and begging, rather than the desired hospital. In that year an order of the Conseil souverain created *bureaux des pauvres* in Quebec, Trois-Rivières, and Montreal. Their aim was to ensure that no one died of hunger, to find work for the able-bodied, and to put a stop to begging, especially begging in groups.

Nevertheless, Bishop Saint-Vallier continued to work for the establishment of an *hôpital général* at Quebec, and in 1689 he decided to use both the house given to the Congregation for "la Providence de la Sainte-Famille" and the sisters of the Congregation themselves to bring the project into being. Obviously, the teaching of women to earn their living accorded with the end for which the Congregation had been established and for which it was authorized by its letters patent and by the approbations granted by Bishop Laval. But now the bishop added a number of old men to the care of the sisters. He also took it upon himself to send Marie Barbier back to Sainte-Famille on Île d'Orléans and replace her with Anne Meyrand. The news of these happenings could only have caused disquiet to Marguerite Bourgeoys and the rest of the Congregation in Montreal.

However, problems within the Congregation were to be completely overshadowed by events in the larger world. In England the "Glorious Revolution" of 1688 had seen the deposing of James II and his replacement early the following year by his daughter Mary and her husband, William of Orange, inveterate enemy of France. The ensuing conflict would embroil the French and English colonies in North America and the Native allies on both sides. For Montreal the war really began on the night of 4–5 August 1689, when, under cover of a severe hailstorm, a party of about fifteen hundred Iroquois crossed Lac Saint-Louis and landed on the island of Montreal, undetected by watchers at the forts. At dawn they attacked the settlement at Lachine, where the inhabitants awoke to the now-unaccustomed sound of war cries. Women and children as well as men were hacked down while their houses and barns went up in flames. Others were taken off as captives. Estimates as to the scale of the massacre have varied. Understandably, the first accounts of the event by the terrified and bewildered survivors were incoherent and confused. It is now believed that the death toll on the day of the massacre was twenty-four and that between seventy and ninety were taken off into captivity. Of these, forty-two never returned. Fifty-six of the seventy-seven houses in the area were destroyed.

The massacre touched Marguerite in a very personal way. The sisters of the Congregation had now been teaching in Lachine for nine years, and her niece Catherine Sommillard was certainly on mission there in 1689. The *Histoire de la Congrégation* records: "Sister Catherine Soumillard ... was there when the place was sacked by the Iroquois, who burned the houses, massacred some of the inhabitants, and took the others into captivity. The sisters, whose dwelling was inside the fort, did not suffer any abuse on the part of the Indians; and, after the massacre, Sister Soumillard brought the pupils to Ville-Marie."[45] The children given refuge at the Congregation house in Montreal were their boarders as well as those whose parents had been killed or taken prisoner. Among the women captured or killed at Lachine were three who had come to Montreal as filles du roi during the time when Marguerite Bourgeoys was offering a temporary home to many of the new arrivals:

Marie Roy had arrived in 1665, Marie Lebrun in 1667, and Charlotte Roussel in 1668. Charlotte Roussel disappeared into captivity, while Marie Roy and Marie Lebrun both died in the massacre, the latter with her husband and nine of their ten children.[46]

During the following weeks, small Iroquois war parties continued to ravage the area. When, in September, a French scouting party overcame one of these at Lac des Deux Montagnes, the fate of their Iroquois captives was an omen of things to come. The three prisoners were slowly burnt alive by the Mission Natives in front of a crowd of the townspeople in Place Royale in Montreal. In his study of this period, the Canadian historian W.J. Eccles has suggested that the sight of the agonies of the three prisoners must have brought the witnesses to a keen realization of the sufferings that their own compatriots who had been captured must have had to endure and of their own likely fate if they fell into the hands of the Iroquois. Consequently, he wrote, "In this war no quarter would be asked or given, and this dictated its tactics: the sudden attack from ambush, swift flight if the enemy appeared in too great strength; fight to the death if escape were impossible. Anything to avoid being taken alive."[47] Montreal had come a long way from that day in 1657 when a mother and daughter had come to the fort with food in a gesture of reconciliation with the Iroquois who had struck down their husbands and servant. The Montreal in which Marguerite Bourgeoys would live out the final decade of her life was not the town for which its founders had worked and hoped a half-century before.

CHAPTER SEVEN

THE DARK YEARS
1689–1694

In 1689 and 1690, I was warned about my state of eternal damnation;
this caused me great suffering, more than I can say. This made me
sadder and less sociable and I had no one to consult.[1]

In November 1689 Marguerite Bourgeoys was some five months short of her seventieth birthday. Almost fifty years had passed since that October Sunday in Troyes when she had been inspired, she said, to give herself to God. Almost thirty-seven years had gone by since her decision to accept the invitation to come to teach the children of Ville-Marie. Arriving alone with nothing but a bundle containing the bare necessities of life, she had built a self-supporting community of women who were offering religious and elementary education not only on the island of Montreal but in many other villages along the St Lawrence. For this community, she had obtained civil and limited ecclesiastical recognition. By the 1680s the Congregation, originally dependent on recruitment from France, was drawing its membership from women born in Canada, both Native and Canadienne.

At the same time, the 1680s had been a difficult decade. After the fire of 1683, the Congregation had had to rebuild itself from almost nothing. It had experienced the deaths of eight of its members, all of them under forty, the youngest only twenty years old. The community became subject to the authority of a bishop who was impetuous and unpredictable in a way that Bishop Laval had not been, and the foundations at Quebec were fraught with difficulties. The people with whom Marguerite Bourgeoys had shared life in Montreal most closely in the era of the foundation, Jeanne Mance and Paul de Chomedey de Maisonneuve, were dead. Gabriel Souart, Montreal's first parish priest, who had joined in their laughter during the "terrible years" and always remained a faithful friend, had returned to France, probably in 1688.[2] Claude Pijart, the Jesuit missionary with whom Marguerite had worked when she first arrived in Ville-Marie, had died in Quebec at the end of 1683. It was perhaps to be expected that she would experience fatigue, loneliness, and sadness as she entered the last decade of the century and what would prove to be the last decade of her life. To the suffering that accompanies the diminishment of powers that is a natural part of aging, to the pain of letting go, was added a quite unexpected anguish. The 1690s – its first four years, at least – were to be the most difficult and costly of Marguerite Bourgeoys's life.

Her account of what happened, like all the passages in her memoirs that deal with her own feelings, is the epitome of reserve and understatement. She writes:

On the night of the third or fourth of November in [1689], a sister who had stayed up beside the fire [told me that she had seen] a sister dead more than sixteen months before and [that she had] said: "I have been sent by God. Tell the Superior of the Congregation that she is in a state of mortal sin because of a sister whom she named ..."

On the third or fourth of January, the deceased appeared a second time and said: "This Superior has still not done what she ought to do. This is the last time I will warn her, for I am going to heaven." The sister came and told me this after dinner.[3]

Thus began a series of events that were to bring about serious conflict in all three of the religious communities in Montreal, the Sulpicians, the Congrégation de Notre-Dame, and the Hôtel-Dieu. Because of the role these played in the society of their time, a serious division in Montreal society as a whole resulted, for the three were responsible for its administrative structure, civil and religious, as well as health and educational services. It was neither accident nor coincidence that this incident began less than four months after the Lachine massacre, for it was closely related to the climate of this time of renewed terror.

In her writings Marguerite Bourgeoys does not identify the sister who made the accusation against her, but other documents do. She was Marguerite Tardy,[4] concerning whom little or nothing is known before these events began except that she was born at Aille-Villiers near Saint-Loup in Burgundy in 1657 and so would have been thirty-two at this time, slightly older than the first Montrealers who had entered the Congregation but younger than the French sisters from the recruitment of 1672. If Jamet's suggestion that she accompanied Étienne Guyotte on his return to Canada in 1682 is correct, then she had been in the Congregation for perhaps seven years. Her reputed visitor from purgatory must have been Madeleine Bourbault, who had died in September 1688.

The author of the *Histoire de la Congrégation* conjectures that a repetition of the apparition was necessary in January 1690 because Marguerite Bourgeoys did not react sufficiently when she was informed about the first visit. This suggestion is very plausible. Although she lived at a time when the existence of supernatural "signs and wonders" was widely accepted and the experience of them much admired, Marguerite does not seem to have shared the general enthusiasm for such events. To the disappointment of her first biographers, she was both reserved and cautious about such experiences in her own life, "fearing illusion," she says. In her early days in Montreal she had displayed the same caution in her approach to stories such as that concerning the severed head of Jean Saint-Père which continued to address its killers.[5] Given the climate of the time and a life spent in close association with a large variety of people, Marguerite Bourgeoys must already have encountered visionaries and dreamers, though not perhaps any who confronted her with personal messages from the beyond.

Sister Tardy's claims might well have passed without incident except for two things: she gained the support of three important Montreal Sulpicians and the attack on Marguerite Bourgeoys was part of a much larger design, a plan to reform the religious communities of Montreal. Marguerite Tardy claimed that she had received a special inspiration from God to achieve this goal and that it sprang from the ideals that had led to the founding of Montreal. Her proposal was rooted in the devotion to the Holy Family of Nazareth that had inspired Jérôme de La Dauversière and the Société de Montréal in the establishment of the colony fifty years earlier. Its aim was to reorganize in a single community and under a single superior the three existing communities of Montreal: the Sulpicians representing Jesus, the Congrégation de Notre-Dame representing Mary, and the Hospitallers of St Joseph of the Hôtel-Dieu representing the foster father of Jesus. To their number could be added the male school teachers attached to the Sulpicians and the newly emerging Charon Brothers, who were beginning the Hôpital général in Montreal. The proponents of the scheme seem to have believed that the creation of this new community demanded the elimination of the superiors of the old communities which it would replace. These were Dollier de Casson at the seminary, Marguerite Bourgeoys at the Congregation, and Catherine Macé at the Hôtel-Dieu. To a large extent their destructive efforts were successful: before the affair was over, both Marguerite Bourgeoys and Sister Macé would have resigned and Dollier de Casson, deeply shaken, would remain at his post only because his superior in Paris insisted upon it.

While Sister Tardy and her project of reform attracted a following at both the Congregation and the Hôtel-Dieu, her most influential support came from three Sulpician priests, all of whom were convinced of the authenticity of her visionary experience and her vocation to reform. These were Guillaume Bailly, Étienne Guyotte, and, most important of all, Joseph de La Colombière. Without the ardent support of these men, Sister Tardy's visions would have caused little stir; they might, in fact, never have taken place. In his 1943 biography of Marguerite Bourgeoys, which contains the first detailed published account of this incident, Jamet advanced the belief that the roots of the whole affair lay, not in the Congregation, but in Montreal's seminary. The source for almost all that is now known of its history is the letters of Louis Tronson, and not even the Sulpician superior seemed to know exactly where it began, although he places much of the responsibility for its development on the three priests.

Of these, the first to have arrived in Canada was Guillaume Bailly, who was in Montreal by 1666.[6] From the beginning and throughout his time in Canada, he worked closely with the Congrégation de Notre-Dame as confessor or ecclesiastical superior and from 1676 to 1680 as director of the Mountain Mission. He was a fervent and cultivated man with an ability in languages that was a considerable asset in his missionary work. This was one of the reasons that made Tronson regret the necessity of removing him from that post and replacing him with François Vachon de Belmont in 1680.[7] The obsession with sorcery that led to his removal from the mission was, of course, already a sign of his fascination with the preternatural. Abbé Bailly's first appointment as ecclesiastical superior of the Congégation de Notre-Dame was as provisional replacement for Claude Trouvé, who had been obliged to return to France on family business. A letter from Louis Tronson to Marguerite Bourgeoys written on 22 June 1682 seems to indicate that she was not happy with the arrangement. This answer to a letter from her shows that she was eagerly awaiting Trouvé's return.[8] In 1689 Bailly was confessor at the Congregation and apparently had not lost his fascination with the preternatural. The rules and customs of the time made possible a high degree of involvement between confessor and penitent. Confession was more frequent than the reception of communion; canon law prescribed at least one confession a week for the sisters, but there was no upper limit to the number of times they could receive the sacrament. The rule to be accepted by the Congregation in 1698 stipulated that, except in extraordinary circumstances, the sisters were not to spend more than half an hour in the confessional, a sure sign that there was a tendency on the part of some to prolong the sessions spent there.

The second of the Sulpician trio was Étienne Guyotte, who was born between 1639 and 1644 and first came to Canada in 1675. The following year, he was responsible for building the first church at Lachine. Guyotte was a man not given to conciliation or compromise: when Bishop Laval placed François Lenoir, *dit* Rolland, under interdict because of his involvement in the liquor trade, Guyotte had him excluded from public prayers. When Rolland turned up at mass, Guyotte ordered the verger to throw him out. There was probably some relief in the settlement and perhaps among some of his Sulpician colleagues when, in 1678, he was recalled to work in France. However, he was determined to return and was indeed back in Montreal by the summer of 1682. Guyotte had spent the intervening years in his native diocese of Besançon, the area from which both Marguerite Tardy and Anne Meyrand came. If indeed he recruited them for Montreal at that time, then Marguerite Tardy was his protégée even before her arrival in Canada. In 1682 Guyotte became parish priest of Montreal, a post he held until his recall to France in 1693, and in 1687 he was made ecclesiastical superior of the Congrégation de Notre-Dame.

If Marguerite Tardy was on the same ship that carried Guyotte back to Canada in 1682, she could also have become closely acquainted with the last and most important member of what has been termed the Sulpician triumvirate, Joseph de La Colombière, who also joined the Sulpician community in Montreal that summer. La Colombière had entered the Sulpician society in 1675 at the age of twenty-four, after several years as a lawyer. He was the youngest of six children of whom the oldest, Claude, was a Jesuit. In the 1670s Claude de La Colombière had become the spiritual director of Marguerite-Marie Alacoque, a Visitation nun whose revelations about the Sacred Heart of Jesus inspired a devotion that profoundly influenced the Catholic Church for most of the next three centuries. Both of these eventually received the official approval of the Roman Catholic Church: Marguerite-Marie was canonized in 1920 and Claude beatified in 1929. From his entry into the Sulpicians, Joseph de La Colombière had greatly impressed Louis Tronson, who admired his qualities and entertained the highest hopes for his future.

So it was that at the age of thirty-one, La Colombière was sent to Canada in the expectation that he would succeed Dollier de Casson as superior of the Montreal mission. On his arrival in Montreal, he carried a letter informing Dollier de Casson that in Tronson's view, this new arrival should be his second-in-command and would eventually take his place: "He is intelligent and shows good judgment and conducts himself well."[9] Two years later, Tronson wrote to Dollier de Casson: "No one is more fitted to replace you in your absence than M. de la Colombière. He is young but he is prudent; and I hope that you will live long enough for him to have the leisure to acquire the experience necessary."[10]

Although later events seem to have taken him completely by surprise, Tronson does show an earlier awareness of some of the personal characteristics of his priests that were to make these events possible. In the same letter to Dollier de Casson, he writes:

M. Guyotte has his troubles and his crosses: since he is faithful, he will sanctify himself. You do well to cheer him up as much as you can and prevent him from communicating his feelings to others when he is in bad humour: for he could lead them into temptation. What you say, that he never finds anything well done, comes often from a great zeal that makes him want to see everything regulated in the way he plans.

At the same time, Tronson was writing to La Colombière himself:

At first, you should think of almost nothing but gentleness and condescension, until hearts and minds won, they do through love what you will never obtain from them by severity. One must gain people's love and confidence to get what one seeks. For this, God has given you a manner of acting that is gentle, open, cordial. You would be well to leave yourself in His hands, so that He might use it, as well as your other talents for His greater glory and for the accomplishment of his plans for you; if you err, I would much prefer it would be by excess of gentleness than by too great a severity.

The young Joseph de La Colombière seems to have met with universal admiration, perhaps even adulation, in Montreal. He appears to have taken over the spiritual direction of the seminary (he had been named spiritual director of the priests), leaving the practical side to Dollier de Casson, who was busy making plans to construct a canal that would bypass the Lachine rapids, a project he saw as extremely important to the economic well-being of Montreal. On seminary lists of the period, La Colombière's name appears immediately after that of Dollier de Casson and ahead of priests who were older and had been longer in the country. He was entrusted with restoring the Confraternity of the Holy Family, which had fallen into neglect since its origins in the 1660s. He was confessor to the sisters at both the Congregation and the Hôtel-Dieu. He was much in demand as a preacher. But quite early, something seems to have gone very wrong. And he and his supporters do not seem to have been ready to wait for the death of Dollier de Casson, who was, after all, only fifteen years his senior and not yet fifty.

Before Saint-Vallier's first visit to Montreal as vicar general in 1685, Tronson had written to the priests of the seminary warning them to be careful about the impression they made and urging them to be discreet about the private business of the house. Instead, some of them appear to have revealed to the bishop "their most secret dispositions." They joined with the bishop-elect in their criticism of Dollier de Casson, whose moderation they found deplorable. So began a campaign to undermine him as superior.[11] With whom did the idea of the new community originate? Faillon says it was with Marguerite Tardy, but he also sees the campaign to prepare the way by eliminating the superiors as already in place long before the revelations of November 1689. Dom Jamet tends to see Sister Tardy as a tool in the hands of the three priests and especially of La Colombière. Perhaps even the four themselves would not have been able to say where the idea began.

Certainly, the months after the Lachine massacre, as the Iroquois attacks continued, were an ideal time for thundering from the pulpit about the wrath of God falling on a guilty people and about the drastic need for reform. From there it was an easy step to look for new and rigorous leaders inspired by God to restore the visionary era in which Montreal had been founded. Soon Sister Tardy and the triumvirate had followers in all three religious communities and among the devout laity in Montreal. The number of these need not have been great. A very small number of persons totally convinced of their own rectitude and of the authenticity of their private revelations from God can be sufficient to bring about a great reform or to completely disrupt the life of a community, depending on one's point of view. Sister Tardy's declarations became more and more extravagent: a number of souls in purgatory brought her revelations, some directly, some in the form of letters left for her to find. She claimed to be able to see into people's inmost dispositions, especially as they approached the communion table. The group called for the excommunication of the governor, Frontenac, who had been reappointed in April 1689, and the placing of New France under interdict. Sister Tardy declared that only eighty people in the colony were not in a state of sacrilege. She probably also said a great deal more to Marguerite Bourgeoys that has not been recorded.

It is apparent that Marguerite was not the only person to whom Sister Tardy carried messages of doom and damnation but she was probably the only one among them who had to live with her, face her across the dinner table, and receive her supernatural comunications afterward. Sister Tardy had hit upon Marguerite Bourgeoys's point of greatest vulnerability: her fear that any faults and weaknesses she saw in the Congregation were due to her failure as superior. She was further saddened at this time by the news that Catherine Joussette, one of the first Montrealers to enter the Congregation and only twenty-four years old, had died at Sainte-Famille on Île d'Orléans on 20 January 1690.

Whatever Marguerite may have thought of Sister Tardy's revelations, the spiritual authorities around her were not only convinced of their authenticity but actively encouraging them. There was, as she says, no one to whom she could turn for advice. Her writings include what is believed to be a fragment of a letter written to Glandelet the following year. It begins, "I was informed that I was in a state of eternal damnation. I had no difficulty in believing this, knowing how greatly I had neglected the duties of my state. With all my heart, I ask pardon of God and offer myself to Him to do with as He pleases, for time and for eternity. I have thought, since, that it seems as if His divine Majesty wishes to destroy this little community. I would not be grieved at this except that it is because of my infidelities. See, over the past ten years approximately, nine sisters have died."[12] It is apparent that the deaths in the community, which she had not had the time to grieve, were taking their toll. Her letter contains the statement that for four months she did not receive holy communion and had returned to the reception of the sacrament only because her confessor had ordered her to do so.

It is difficult to see how Marguerite Bourgeoys was able to continue the day-to-day business of the community under these conditions, yet all the indications are that she did so. Nor do those with whom she dealt outside the community seem to have had any idea of her profound desolation of spirit. The letter just quoted gives some hint as to the source of her continued strength: "I have never doubted the mercy of God. I will always hope in Him, even when I see myself with one foot in hell ... I have still another recourse which the merciful God has been kind enough to give me; it is the help of the Blessed Virgin. If I am the object of God's mercy. I am at the same time a proof of the Blessed Virgin's help."

In the summer of 1690, Bishop Saint-Vallier visited Montreal, but Marguerite Bourgeoys certainly received no help from him. In fact, he was very favourably impressed by La Colombière and seems to have been ready to support the idea of the new community. Marguerite approached the bishop with a request to resign: "During these trying times, I found by certain signs that my sisters had lost the confidence they used to have in me and that I had lost the freedom to speak to them. When Bishop [Saint-Vallier] came to Montreal, I asked his permission for the election of a Superior, indicating to him the reasons for such an election."[13] The bishop offered her neither reassurance nor consolation, and when he left Montreal for Quebec, La Colombière went along as a member of his retinue.

Meanwhile, the war continued. Raids on their border settlements in January 1690 spurred the English colonies to plot a massive attack on Canada by land and sea. A militia force from New

York, New England, and Maryland, planned to join the Iroquois
in an attack on Montreal, while a fleet from Boston would attack
Quebec. The intended attack on Montreal collapsed because of lack
of organization and an epidemic of smallpox, and Frontenac, who
had come to Montreal to confront it, was able to return to Quebec
and concentrate his forces on the successful defence of the capital. There he reportedly made one of the most famous utterances
in the history of New France in answer to the emissary sent by
Admiral William Phips: "I have no reply to make to your general
other than from the mouths of my canons and muskets." The English withdrew after some half-hearted skirmishing and at the great
victory celebration that followed, it was La Colombière who was
given the honour of preaching the sermon. Jamet's biography of
Marguerite Bourgeoys describes La Colombière's triumphal progress: "He returned to Montreal crowned with the glory of a success
that made him the most important ecclesiastical personage in the
town. In fact, he would now be the true head of the Seminary and
of the religious communities, where with his lieutenant, his proph-
etess, and the correspondents from the other world, he could at last
ensure the triumph of his ideas and his person."[14]

The situation so alarmed François Vachon de Belmont that he
took time from his duties at the Mountain Mission to write, in
rapid succession on 31 October and 10 and 12 November, three
long letters to Louis Tronson. These might not have arrived in Paris
until the following summer, but that year the ships were delayed at
Quebec by the weather, and the letters were able to reach the French
capital before the end of the year. Belmont's letters, with others he
received from Montreal, gave the Sulpician superior a comprehen-
sive picture of what was happening. Tronson was appalled by what
he read and acted with decision and alacrity to remedy the situation. However, his reply could not reach Montreal until the following summer.

Somehow Marguerite Bourgeoys got through that terrible winter
as she continued plans for her resignation and sought a successor
who might take over responsibility for the Congregation in these
difficult circumstances. The *Histoire de la Congrégation*, following
Glandelet, suggests that the person considered for the office was
Anne Meyrand and that it was for this reason that in May 1691 she
returned to Montreal from Quebec, accompanied by Marie Barbier.
In some ways, she seems a strange choice. Marguerite's first com-

panions were no longer young or in good health, but there were
women from the recruitment of 1672 and some of the first Canadians who already had experience in administration. Anne Meyrand
had been in the Congregation for less than ten years and had been
out of Montreal for six of them. There is a possibility that she was a
compromise candidate. Like Marguerite Tardy, she may have been
a protégée of Étienne Guyotte and therefore more acceptable to
the Tardy faction. On the other hand, she seems to have acquitted
herself successfully of her responsibilities on Île d'Orléans and at
Quebec and might have been more acceptable to the rest of the
community than Marguerite Tardy herself. In any case, it was not
to be: Anne Meyrand had returned to Montreal in poor health and
died on 2 September 1691 at the age of thirty-two. Meanwhile,
Louis Tronson's letters had reached the seminary in Montreal.

The superior minced no words in his response to the communications that, Jamet says, had struck him like a thunderbolt. His first
letter, written in code to "Monsieur Dollier de Casson et Mr de Belmont seuls," begins, "The letters I have received this year inform me
about the Wild Visions, the ridiculous prophecies and the extravagent plans of M. Bailly and M. de La Colombière and their spiritual
daughter and strayed mystic ... I would never have believed them
capable of getting into such obvious aberrations." He articulates
his assessment of the situation and states the action to be taken
unequivocally and succinctly:

I am therefore persuaded 1. that these persons are deceived by false visions;
2. that you must put nothing forward, do nothing and believe nothing of
anything they say on such wretched foundations; 3. that the union of the
communities is impractible, and that the plan for a third is even more
ridiculous; 4. that the best one can do for M. de La Colombière is to send
him back to France, and that it would be better to lose him than to leave
him in Canada any longer; 5. that I am amazed that they dared to forbid
M. Dollier his confessional and his holy mass one day a week; I would
have wished to be given the reason so that I could explain myself effec-
tively; 6. that M. Dollier must continue to act as he has in the past without
thinking of resigning as superior, for, no matter what the "tempted persons" say, another would not do as well as he.[15]

The fifth and sixth items make it clear that Marguerite Bourgeoys
was not the only superior targeted by the group. Tronson expresses
his confidence in the embattled superior of the Montreal seminary

in another letter written in March to a Sulpician who had arrived in Canada in 1688: "Neither M. Bailly nor M. de La Colombière will give you advice as good or as sound for the conscience as M. Dollier, and I am pleased that you go to confession to him."[16]

Nowhere in these letters is there mention of the attack on Marguerite Bourgeoys. But a long letter directed to Belmont in answer, apparently, to a series of questions posed in his letters to Tronson gives a fairly detailed picture of the extent of the affair. Among his answers: "The excommunication of M. Frontenac and the interdict would have done damage that could perhaps never be repaired ... That there are in Canada only 80 persons not in sacrilege is a paradox that would have to be said by someone from the next world to make it credible ... For Sister Tardy when she says that she knows the state of those going to communion, I say that one does great wrong to believe her and that in my opinion one would do well to regard her as a visionary." A certain dry humour enters Tronson's voice when he says that it would take a great many souls from purgatory to make these visions believable and speaks of letters purporting to come from the beyond: "Nobody would imagine that the letters come from a soldier and are not the work of the authors of the comedy ... If M. Certain had spoken he would have done it better." His considered judgment is that the scheme for the new community, which seems even to have had plans for a multicoloured habit, is the production of a "cracked brain and overheated imagination." Bitterly disappointed in his former favourite, who was a native of the Dauphiné region in France, Tronson played on the title traditionally used to describe the heir to the French throne when he wrote, "I can only say, Adieu to the Dauphiné in Canada ... For the lost sheep, he needs the air of the region, for I do not believe there is any other remedy. It is to be hoped that time will cure him. He was a good subject with a good mind and a good heart; but I fear that too much mortification, or a too intense application has worn out his head."[17]

Not only La Colombière but Guillaume Bailly too received a letter calling for his return to France:

A longer stay in Canada would not be useful to you and could harm many others. For, as you have not more confidence or esteem for your bishop and for M. Dollier, that I even see from your expressions that you have developed a great contempt, you can only follow your own views and expose yourself to frequent illusions, no longer having obedience to guide your conduct. You must, then, dispose yourself to return this autumn and if, before your departure, you could return the visionary sister to the common way and not continue to play around with her visions, you would do her a great service of charity.[18]

There is one other statement among the answers given by Tronson to the questions posed by Vachon de Belmont that concerns Marguerite Bourgeoys at least indirectly but remains something of a mystery. It is: "The conduct of M. Bailly toward the niece of the Superior of the Congregation appears quite extraordinary." Not only is there no clue as to what the conduct was – though to merit mention among all the points raised by Vachon de Belmont, it must have been something notable – but there is also no indication of which of Marguerite's surviving nieces is concerned. Catherine had been at the house in Montreal since the Lachine massacre, but Louise, the married niece, had also been in Montreal in the summer of 1690 just before the letter was written. Louise, her husband, François Fortin, and their family had been living at Rivière des Prairies since at least 1687. The region around that settlement was the scene of a great deal of Iroquois activity in the months after the Lachine massacre. Sometime in 1690 Louise's husband died. Because the parish records for that time are missing, neither the cause nor exact date of the death can be determined, but he might well have been killed in one of the attacks. On 25 July a three-year-old child belonging to the Fortins was buried from Notre-Dame parish, indicating perhaps that Louise had come to her aunt and her sister in Montreal.[19] In November of the same year, she married Jean-Baptiste Fleuricour, and the contract in which he agreed to adopt her seven children indicates that her first husband had died several months before.[20]

La Colombière must have left for France immediately after the reception of Abbé Tronson's letter since both he and Bishop Saint-Vallier were in Paris by the middle of July. Abbé Bailly and Sister Tardy also set off for France that summer, and they left in high spirits convinced that they would be vindicated, that Tronson would only have to meet Sister Tardy to be convinced of the authenticity of her mystical experience. In February 1692 Tronson wrote to Dollier de Casson and Belmont telling them that after La Colombière had refused any appointment offered to him other than that of Montreal, he had left the Sulpicians and retired to the Séminaire des Missions-Étrangères. "This then," he wrote sadly, "is the fruit of his beautiful and chimerical visions." It was rumoured that Bishop Saint-Vallier would take La Columbière back to Canada with him. Tronson had advised against it but, he feared rightly, without success.

Tronson's letter also contained news of the other two travellers from Montreal: "Sister Tardy has gone to her own region. I don't know if it will be for long: please God she will stay there. Her director says little and does not explain himself. There is no one here he trusts."[21] Tronson repeats his assurances to the two priests and then adds: "The superior of the Congregation must reassure herself as well as you; that you work in peace as in the past; that you maintain order and subordination in the house; and that you remain certain that when God asks something of you, He will make it known to you by ordinary means, without recourse to people from the other world ... Faith and the common rules the Church gives us are sufficient." Tronson's insistence on repeating his reassurances to the two priests indicates that it was not just Marguerite Bourgeoys whose confidence had been shaken by the affair.

One incident involving Marguerite Bourgeoys has been recorded from that summer of 1691. Fighting continued in the Montreal region, and on 11 August a skirmish with an English force took place near Laprairie. The French were successful in repulsing the enemy but not without losses. Among the dead was Nicolas Barbier, the brother who had helped Marie to enter the Congregation. An entry in the registers of Notre-Dame parish for 11 August reads, "Nicolas Barbier, Louis Ducharme, Pierre Cabasier killed by the English at the battle of La Prairie de la Magdelaine in the woods where the bodies have remained."[22] Two days later another casualty was buried. This was Jean-Vincent Le Ber Du Chesne, Jacques Le Ber's third son, who had been carried back to his father's house mortally wounded. Marguerite Bourgeoys went to the house to wash the body and prepare it for burial. She was accompanied in this task by Marie Barbier, not by one of the Le Moyne sisters in the Congregation, who were first cousins to the dead man. Perhaps Marie Barbier found comfort in performing a service she could not perform for her brother. Perhaps her presence reflects her increasing role in the Congregation as assistant to Marguerite Bourgeoys. Jacques Le Ber's wife had been dead for some years, and his only daughter, Jeanne, had felt called to a vocation that awakened wonder and dismay in those around her. The heiress had chosen the life of an anchoress or recluse, though she remained at this time in her father's house. She obviously knew about her brother's death and emerged from her quarters to give the two women what they needed to prepare him for burial, but she spoke neither to them nor to her father.[23]

If Marguerite Bourgeoys still thought that the deaths in the Congregation were due to her failings, she had more to grieve her that autumn. Anne Meyrand's was just the first of three more deaths in the little community. On 5 October Marguerite Bourgeoys lost one of her first companions, Marie Raisin, whose family had been neighbours of her own in Troyes. Marie Raisin had been the first member of the Congregation to go out on the travelling missions. Marguerite had relied on her to take responsibility for the community and the construction of the new house during her own absence in 1670–72. At fifty-five, Marie Raisin was sixteen years Marguerite's junior, but thirty-three years on the Canadian missions had taken their toll. Before the end of 1691 the Congregation also lost one of its two Native sisters, Marie-Barbe Atontinon, who had been baptized at the Mountain Mission and then, Marguerite wrote, "lived with us in order to join the community. She was received there and took the habit and made promises as they did at the time."[24] Marie-Barbe was about thirty-five years old at the time of her death on 29 November.

It was now two years since Marguerite Tardy had first carried her messages from the other world to Marguerite Bourgeoys, but the affair was by no means over. She and her supporters still had disciples in Montreal, and Tronson's letters continue to reflect the efforts being made in France to bring about her return to Montreal.[25] However, visitations from souls in purgatory, multiple deaths, and a war raging around them were not the only trials besetting the Congregation in the autumn of 1691. There were new and serious difficulties at the mission in Quebec, where Ursule Gariépy had replaced Anne Meyrand. The house given to the Congregation by Bishop Saint-Vallier was inadequate for all the demands now imposed upon it. What is more, its location in the Upper Town, where the Ursulines already had a school, was unsuitable for the principal work of the Congregation, the education of children of the poor. Most of these lived in the Lower Town, where there was no school; nor were they able to make the climb to the Upper Town in winter. The original deed of gift had given the Congregation the right to sell the house bought by Bishop Saint-Vallier, provided the proceeds were to be used in the work for which it had been destined. Accordingly, in the autumn of 1691, arrangements were made to sell the house in the Upper Town and to buy another in the Lower Town.

Unfortunately, the sisters making the arrangements in Quebec did not have the business acumen of their superior. Marguerite Bourgeoys explains:

The house in Quebec, given by Bishop Saint-Vallier, had been purchased for a capital sum of 3,500 livres and the sisters sold it with the approval of the Seminary for 2,500 livres, and 10 livres for pins [a customary fee when the agreement was signed], 2510 livres in all. The purchaser paid 1,000 of this when the contract was signed. In October 1691, they bought a house from Descareaux for a capital sum of 2,300 livres and for the costs, the lots, sales and revenues, 215 livres; in all 2,515 livres he was to receive. The 1,000 livres we had received from the house we had sold ... was available for the down payment but the seller was to receive his second payment sooner than the buyer was to pay his. The matter was very badly co-ordinated.[26]

The situation was so serious that, according to an oral tradition in the Congregation reported by Montgolfier, the sisters and their pupils, forced out of both houses, were compelled to spend the winter of 1691–92 in a stable.[27] Marguerite Bourgeoys writes of rented lodgings rather than a stable, but certainly these sound wretched enough: "The sisters still had two rented lodgings to pay for, 40 écus each: one, where they had not been able to live and for which the Seminary of Quebec paid 20 écus and the other in which they did live that they paid for by keeping several boarders and by renting the Descareaux house. They were so poorly housed that when they left this lodging they left destitution."[28] Once more, then, Marguerite Bourgeoys undertook the challenge of a journey down the St Lawrence in early spring, reaching Quebec on 8 May. This time she faced the hazards not only of the weather but of a country at war, and she can have found little to comfort her when she attained her destination. It was to be her last trip to the capital. Because of the compexity of the problems she encountered there, it was also to be perhaps her longest stay in the region, for she was still there the following 8 September.

On her arrival, Marguerite found that the sisters had been hauled before the court and before the intendant, that the buyer of the first house had refused to advance his date of payment, and that the seller of the second had refused to retard his. However, the sisters had found a technicality by which they thought they could delay payment: "It was discovered that he had sold the property free and clear and that whenever it was a matter of money he was required to post a notice on the door of the church to see if anyone opposed the sale of the property." This ploy was not effective because "there was no opposition." Still further delaying tactics were suggested to the sisters, so that the seller became infuriated and declared "that he would never forgive the wrong that had been done him." At this point, disagreement arose between Marguerite and the sisters. The sisters were ready to continue the attempts to delay payment, but Marguerite would have no part of them. "It was unjust," she says. The sisters did not want her to get involved, but, she says, she believed herself responsible "before God" because "I had to give the consent for the community."[29] She believed that the man's anger was justified in the circumstances and that it was time to put into practice one of her own most deeply held convictions: "God is not satisfied if we preserve the love we owe our neighbour; we must preserve our neighbour in the love he ought to have for us."[30] How this was to be achieved was, of course, the question.

Marguerite tried to borrow money, but the best offer she could get was for 300 livres for a month, and she needed more than 1,500 until 26 July. Totally spent, she went into the Lady Chapel of the Jesuits, where, perhaps remembering Mary's promise of forty years earlier, "Go, I will not abandon you," she made the only prayer she could utter. Her words are perhaps best rendered in English as "Holy Virgin, I can't take any more," to which she added a Hail Mary. Her account of what happened next parallels her description of events in Paris when she arrived there penniless in 1672:

Going out the door, I met someone I had not thought of at all. He asked me how our case was coming on and said that he could lend me 1,000 livres in French money for which we would not pay interest. "Perhaps you can keep it, if our business in France prospers. Do not tell anyone about this; you can make use of this money." All that was fine, but we gave him a promissory note, payable upon demand. Without returning to the house, I sent for the sisters. We gave him a note payable on demand and received the 1,000 livres in French money in louis d'or, Sisters Ursule [Gariépy] and [Catherine] Saint-Ange and I. I came upon the seller and his wife in the street; they were as meek as lambs.[31]

The unnamed benefactor was not so fortunate. His affairs in France did not prosper, and he was forced to call in his debt there the following year.

That was not the end of the business to which Marguerite attended in Quebec. There were other unsatisfactory features about the Descareaux house besides the date on which payment for it was due. Marguerite found it quite unsuitable for the purposes of the Congregation. Whatever emotional burdens she was carrying and however much she may have urged the sisters toward greater simplicity of life, her activities at this time show confidence in the future of the Congregation and concern for the physical well-being of its members. They also demonstrate that at seventy-two she had lost none of her practical abilities. She sought the help of Father Glandelet and of François Hazeur, a Quebec merchant and trader who was very generous toward the religious communities, in finding "a place in the Lower Town to set up a school" and also to answer other needs of the Congregation: "M. Hazeur offered me two buildings to choose from. We bought the one with the platform which had been used as a storehouse for 1500 livres. We had to be sure of the money from the sale of the bishop's house and we had to have a lodging for the sisters. My strongest intention was to have a shelter in Quebec for those who were and who would be on mission in all parts of the environs of Quebec and for those who would come and go from Montreal." The conditions of this sale were so generous that Marguerite signed a document giving Hazeur "a share in all the good works that would be done in our house."[32] The successful resolution of these difficulties was due, in Marguerite's opinion, to "the providence of God and the help of the Blessed Virgin."

In August, Bishop Saint-Vallier was back in Quebec, accompanied, despite all the objections of Louis Tronson, by Joseph de La Colombière. Marguerite Bourgeoys records, "Upon his return from France, the Bishop disapproved of [the sisters] having sold the house for so little, even though it was with the consent of the seminary [of Quebec] that they had bought the Descareaux house."[33] The approval of the seminary would not have been any great recommendation to the bishop at this time. Since he had demanded its complete reorganization in the autumn of 1688, the bishop and the seminary had been involved in an escalating and acrimonious dispute that had caused Bishop Laval to take refuge at Cap Tourmante. Saint-Vallier had gone to France in 1691 to seek arbitration in this dispute. The decision was almost completely in his favour, and he returned in triumph ready to demonstrate "who was bishop." There followed a terrible year of ecclesiastical quarrels that, by December, had even Joseph de La Colombière writing letters seeking Saint-Vallier's removal for the sake of the Canadian church. Presumably, this controversy would have distracted La Colombière's attention from Montreal, though references in Tronson's letters indicate that he continued to hope and even work for Marguerite Tardy's return to Canada.

Sometime in the summmer of 1692, Marguerite Bourgeoys received a letter from Abbé Tronson replying to one she had sent the previous year. He wrote:

I hope that the minds of all your daughters are calm; that the causes of distress you were given are dissipated and that all of you returning to the common path of obedience, you can again experience the establishment in your house of the holy peace Jesus Christ earned for you by his death. I do not believe that Sister Tardy will return there, nor that M. Bayly and M. de La Colombière will come back to Montreal. However holy these three persons may be, and whatever services they remove from your house, you must not regret their absence; and there you know better than I convey.[34]

Faillon thought this letter implied that Marguerite Bourgeoys had requested the return of the persons in question. If that interpretation is correct, and it does not necessarily follow from what Tronson wrote, she must have been very demoralized indeed and in need of all the support the Sulpician superior could give. In fact, his words sound more like a reassurance that the three would never be back.[35]

Evidence of Marguerite's continued presence in the Quebec region can be found in the accounts of the seminary cobbler, who on 13 August mended her shoes for free, a fact that is sometimes taken as proof that this was the occasion of the famous walk to Quebec. Jamet believed that the mission at Château-Richer was probably founded at this time. Marguerite certainly visited the mission at Sainte-Famille on Île d'Orléans, and a document she signed there on 8 September is the last evidence of her presence before her departure for Montreal.[36] She seems to have left soon afterward and before great changes took place at the Hôpital général.

Bishop Saint-Vallier had returned from France not only with a favourable decision in his dispute with the seminary but also with letters patent for the Hôpital général, to house which in September he bought the Récollet monastery on the Petit-Rivière Saint-Charles. The *Annales de l'Hôpital général*, whose composition was begun in 1706, records the move to the new quarters: "It was the 30 October of that year 1692 that they were led by the sister of Sainte-Ursule, Congreganist and Madame Denis who cared for them."[37] The reference is to Ursule Gariépy, but the Congregation would not remain much longer in this work which would be assumed, under protest, by the Augustinians of the Hôtel-Dieu in Quebec at the beginning of 1693. Certainly, this was not a work that accorded well with the purpose for which the Congregation was founded. Indeed, if the letters patent granted the hospital in 1692 had ever been followed with exactitude, it is doubtful that the institution would have accorded with the spirit of any religious community, for they describe a prison rather than a charitable endeavour. However, Bishop Saint-Vallier was not conspicuous for his consideration of the ends and purposes of others when these did not correspond with his own, and the *Annales de l'Hôtel-Dieu de Québec* says that the bishop wanted to "remove" the Congregation from the work. Marguerite may have been able to convince him that the Congregation sisters would be more usefully employed setting up schools in the diocese, but their departure from the Hôpital général may not have been entirely amicable.

Back in Montreal, Marguerite Bourgeoys continued to direct the business of the community and to receive new members into the Congregation. Among the entrants in 1692 were Catherine and Marguerite Trottier, two sisters from Batiscan with deep roots in New France, for they were great-nieces on their mother's side of Pierre Boucher, the first governor of Trois-Rivières. Catherine would die in 1701 at the age of only twenty-seven, but Marguerite survived her by forty-three years and became, in 1722, the fifth superior of the Congregation. Marguerite Trottier recorded a gentle and affectionate memory of Marguerite Bourgeoys in a passage where the closing simile has the authentic sound of the founder's style: "At the giving of the habit or headdress at receptions or professions our revered Mother Bourgeoys repeated often as the secular clothing of the sisters was removed and they put on that of religion: 'My dear sisters, be always little and poor.' When I took the habit with my sister Catherine she was still superior and she said to us in laying her hand on our heads: 'All your lives, keep the humble opinion God gives you of yourselves. Be always little, humble like cabbages and pumpkins.'"[38]

After the Trottiers made their promises in 1694, Marguerite Trottier was sent to Château-Richer, while the more delicate Catherine remained in Montreal. The fact that she was no longer superior did not prevent Marguerite Bourgeoys from intervening when she saw the unhappiness of the two sisters at their impending separation. Marguerite Tottier's remembrance of Marguerite Bourgeoys's efforts to comfort her contains words that evoke the image of the mystic winepress in the great stained glass window of the cathedral of Troyes which had inspired Marguerite Bourgeoys so many years before. She writes:

Noticing how greatly I was grieved and distressed, [Marguerite Bourgeoys] was kind enough to speak to me so as to encourage me to make well this step that cost me so much. She said, "Think, my child, that in going on mission you will be fortunate enough, in removing the children from ignorance, to gather up the drops of Our Lord's blood that are being lost." These words made so lively an impression on me that, in a moment, I no longer felt my great sorrow. They have often helped me to fulfill well my duties to the children, and I cannot tell you how much strength I have derived from them in my work.[39]

The incident suggests that Marguerite Bourgeoys was neither so cut off from the sisters nor so lacking in influence as she felt at this time.

There were other new inhabitants in the Congregation house in Montreal in 1692. On 25 January of that year Abenaki allies of the French made an attack on the English settlement of York in a raid that was much like the one made by the Iroquois on Lachine in 1689. As was frequently to happen, some of the survivors were taken to Montreal for ransom. Among these were Mary Rishworth, widow of William Sayward, and her two daughters, Mary Genevieve and Esther. The mother was about thirty-two and the daughters eleven and seven years of age. The family went to live with the Congregation. There they quickly learned French, and in December 1693 the mother was received into the Catholic Church. The family later chose not to be repatriated, and Mary became a sister of the Congregation, where she died in 1717 while her younger sister married a Montreal merchant and saw the fall of New France to the English before her death in 1770.

During these years there were more deaths at the Congregation. On 4 September 1692 Marie-Anne-Françoise Charly, Marie Dumesnil's youngest daughter, died three months short of her seventeenth birthday. This news would have been waiting for Marguerite Bourgeoys on her return from Quebec in that year. On 1 February 1693 another of the young Canadians, Françoise Letourneau, became the first person to be buried in the church of Saint-Famille on Île d'Orléans. Then on 19 March Marguerite had to close the eyes of another of her first companions, Anne Hiou, who had died, like Marie Raisin, at the age of fifty-five. Her passing must have been another reminder to Marguerite of her own mortality and increased the urgency of her desire to secure the future of the Congregation. Of the recruits of 1658, only Catherine Crolo remained. These deaths were followed by another material catastrophe: the burning of the farm house in Pointe-Saint-Charles, which Marguerite says took place "about three months before the election."[40] Though that summer saw the departure of the last of the Sulpician triumvirate when Étienne Guyotte was recalled to France, the darkness of spirit that oppressed Marguerite Bourgeoys continued.[41] Bishop Saint-Vallier came to Montreal late in the summer of 1693, and while there, he accepted her resignation and called for an election to replace her. According to Glandelet, the election took place on 5 September.

For Marguerite Bourgeoys this was not a peaceful laying down of the burdens of office accompanied by some sense of satisfaction at past accomplishments. Instead, she was torn by conflict and by doubts about her own motives: "I did not tell [the bishop] about the thought that came strongly to my mind that I had promised God that I would never give up, whatever the suffering I would have to endure. The fear that I might love authority made me disregard this."[42] On a less personal and more objective note, the fiasco she had had to deal with in Quebec the previous year might well have given her reservations about the readiness of any of the sisters to take over the business of the Congregation from either a practical or a moral point of view. But at the same time, the realization that she was still needed in the Congregation strengthened her in the hope that "perhaps God would still give me some time to live and that I would share with the new superior all the experience I had gained over more than forty years."[43]

Marguerite Bourgeoys says that she had been told she could simply name a new superior but that she chose instead to ask the bishop to call an election. This does not mean, however, that she took no hand in the selection of her successor. "I tried to bring it about that it would be Sister Barbier," she wrote; and "As soon as she was elected, joy spread through the house."[44] She does not specify how many ballots had been required to bring about this result. Nor is it known who the alternative candidate or candidates were. The other members elected to the council were Catherine Charly, assistant superior, Marguerite Le Moyne, mistress of formation, and Marguerite Gariépy, bursar. A fifth position was created on the council for Marguerite Bourgeoys herself: she was to be *admonitrice*, or "admonisher." Marguerite Gariépy, the oldest member of the new council, was thirty-three, Marie Barbier, thirty, Marguerite Le Moyne, twenty-nine, and Catherine Charly, twenty-seven. All of them were Canadians.

In his biography of Marguerite Bourgeoys, Jamet expresses surprise that all the French sisters were passed over since some of those who survived from the recruitment of 1672 had already held office in the Congregation. He speculates that the machinations of Saint-Vallier may have lain behind this election, that the bishop might have thought that the young Canadians would be easier to manipulate than the French sisters who had a longer experience in the community.[45] If this was his hope, he was in for severe disappointment, as his relations with the Congregation the following year were to prove. By 1693 Canadians were in the majority in the Congregation, and that same year the sisters at the Hôtel-Dieu would also elect their first Canadian superior in the person of Marie Morin. What is perhaps more difficult to understand than the election of a Canadian as superior is Marguerite Bourgeoys's recorded support for Marie Barbier.

Its subsequent history would indicate that the real leaders who were emerging in the Congrégation de Notre-Dame at this time were Marguerite Le Moyne and, to a lesser extent, Catherine Charly, *dit* Saint-Ange. Marie Barbier was to have only one term as superior, although she obviously always had a following in the Congregation and was elected to a lesser position in several councils. Marguerite Le Moyne, who succeeded her as superior, was elected to that office four times and Catherine Charly twice. In this election to choose a successor to Marguerite Bourgeoys, age was almost certainly a factor. The Congregation would soon have a rule that prescribed that the superior must be at least thirty years of age, the assistant and the mistress of probation at least twenty-five. This requirement was in accordance with the norms of other communities, including the Filles de la Croix and the Filles de Sainte-Geneviève. Marie Barbier was the only one of the Montrealers to have attained the age of thirty at this time.

Glandelet's notes on the life of Marie Barbier describe a personality, outlook, and spirituality very different from Marguerite Bourgeoys's. Marie's naïveté has already been remarked. Nowhere in the letters and conversations he quotes does Glandelet give any hint that she had understood or responded to Marguerite's primary inspiration, the imitation of Mary as the first disciple of the Lord in building the early church alongside the Apostles. While Marguerite Bourgeoys was able to relate easily to all kinds of people, constantly to find good to admire in them, and to make excuses for those in whom it was harder to discover, Marie, at least as she is portrayed by Glandelet, was uncomfortable with people, in whom she tended to see sin and evil and over whom loomed the threat of damnation. He says that at one point Marie hoped to go on mission to Champlain, where she would be the only missionary and so "alone with the great Alone."[46] This is a long way from going out to gather up the drops of Christ's blood being spilled through the ignorance of the people.

Nothing Marie Barbier is reported to have said resembles Marguerite Bourgeoys's statement about teaching: "It is the work [most] suited to draw down the graces of God if it is done with purity of intention, without distinction between the poor and the rich, between relatives and friends and strangers, between the pretty and the ugly, the gentle and the grumblers, looking upon them all as drops of Our Lord's blood. When we must correct we must be very moderate and act in the presence of God."[47] Glandelet gives a complete report of an account that Marie Barbier provided him toward the end of the century of her practice concerning the vows the sisters were making at that time. In regard to the fourth of these, the instruction of persons of their sex, she told him that she "had always felt a strong inclination and a particular desire to contribute to the salvation of souls; that when she left Ville-Marie, she had felt real regret at parting from the members of the extern congregation with whom she was charged, about sixty in number; that these girls both feared and loved her, that she excused them nothing and that they did what she wanted."[48]

In passages already cited, it is clear that while she was much given to self-afflicted penances, Marie Barbier was very willing to complain to Glandelet about the unsought hardships she encountered in her travels and her way of life. In this, too, she is very different from Marguerite Bourgeoys. When Glandelet wrote his accounts of the life and virtues of the founder, he was unable to report anything resembling the practices he attributes to Marie Barbier. He says that while Marguerite did not spare herself in the penitential practices approved by her spiritual director, they were not her primary focus:

She gave free and loving acceptance to ordinary inconveniences. These were always part and parcel of her life of poverty, and would be enough to identify her as one given to penance, austerity and mortification. It was indeed a most severe mortification to refuse constantly to pamper herself in regard to food, drink, clothes, sleep, warmth and many other conveniences which the poor and needy are obliged to forego. Sister Bourgeoys considered herself a poor person and used all things sparingly, taking only what was necessary to sustain her life.[49]

Like Marguerite Tardy, Marie Barbier experienced visions, or what Glandelet calls "a kind of vision." This, he says, caused her to be regarded with some suspicion when she returned to Montreal in 1691 at the height of the Sister Tardy affair. His comments make it clear that while Sister Tardy had her supporters, her claims were also as strongly rejected by others in the Congregation:

A rumour which had run through the Community that [Marie Barbier] had experienced visions on the Quebec Missions, added to some rather unfavourable reports which had been made of her conduct, had rendered her suspect to her Sisters and to others. When she returned, she was put to the most lowly tasks in the house thinking to humiliate her in this way; but they were mistaken, for they could not have given her greater pleasure.

This became clear to one and all who forthwith changed their opinions and the blame they had placed on her and the distancing they had shown her into feelings of esteem and confidence.[50]

In a divided community Marguerite Bourgeoys sought a conciliator in her successor. She must have hoped that in Marie Barbier she had found someone who could bring together both sides in the Sister Tardy affair and heal the divisions. Her own most powerful desire for the community remained what it had always been: "We must live together in perfect unity in the Congregation. Without this union, there is no community. Above all, this must be a union of hearts and minds, conforming to the same spirit of grace which ought to animate us. It is a spirit of simplicity, littleness and poverty, of detachment from all things and abandonment to God who would draw us all toward the same good. Without this union, it is impossible for a community to be whole and at peace."[51]

Marie Barbier must also have had personal qualities that made her attractive to others and inspired their confidence, even though Glandelet does not succeed in conveying them. He quotes from a letter written by Sister Ursule Gariépy in 1706 in which she says of Marie Barbier: "I cannot tell you enough ... how great a grace I think it for our house that Our Lord preserved her for us. It seems to me that she is its soul. She is an example of fervour and of all the virtues, and a treasure that is scarcely known."[52] Even if the extent of the praise heaped on Marie Barbier by Glandelet is regarded with a touch of skepticism, there is one powerful piece of written evidence about her influence on others in another source.

In 1700 Marie Barbier underwent a cancer operation at the Hôtel-Dieu in Quebec. The sisters of the hospital obtained permission to take her into their cloister, and the annalist records:

In the early spring of the year 1700, dear Sister Marie Barbier de l'Assomption, Congréganiste, came down from Montreal to seek a cure in our house for a cancer she had in her breast. She had already stayed with our Community for four months in 1698 where she was treated for this disease but because it had considerably increased she had to come back. After some preparation, M. Sarrazin, as skilled a surgeon as he was a learned doctor, operated on her successfully on 29 May; it was the only treatment that could prevent her death. We took great care of her: all the time of her illness she stayed in one of our infirmaries, and all the nuns of this House, who already knew the virtue of this devout woman, were greatly edified by her conversation and rushed to stay with her and to help her in order to profit from her holy conversation. She returned to Montreal in the autumn, perfectly cured, very satisfied with us, and full of gratitude, esteem, and friendship for our community where she has also always been greatly loved and highly regarded.[53] .

When it is remembered that Marie Barbier was charming these visitors to her sickroom in the days immediately after the removal of her breast without modern anaesthetic or painkillers, this is no small tribute.

Indirectly, even in Glandelet, there is a clue that, despite her apparent obsession with physical mortification, Marie's deepest religious values lay elsewhere. She told Glandelet of a dream she had had when she was very ill. In it she saw her mother, who had been dead for some years, being led from purgatory into paradise by her guardian angel. When asked how it was that she was being admitted to paradise so soon, her mother replied that it was because of her charity toward the poor and in even accepting mockery for her good works. Marie then saw her sister-in-law, who had recently died in childbirth and now was also ready to enter heaven because of the care she had taken of her mother-in-law during her final illness.[54] This insistence on the primacy of charity brings Marie closer to the values proposed by Marguerite Bourgeoys than her obsession with physical penance.

There is another consideration to be made in regard to Marguerite's choice of Marie Barbier as her successor. One of Marguerite's preoccupations in her last years was the practice of poverty in the Congregation or, rather, what she saw as a decline of that practice in the abandonment of the simple life in which the community had its beginnings. Here she would have found an ally in Marie Barbier, for in one of the very few references to Marguerite Bourgeoys in all that she said or wrote to Glandelet, she expressed her regret at seeing "that we have things that are too nice or abundant in comparison with the past when we used patched-up things." When someone reproached her for wanting "to be and act like Sister Bourgeoys," she replied that "she would very much like to resemble her."[55]

Finally, Marguerite Bourgeoys would not be the first leader to make an unwise choice of successor. A recent study has suggested that exceptionally gifted and effective leaders are often led to such choices because they are all too aware of their own limitations.[56] In their successors they look, not for the qualities they possess, but for those they think they lack. Marguerite Bourgeoys had been accused of laxity by Sister Tardy and her supporters. Besides practising a high degree of personal asceticism, Marie Barbier was strict in her dealings with others and apparently had her own communication with the other world, characteristics Marguerite herself had been accused of lacking.

The following years were to be difficult for everyone, not least for Marie Barbier herself. Marguerite Bourgeoys was to find the experience of surrendering authority very painful and her relationship with the new council far different from what she had anticipated. Nor did laying down the burden of office bring any immediate relief from the oppression of spirit that had now affected her for nearly four years. Yet finally the darkness did pass. She says that the experience of desolation lasted fifty months, so the release came sometime in 1694: "As suddenly as an enclosed light, on which one opens a window. I cannot explain myself otherwise."[57] Glandelet records her description of that release: "The calm succeeded the storm, and she found herself in great tranquillity of spirit. Our Lord, wishing to make up for the apparent loss that she felt she had incurred during the time of darkness and horror, filled her soul with an abundance of light and consolation. She was amazed, as she frequently told the same confident."[58]

The moment in which the cloud lifted from her spirit seems to have corresponded very closely with her need to respond to a new crisis facing the Congregation. In the spring of 1694 Bishop Saint-Vallier arrived in Montreal once more. This time he brought a special gift for the Congregation, a rule that he had personally prepared for the community. A reading of this document filled the sisters with dismay, for they saw in it an attempt to destroy their identity and way of life as an uncloistered community of secular teaching women. As in the aftermath of the fire of 1683, Marguerite Bourgeoys seemed to be able to draw on new depths of strength and courage to defend the Congregation. This was to be the last great struggle of her life.

CHAPTER EIGHT

THE QUESTION OF THE RULE
1694–1698

Since you made it so easy for me to write to you last year, I feel at liberty
to inform you of the motives that led to the establishment of the
Congregation in Montreal. And since I understand that you are kind
enough to work on the rules which are to serve this Congregation, I am
setting my repugnance aside, to inform you of the motives and purpose
which you may judge appropriate to mention in this Rule.[1]

The elections of 1693, the surrendering of authority, even the disappearance of her sense of separation from God, were not the end of
the struggles Marguerite Bourgeoys faced in the last decade of her
life, struggles that were both internal and external. As she does not
seem to have anticipated, she found the loss of power a very difficult experience. She expected, as have so many others accustomed
to the exercise of authority, that though she would be relieved of its
burden, her successor and the new council would consult her and
follow her advice. She quickly discovered that this was not to be the
case: "Once the election had taken place, I found myself stripped
of everything; I no longer had the liberty to look at the sisters or to
speak a word to them ... the change of superior did not give me the
power to have confidence in her ... I was elected admonitress, but
I had no role to play ... No one asks my opinion and I never offer
any; I must remain in my anxiety."[2] Marguerite's sense of reponsibility for the Congregation she had founded remained undiminished;
the power to exercise that reponsibility was gone, even though, she
says, "No one knew this community so deeply."[3]

According to Glandelet, the situation was no easier for Marie
Barbier, the new superior, although she was able to give a much
more dramatic and colourful account of her sufferings than Mar-

guerite Bourgeoys ever permitted herself. Glandelet continued to direct Marie, corresponding with her from Quebec. He recalls: "It would be difficult to describe the painful and anguished states she experienced during the time she was responsible for leading the Congregation ... often suffering appalling agonies, vivid impressions of all the vices, horrible temptations to despair that made her sigh, weep, and cry out without being able to prevent herself and which made it for a long time impossible for her to fulfill many of her duties and powerless even to approach Communion."[4] If Marguerite Bourgeoys could not confide in Marie Barbier, the situation was mutual, for Marie "felt herself deprived of any kind of support or help divine or human." During these years, she gave herself up to the performance of many extreme kinds of physical mortification, to one of which, the wearing of a barbed cross against her skin, she was later to attribute her cancer. Because she chose not to take any of the priests in Montreal as her spiritual director, Catherine Charly, her assistant, wrote a desperate appeal to Glandelet in Quebec. He responded by forbidding Marie to undertake any kind of penance not directly ordered by her confessor. Meanwhile, the Congregation was facing a situation that called for strong and united leadership.

Since his return from France in 1692, Bishop Saint-Vallier's determination to assert his authority in his diocese had led to quarrels not only with the secular authorities in the persons of Frontenac and Louis-Hector de Callière, the governor of Montreal, and of some of the military officers in the colony but also with the cathedral chapter, the seminary, the Récollets, the Jesuits, and the nuns of the Hôtel-Dieu at Quebec. The bishop was certainly not always in the wrong in his many quarrels, but his manner of making his opinions known and of attempting to impose them could usually make him appear so. Nor had he learned that it is better not to make too many enemies at the same time. In 1694 it was the turn of the Congregation to enter into his bad graces.

There is evidence that Marguerite Bourgeoys was neither so inactive nor so lacking in influence in the Congregation as her remarks quoted earlier would suggest. One of the tasks she wanted to see completed before her death was the obtaining of ecclesiastical approval of the rule of the Congregation. The *Histoire de la Congrégation* says that she feared a rule given after her death "would change the purpose and the spirit of her institute."[5] To this end, she sought the help of the Sulpician confessor of the Congregation,

Antoine-Aimable de Valens, to put in writing in acceptable canonical form the rule then practised in the community. This presumably had as its basis the rule submitted to the theologians of the Sorbonne by Antoine Gendret some fifty years earlier in Troyes, as it had been developed to correspond with conditions in New France. Modifications had also been made in accordance with the rules examined by Marguerite Bourgeoys in 1680.[6] Abbé de Valens was very hesitant about undertaking the project, judging that it was not within his sphere of competence. In March 1694 Abbé Tronson wrote about the project to Marguerite Bourgeoys as well as to Dollier de Casson and to Valens himself. The *Histoire de la Congégation* suggests that it was in order to circumvent these efforts on the part of Marguerite Bourgeoys and the Sulpicians that Bishop Saint-Vallier demanded a copy of the existing rule and practices of the Congregation when he was in Montreal at the time of the 1693 elections. A copy was accordingly made for him by Abbé de Valens.

When the bishop returned to Montreal in the summer of 1694, he presented the Congregation with a rule he himself had drawn up for them. The document, entitled "Constitutions Pour les Soeurs de la Congregation de nostre dame de Ville Marie," contains a profession formula and eighteen "constitutions" that enter, sometimes, into minute detail.[7] Although there are some elements that clearly reflect what must have been Congregation practice at that time – for example, the role of Notre-Dame-de-Bon-Secours chapel in community ceremonial – the sisters of the Congregation saw little evidence of their current rule and customs in the document presented to them. Of necessity, it would have to have been read aloud to the assembled community, and the indignant reactions it must have provoked are not difficult to imagine. Jamet holds the bishop responsible for the eclectic nature of the new rule proposed to the Congregation, but elements deriving from the rules of Fourier's Congrégation de Notre-Dame and of the Filles de la Croix could very well have already found their way into the rule practised by the Congregation. The bishop had incorporated many elements from the rules of cloistered communities and chiefly, the sisters believed, from that of the Quebec Ursulines, who, he believed, would eventually absorb the Congregation.

The members of the Congregation perceived in this document a threat to its most basic identity, but the sisters also knew that they had to deal with a bishop who was impulsive and unpredictable and had the power to destroy their community. They did not dare to reject the rule outright; so, instead, they asked for time to consider. This response was not enough to mollify the bishop. He had expected ready, even grateful, compliance. Perhaps he even thought he was bringing the community a delightful surprise. Their resistence infuriated him. His mood was not made more complaisant by the eruption of one of those fights over precedence that were so common in the history of New France. In 1692 the bishop had not only authorized the return of the Jesuits to Montreal but had also established the Récollets there. Now the bishop and the governor of Montreal became involved in a dispute about precedence in the chapel of the Récollets that resulted in the placing of the Récollet chapel under interdict.

Relations between the bishop and the Congregation had already been exacerbated by the decision of the community to close the trade school for women known as La Providence. The community cited financial reasons for the closure, but it might have been another casualty of the Tardy affair since the name of Étienne Guyotte is closely associated with that of such an institution at this time.[8] The decision of the new council to discontinue the work done there had been a sad lesson to Marguerite Bourgeoys on the consequences of a loss of power. Glandelet comments:

[Marguerite's] confidence in God was so great that even in destitution and in the most hopeless cases she was serenely confident that He would come to her assistance. A typical example of this was "La Providence" of which the sisters in Ville Marie were in charge – a house which had been established by people from outside the Community to receive gratuitously young women in need. In 1694 it was forced to close because charitable donations had ceased and the Congregation could no longer provide sisters. They were forced to abandon the house and send the girls away. Sister Bourgeoys offered to maintain it without any other help, she said, than that of Divine Providence, but it was not considered advisable to accept the offer.[9]

There can be no doubt that this was one of the occasions when Marguerite Bourgeoys felt that her inclusion in the council of the Congregation was largely a polite formality. Ironically, the consequences of the decision made in face of her strong objections were to demand that she return to playing a central role.

Bishop Saint-Vallier's reaction to the closing of La Providence began with name-calling and threats but did not stop there. He then resorted to a method he had perhaps used to send that unknown sister to Port-Royal and was certainly to use later in sending a sister of the Congregation to Louisbourg. The new council wrote to Abbé Tronson the following year:

He said that we were pigheaded, that we wanted to make ourselves ladies; he even threatened to prevent us from receiving boarders or candidates. He wanted to detach some sisters from the commitment they had made to the Congregation, telling them that they would have nothing more to do with the community, but with him alone; this is what he told one of our oldest sisters, that he wished to remove her altogether from the state of sister of the Congregation to place her in the house of Providence against the feelings of the whole community.[10]

Fortunately for the Congregation at this juncture, complaints about the many quarrels in which the bishop was embroiled had reached France in the autumn of 1694 and resulted in his being summoned to the home country to account for himself. He would not be able to return to his diocese until the summer of 1697. This absence gave the Congregation some breathing space, some time to seek the help and intercession of Louis Tronson. The correspondence between Abbé Tronson and the Congregation is invaluable for the light it sheds on the practices of the Congregation prior to this time, information that would have been lacking had only the rule given by Bishop Saint-Vallier survived, in the 1694 form or in the version in which it was accepted by the Congregation in 1698.

The sisters of the Congregation and their Sulpician advisers in Montreal were not alone in their desire to have Tronson examine the new rule. On his arrival in Paris, Bishop Saint-Vallier also was strongly insistent that the Sulpician superior do so, even though Tronson, suffering from a severe eye ailment at the time, had intended to delegate the task to his assistant, Abbé François Leschassier. Louis Tronson himself, then, became the intermediary between the bishop and the Congregation. His first piece of advice was that they must consider the document clause by clause, explaining what points they found unacceptable and why. It is understandable that at first the sisters had some difficulty in formulating their objections to this rule. Where could they begin when faced with a document whose entire spirit appeared contrary to that of their community? Given that basic dilemma, individual articles, pre-scriptions, and prohibitions within the document seemed of little importance. Eventually they crystallized their objections as best they could in the form of letters written by Marguerite Bourgeoys to Louis Tronson and a series of remonstrances that Abbé de Valens helped formulate and write and that were signed by the council of the Congrégation de Notre-Dame.[11] The united front presented by the sisters of the Congregation and their determination to resist the imposition of this rule lead to certain conclusions. They show that the young community had a strong sense of its own identity and the courage to fight to maintain it and that the influence of Marguerite Bourgeoys was still much more powerful than she realized. They also suggest that Bishop Saint-Vallier's actions may have led, inad-vertently, to the healing of whatever breaches still existed as a result of the Sister Tardy incident. There is nothing like an external threat to promote unity in a group.

At its deepest level, the conflict between Bishop Saint-Vallier and the Congregation about the rule was a conflict about cloister. The sisters of the Congregation were convinced that it was of the essence for their community to be uncloistered; the bishop saw it as a tem-porary condition. He has been accused of inconsistency in, on the one hand, disposing so freely of the Congregation in various proj-ects in his diocese that they were able to undertake only because they were uncloistered and, on the other, attempting to impose conditions of cloister upon them. The apparent inconsistency is, however, easily resolved. The bishop did find in the Congregation a very useful group of women, but he believed that usefulness was contingent on time and place. He thought that as time brought more settled conditions to New France, an uncloistered community would no longer be necessary and the Congregation could simply be absorbed by a traditional religious community.

So the first and pre-eminent objection to this rule, at least on the part of Marguerite Bourgeoys herself, was not so much what was in it as what was absent. Nowhere is there evidence in the 1694 constitutions of any understanding of the basic inspiration that had led to the founding of the Congregation and determined its nature. Nowhere is there mention of the most important model proposed by Marguerite Bourgeoys for her community: the role of the Virgin Mary and the other women disciples in the the early Christian church. Marguerite's own defence of the Congregation is contained in two letters to Louis Tronson which have survived and are included in her published writings and which she clearly hoped might, at least in part, be included in the rule.

Her letters to Tronson do not begin with abstract statements of principle; they are firmly grounded in history – her personal history and that of Montreal. First, she states that the purpose of the letter is to inform Tronson "of the motives which led to the establishment of the Congregation in Montreal," and she makes it clear that she is providing him with material she believes "appropriate to mention in this Rule."[12] What follows then, written almost halfway through the last decade of her life, is Marguerite Bourgeoys's own recapitulation and interpretation of the events of that life.

She begins with the "touch of grace" that she had experienced when she looked at a statue of the Blessed Virgin on Rosary Sunday 1640, "which I have since learned was the year of the first arrival in Montreal." She further associates her special moment of grace with the founding of Montreal through adding that "at the same time M. de Maisonneuve's sister ... gave her brother a picture on which was written in letters of gold: 'Holy Mother of God, pure Virgin, with a faithful heart, keep us a place in your Montreal.'" She describes her entry into the lay outreach group attached to the cloistered Congrégation de Notre-Dame of Troyes, where she learned of the hope of that community to go someday to Montreal: "I promised to be one of the company."

She next deals with her first attempt to found a new kind of community in her native Troyes:

M. Gendret agreed to take me under his direction, he told me one day that Our Lord had left three states of women to follow Him and to serve the Church: the role of Magdalen was filled by the Carmelites and other recluses; that of Martha, by cloistered religious who serve their neighbour; but the state of life of the journeying Virgin Mary, which must also be honoured, was not yet filled. Even without a veil or wimple, one could be a true religious. This was very acceptable to me because I had compassion on the young women who for lack of money could not enter the service of God. He and the Theologian of Troyes drew up some rules which they had approved by the Sorbonne in Paris. Three of us young women were brought together to try them, but the attempt did not succeed.

For the moment, the dream had to be set aside. Then came the moment when her own story and the story of Montreal came together. De Maisonneuve returned to Troyes in 1652, when he refused the pleas of his sister and her companions to accompany him back to Montreal but instead accepted the presence of Marguerite herself "without a single companion." M. Gendret urged her to go with the assurance that "what God had not willed in Troyes, He would perhaps bring to pass in Montreal." Any lingering doubts were dispelled by the Blessed Virgin herself: "One morning, when I was fully awake, I saw before me a tall woman dressed in white who said to me: 'Go, I will not abandon you.' And I knew it was the Blessed Virgin, although I did not see her face. This gave me confidence for the voyage. I said within myself: 'If it is the will of God, I shall want for nothing.'" This part of the story ends with Marguerite's arrival in Montreal, her discovery of the picture sent by de Maisonneuve's sister, and her realization that from the beginning the place the Virgin had been asked to keep in Montreal had been kept for her.

As the letter continues, rather than stating what the sisters of the Congregation should *not* be, that is, cloistered, Marguerite describes what they *should* be. They are to be what she calls *filles de paroisse* (women of the parish), whose life of worship should not be conducted separately from that of the church as a whole in their own private chapel but alongside and among the rest of the faithful, in the parish church. Secular priests, in Montreal the priests of Saint-Sulpice, should be their spiritual directors. The attachment to the parish would extend even beyond death, for the parish church was also to be their place of burial.

Marguerite further insists that all the sisters in the Congregation should be equal. Bishop Saint-Vallier's second constitution, "Concerning the persons who can be received in the Congregation," distinguished three categories of member, the third being the permanent boarders referred to as *soeurs associées* without voting rights in the Congregation. Of the other two, the first were those able to undertake the work of teaching, and the second, those who would do the manual labour of the community. While both of these would be able to vote in elections in the Congregation, only those in the first group would be eligible to hold major office. Marguerite expressed her objections to this provision in the strongest possible terms: "In the house, the sisters should be equal so that after her demission, the superior can be the cook or serve in any other capacity in which she is thought capable. The cook may be superior or spend all her life in hard manual labour – and all this to imitate the life of the Blessed Virgin." In this insistence on the equality of the sisters, Marguerite Bourgeoys would have had the Congregation differ sharply from the two communities whose rules she had examined in France in 1680, for both the Filles de la Croix and the Filles de Sainte-Geneviève do provide for a "servant class" of sisters.[13]

When he reached the question of the 1694 rule in his biography of Marguerite Bourgeoys, Étienne Faillon inserted, very convincingly, a defence of the Congregation from the writings of Marguerite Bourgeoys, putting together, as Montgolfier had done before him, answers that appear in various parts of the writings to a series of questions he believes were those posed by the bishop. Marguerite responds:

We are asked why we prefer to be vagabonds[14] rather than cloistered, the cloister being a protection for persons of our sex. Why do we not make solemn vows which are conducive to greater perfection and which draw women to religious life? Also, that is more honourable. Why do we prefer to be women of the parish rather than to live our lives in our own institution and not have to submit ourselves to the parish? Why do we go on missions that put us in danger of suffering greatly and even of being captured, killed or burned by the Indians? Why do we wish to be directed by the Seminaries? Why do we not take a protector and a Rule from one of the founders of the Church?[15]

To the first question Marguerite replies, "The Blessed Virgin was never cloistered. She did indeed withdraw into an interior solitude, but she never excused herself from any journey on which there was good to be done or some work of charity to be performed. We wish to follow her in some way." Faillon gives depth and context to this answer by associating it with other passages in Marguerite Bourgeoy's writings where her vision is very clear: the Congregation continues in Canada and in Montreal, in particular, the mission of the Apostles, of the Virgin Mary, and of the other disciples, men and women, in the early church. She says:

The state we embrace and to which we commit ourselves in this uncloistered community is the same as that of the Blessed Virgin, our foundress, our mother and our queen. Having received from God this country as her domain in accordance with the prayers of the first settlers she planned to have the little girls taught to be good Christians so that they would later be good mothers of families. For this she chose the poor women of the Congregation without brilliance, skill, talent or goods; just as Our Lord chose men who were not refined or held in high esteem by the world to teach everyone his doctrine and his Gospel. Different signs show that the Blessed Virgin was pleased that a group of women came together on the island of Montreal to honour the life that she lived on earth; also that there be a seminary under her protection; that, at last, a church be built here dedicated to her and a town called Villemarie. All this was accomplished[16] ... If, then, the Blessed Virgin has favoured us by giving us a small place among her servants, should we not use all our strength, our industry, our life itself, to contribute in some way to the instruction of girls ... ? For, after the resurrection of Our Lord she gave all her care to the establishing and strengthening of the church. She taught the first Christians to know and love Our Lord in every way she could, never refusing to go anywhere that charity or need called her.[17]

Marguerite's answers to the questions about seminary and parish also spring from her perception of life in the first Christian community: "The seminaries represent for us the college of the apostles ... The parish church represents for us the Cenacle where the Blessed Virgin presided, as a queen governs the state during the minority of her little prince, for the apostles were not yet capable of leading the Church. The Blessed Virgin sustained it from the death of her son until the descent of the Holy Spirit."[18] To the questions about founders and patrons she poses her own: "Can we have a greater protectress than one who was, as it were, a shoot of the purity in which God created the world? Although she was only a creature, the eternal Father confided to her the most holy humanity of His Word to be nourished and reared in His human life."[19]

There is, in fact, a section in the writings of Marguerite Bourgeoys that could have served very well as a part of the rule. It reads:

This community was founded to honour the third state of women which Our Lord Jesus Christ left on earth after His resurrection. These are [represented by] Saint Martha, St Mary Magdalene and the Blessed Virgin. It is clear that Martha's role is fulfilled by cloistered religious who are engaged in the care of the sick and in other services to their neighbour. The role of Magdalen is fulfilled by women recluses; austere and penitential, they have no dealings with their neighbour but are given wholly to contemplation.

But the life led by the Blessed Virgin throughout her time on earth ought to have its imitators. Therefore, it is she whom we regard as the foundress of this little company of women who, although they live in community, are not cloistered, so that they may be sent for the instruction of girls to all the places judged suitable by those who direct us.[20]

The sisters of the Congregation must have come to the realization that, given the personality and mood of Bishop Saint-Vallier, there would be no question of sending his rule back to the drawing board. They therefore attempted to formulate specific objections to precise points in the suggested constitutions, as Tronson had suggested. These were drawn up by the council and signed by all its members, including Marguerite Bourgeoys. The references in these "Rémontrances" to practices in the newly founded uncloistered communities in France indicate that Marguerite Bourgeoys participated in their preparation. Dealing with some of the petty details that had found their way into these constitutions must have been a disheartening experience for someone who believed: "The Constitutions are Our Lord Jesus Christ who having come down from heaven, was made man to reveal to the human race both by His example and by His words, even by dying on a cross, the means of fulfilling the commandments of God which read: 'You shall love God with your whole heart, with your whole soul and with all your strength and Him alone will you adore.' To this commandment is added: 'And your neighbour as yourself; do not do unto others what you would not have done to you.'"[21]

From the outset, the memorandum prepared by the Congregation makes it clear that the sisters were convinced it was actually an attempt to impose the Ursuline rule upon them as a first step toward their absorption into the older community:

The bishop, wishing to favour the intention the Reverend Ursuline Mothers of Quebec have stated of establishing themselves at Ville-Marie, where they have recently bought property for this purpose, and seeing well the uselessness of a second community for the instruction of the girls in this area, has spoken to us several times of uniting and merging us with the said Ursuline Mothers, who have also expressed the same desire to us. We have always told the bishop that we could never consent to this given that we had no intention in joining the Congregation of embracing the life of which the Ursulines make profession. However, the bishop wants to give us rules and constitutions that tend for the most part to make us nuns. He has told us that we must live under the rule of some holy founder of an order, and has placed at the beginning of the said constitutions the rule of St Augustine, which can be found printed at the beginning of the constitutions of the Reverend Mothers Ursuline, and enjoins us in formal terms to observe the said rule. Although we can draw several good things from it, we do not believe that this rule is suitable for our institute since it is expressly given to nuns and we are established as the secular women of the Congrégation Notre-Dame, without being able, in the future, to claim to change into the religious life.[22]

The last point is a strong one to which the sisters of the Congregation would return: all previous authorizations received, whether from Bishop Laval or from the king, were for a community of secular women, not of a traditional religious community. In fact, Bishop Laval's earlier authorization had expressly forbidden the transformation of the Congregation into such a community.[23]

The fear that the the bishop intended to use these constitutions to destroy their identity as secular women lay behind the sisters' objection to the third article of the third constitution, regarding obedience. This contained the statement "The sisters will regard as their most important obligation to obey all those persons who for them take the place of Our Lord on earth, they will be entirely submitted to the authority, jurisdiction, correction, and government of the bishop as to their first and only superior and by whom they should know the will of God in all the occasions he chooses to pronounce himself."

This fear of having cloister imposed upon them also led to the sisters' objection to some of the terminology used in the constitutions: they preferred the terms "candidate," "probation," and "reception" to "postulant," "novitiate," and "profession," which they saw as the vocabulary of the cloister. Until this time they had made "promises" binding as long as they remained in the Congregation. These constitutions proposed that they make "solemn promises" to observe poverty, chastity, and obedience and to teach persons of their sex, promises that only the bishop could dispense them from. The sisters questioned whether there was any distinction between solemn promises and solemn vows and proposed instead simple vows binding "for the time one wished to remain a sister of the Congregation." After six years of reception, a sister could make a vow of stability, not in the monastic sense but in the sense of remaining in the Congregation for life. "For the rest," they wrote, "we ask you to regulate things so that we will always have the freedom to open the door of our little Congregation to those who want to leave, or whom we judge suitable to send away; we want no prisoners among us nor any other chains than those of pure love."[24]

In the same spirit, there are objections to the existence of article nine of the tenth constitution, entitled "Concerning cloister." The sisters objected to the word "cloister" itself, as well as to some of the provisions falling under its heading, such as the one that they should never speak to anyone in the street. (Did it occur to Marguerite Bourgeoys that had she been bound by that provision, she would not have been relieved of financial embarrassment in Paris in 1670 or in Quebec in 1692?) The community found some of the provisions in the article on silence unrealistic for a group such as theirs. Whatever may have been her own practices, Marie Barbier, as superior, was the first signatory of this document, which states that as secular women, the sisters should not be bound to any particular penances beyond those prescribed for the church in general unless with the advice and consent of their director.

Among the other objections raised is one in which the voice of Marguerite Bourgeoys can clearly be heard:

The bishop wants us to exact a dowry of two thousand livres. We beg His Excellency to leave us the freedom we have had until now to receive among us the women who present themselves, without exacting a dowry from them. It is true that our Congregation is poor; but we have good reason to hope, from the experience of the past, that this poverty will draw on us the blessings of God. We live by our industry, with grants His Majesty has kindly accorded us, without being a burden on anyone. If we are obliged to take a dowry, it will keep very capable subjects away from our institute and finish by destroying our establishment.[25]

While all these discussions so vital to the Congregation were taking place and while Abbé Tronson was doing his best to intervene on their behalf in France, life was, of course, not standing still in Montreal. To the distress occasioned by the continuing war around them came a new disaster within the town: on the night of 24–25 February 1695 the Hôtel-Dieu burned to the ground. There the Sister Tardy affair had resulted in the resignation of Sister Catherine Macé and the election as superior of Marie Morin, who had been the Hospitallers' first Canadian postulant in 1662. Sister Morin had just completed a very demanding term as community bursar. The Hospitallers had never recovered financially from the loss, at the time of Jérôme de La Dauversière's death, of the funds given by Madame de Bullion for their foundation. With great difficulty and at the cost of considerable sacrifice, they had succeeded in rebuilding their crumbling hospital in the early 1690s. The new building had been opened barely three months before it was destroyed.

Sister Morin has given a detailed and vivid account of the events of that night: the difficulty of giving the alarm and waking up the inhabitants of the hospital, the noise and confusion, the attempts to save what could be removed from the building, first from the fire and then from the looters.[26] She describes the frustration of being unable to get the help that might have saved at least the new building, for the fire had started in the chapel attached to the old building. There were comic moments, as when some of the looters consumed what they hoped might be fine wines or syrups from the pharmacy but were in fact purgatives. There were dramatic moments, as when Dollier de Casson, followed by his clergy and by much of the population of Montreal, arrived carrying the Blessed Sacrament and at that very instant the wind changed direction, removing the threat that the conflagration would spread to the surrounding buildings. One of the most moving moments comes in Sister Morin's description of her own actions that night: "The superior did all she could to engage some of these persons, earnestly begging them to get on top of the house and make a firebreak to save a part, which could have been done by carpenters, but none could be found and no one else was willing to risk it, which made her realize that it was God's will that all pass by fire. And throwing herself to her knees, she offered Him the sacrifice of this dear convent whose building had cost her so much trouble and care and which had been finished only four months."[27]

Sister Morin says that this was the biggest fire yet seen in Canada, for the convent was 190 feet long by 32 feet wide and four storeys high, and the hospital and chapel 200 feet long. The fire was reportedly visible as far as Sorel as well as in Laprairie, Longueuil, Boucherville, and Pointe-aux-Trembles. The break of day found the sisters and their patients assembled in what was left of their garden, some without shoes or adequate clothing. There, as the fire began to die away, a priest came to bring them the message that a room in the seminary had been made available for the patients, while the nuns could take refuge at the house of the Congregation. As the flames diminished, the bursar and the pharmacist went to salvage what they could from the wreckage, especially grateful for what remained of the contents of the pharmacy.

The Hôtel-Dieu sisters remained with the Congregation for several months, occupying the space usually used by the Congregation boarders, two medium-sized rooms on the second floor with an attic above, as well as three small cells in the sisters' dormitory for the superior, assistant, and bursar. As she struggled with the immense task of rebuilding the hospital and convent, Marie Morin must have found sympathetic support in Marguerite Bourgeoys, who had faced the same sort of challenge less than twelve years before. These months must have strengthened that respect and affection for Marguerite Bourgeoys so conspicuous in Sister Morin's *Annales*; perhaps, also, it gave the two women time to recall and share some of the anecdotes about Montreal's beginnings included in that work. The presence of the Hospitallers in her house at a time when the inspiration for the Congregation was very much in the forefront of her thoughts made possible an event that Marguerite described in a letter to Abbé Tronson as one of the "signs" confirming the inspiration for the Congregation. She observes, "When M. Le Ber's daughter entered our house where the Hospital Sisters have been staying since their fire, I had the great joy of seeing the three states of religious women gathered together in the house of the Blessed Virgin."[28] The reference to "M. Le Ber's daughter" points to new developments at the Congregation and introduces the most unusual of all the religious heroines of New France.

Jeanne Le Ber was born in Montreal in January 1662, the only daughter of Jacques Le Ber and Jeanne Le Moyne and therefore a member of two of the wealthiest and most influential families in New France. One brother had preceded her in the family; four more would follow. Her godfather was Paul de Chomedey de Maisonneuve, her godmother, Jeanne Mance, after whom she was named. Jeanne Le Ber's first biographer was François Vachon de Belmont. Since he had not arrived in Montreal until 1680, he relied on two sources for his information about Jeanne's early years, the memories of Marie Morin and those of the nuns of the Ursuline convent in Quebec, where Jeanne Le Ber completed her education. The house shared by the families of Jacques Le Ber and his brother-in-law Charles Le Moyne was adjacent to the property of the Hôtel-Dieu, where the small Jeanne was a frequent visitor and a great favourite among the nuns at recreation. One of the anecdotes shows that the five- or six-year-old Jeanne had both an inquiring mind and an ease in spontaneous prayer. When told of the flight into Egypt, she demanded: "O good Jesus, why didn't you make Herod die, who was so wicked, instead of giving so much trouble to your blessed Mother and to Saint Joseph to take you so far?"[29] The word translated here as "trouble" was *peine*, whose primary meaning is sorrow or sadness, something Jeanne would certainly one day bring to her own parents. Jeanne may have gone to the Congregation school like her cousins, for she appears to have been friendly with the Charly sisters. It is strange that no one in the Congregation seems to have supplied Abbé Belmont with any memories from Jeanne's childhood, for Marguerite Le Moyne, Jeanne's first cousin, was certainly still alive at the time he wrote.

In 1674 the twelve-year-old Jeanne was sent to the Ursuline boarding school in Quebec. Not everyone there would have been a stranger to her: her aunt Marie Le Ber, who had lived in the Le Ber house in Montreal from the time of her arrival from France in 1666 until her entry into the Ursulines in Quebec in 1668, had made profession there in October 1670.[30] Jeanne's parents seem to have been very indulgent toward her: they commissioned one of their friends in the capital to make sure that their daughter lacked nothing, even to providing her with special treats. The Le Ber family fortunes were already on the rise, and these years in the capital would not just provide an education in keeping with her station in life; they would also give Jeanne the opportunity to make suitable friends and contacts among her fellow boarders. It has been suggested that her seriousness, maturity, and religious spirit awakened in her teachers the hope that she would become a member of their community. If that is so, they must also have realized that the parents almost certainly had other ambitions for this girl, who would some day be one of the most notable heiresses of New France. One of the accomplishments the Ursulines taught the girls in the boarding school was embroidery, whose techniques and patterns they had brought from France. Jeanne, it is said, soon proved herself more expert than her teachers, and indeed, the examples of her work that still exist, bear this out. What else did she learn during these years? Besides the grounding in secular subjects, besides the usual religious intruction and formation she received, where did she find the inspiration for the extraordinary spiritual journey on which she was soon to embark? Not even her first biographer, who had actually known and questioned her, could provide the answer to that question.

When Jeanne returned to Montreal in 1677, it was not to the social round her parents expected. Devout though she undoubtedly was, her mother must have anticipated with pleasure the launching of an only daughter in society. Jeanne was reportedly attractive, lively, and charming. Even if she was none of these things, her social position would have guaranteed her popularity. But Jeanne chose to observe a rule of life similar to the one she had followed in boarding school, with daily mass and regular periods of prayer and work. Some of her practices resemble those of earlier saints who attempted to reconcile a privileged life with Christian asceticism: like Thomas More, who wore a hair shirt beneath the robes of the lord chancellor of England, Jeanne redoubled her penitential practices when she wore the fashionable clothes that pleased her mother. She felt herself increasingly repelled by what she saw as earthly vanity. Her biographer says that she was also much impressed by the sight of the dead body of one of her companions, who had died young. Traditionally, this companion has been identified as Marie Charly of the Congregation, born, like Jeanne, in 1662. If so, the event did not take place until the spring of 1682, after Jeanne had already begun her chosen way of life.

It seems that matters were brought to a head when Jeanne received a proposal of marriage and she made clear her rejection not only of this but of all suitors. One can only imagine the struggle with her parents, their arguments, their incredulity, perhaps, at the step she hoped to take. Jeanne must have been both strong-minded and persuasive. In 1680, at the age of eighteen, she won the consent of her spiritual director, the Sulpician François Seguenot, and, through him, of her parents to attempt the way of life to which she felt drawn: like Catherine of Sienna, the fourteenth-century saint, she became a recluse in her parents' house.

It has sometimes been suggested that Jeanne Le Ber's decision to become a recluse, a way of life rare in any age and almost unknown in seventeenth-century France, was a consequence of the absence of contemplative communities in the New France of her time.

Although the Ursulines and the hospital sisters in Quebec and Montreal were cloistered, they were not devoted to pure contemplation. However, Jeanne had both the connections and the means – her father gave her a dowry of 50,000 écus – to enter a contemplative community in France, and there were people around her who could have told her about the Carmelites, the Poor Clares, and other such groups. Belmont says that Jeanne had two objections to entering a religious community. In the first place, she did not want to make a vow of poverty since this would take away from her "the means of helping the poor and, especially, of providing for the education of little girls, an endeavour for which she felt a wonderful attraction and that, on the contrary, the free disposal of her goods would give her the means of contributing to many good works." Secondly, her biographer says, she wanted a life of silence and seclusion impossible in any kind of community: "She considered ... that although the cloister separated the nuns from worldly conversations, it did not dispense them from the administration of the duties of the community and would involve her in an infinity of cares and speeches, finally that obedience would not dispense her from the conversations that must be inevitable and regular among sisters of the same community. These engagements, then, did not satisfy her attraction for solitude, strict silence, and a continuous attachment to the presence of God."[31]

Initially, Jeanne Le Ber was permitted to make a vow of reclusion for a period of five years. Her parents might well have thought that before that period was over, their daughter would have tired of this strange way of life. Indeed, the death of her mother two years later would certainly have given her an acceptable reason for asking for a dispensation even from the remainder of the five years. However, she resisted all pressure to leave her seclusion and take over the running of her father's household and remained faithful to the rule of life drawn up for her by her director. If the pattern she followed in her later life had already begun, her days started with an hour of prayer at four in the morning and attendance at the first mass of the day at five and continued with periods of mental and vocal prayer, spiritual reading, and manual work. This work was devoted to the service of Christ present in the Eucharist, through the creation of exquisite embroidered liturgical vestments and other articles for use in chapels and churches. It was also devoted to Christ present in the poor, through the making of clothing to be distributed among them.

At first, the reclusion was not complete. Jeanne attended mass at the chapel of the Hôtel-Dieu and then, after its completion in 1683, at the parish church. She twice acted as a godmother in 1681. She continued to visit and converse with Sister Catherine Macé at least occasionally. If, indeed, the death of a companion that so moved her was that of Marie Charly, the two may have continued their friendship during the first years.

During this time Abbé Seguenot came in weekly from his mission in Pointe-aux-Trembles to hear Jeanne's confession and instruct and counsel her and, as the years passed, to limit her visits to the parish church and to modify her rule. He and the other Sulpicians in contact with her watched carefully for signs of mental or emotional imbalance. What they saw convinced them to allow Jeanne Le Ber to pronounce perpetual vows of chastity and reclusion on the feast of St John the Baptist, 24 June 1685.

In her room in her father's house, Jeanne must have learned of the Lachine massacre in 1689 and of the opening events of the war that claimed the life of her brother Jean-Vincent in 1692, when she emerged to give Marguerite Bourgeoys what was needed to prepare him for burial. There she would have witnessed the fire that destroyed the Hôtel-Dieu. (Despite the strict asceticism of her own life, it was a luxury she sent for the hospital patients the next day: four jars of jam.[32] Her father would be the most important financial contributor to the rebuilding of the hospital.) At some point Anne Barrois, a daughter of Anne Le Ber, Jeanne's first cousin, became her go-between, the one person permitted to enter her room to bring her what she needed from the outside world and to take away whatever required removal. Through her or in some other way, Jeanne Le Ber learned of the desire of the Congregation for a larger chapel.

Jeanne's first biographers say that she had three principal devotions: to Christ in the Blessed Sacrament, to Mary his mother, and to the angels. Of these, the most important was the first, but until this time, Jeanne could only direct her prayers toward the glow of the sanctuary lamp in the church visible from her window and marking the presence of the consecrated host in the tabernacle. Now the idea came to her that she could finance the building of a chapel for the Congregation with a condition attached: that adjacent to this chapel there would be an apartment where she could live in seclusion in close proximity to the sanctuary and to the tabernacle containing the Blessed Sacrament. The arrangements were made and the chapel and apartment completed by August 1695.

Montgolfier places in 1692 the origin of the idea of building a large chapel within the grounds of the Congregation where mass could be celebrated and the Blessed Sacrament reserved. If the date is accurate, then it would have been while Marguerite Bourgeoys was still superior. In some ways it seems strange that this chapel should had been planned and built during the very years when the sisters of the Congregation were fighting to remain *filles de paroisse*. In fact, the new chapel did not replace the parish church in the life of the Congregation. Writing in 1697, Marie Morin says that the sisters of the Congregation "always attend the divine worship of the parish even though they have a chapel in their grounds built by Mademoiselle Le Ber."[33] However, the chapel within their building where they assembled for common prayer was already too small: Sister Morin describes it as inadequate for one of the hospitallers' clothing ceremonies, which had to take place in the unfinished new chapel during their sojourn with the Congregation.[34] Also, by the 1690s, for the first time, the Congregation numbered old people among its members in the persons of Marguerite Bourgeoys and Catherine Crolo; it also included some not-so-old sisters whose health had been broken by the hardships of mission life. A chapel in their own grounds would make it easier for them to attend daily mass, especially in bad weather, and also to pray in the presence of the Blessed Sacrament, a practice very important in Catholic piety until the Second Vatican Council shifted the focus of eucharistic piety.

On 4 August 1695 Jeanne Le Ber signed a notarized agreement with the Congrégation de Notre-Dame. This stated that she had already advanced the sum of 4,000 livres, the major cost of the construction of a chapel in the grounds of the community with a small apartment at the rear where she could live "in retirement as long as God will give her the perseverance." The document went on to provide for the payment of her board and to arrange that Anne Barrois also would be able to live at the Congregation as long as the arrangement was acceptable to the two cousins.[35] Besides that of Jeanne Le Ber, the document carries the signature of Dollier de Casson, acting as vicar general for Bishop Saint-Vallier, and of Marie Barbier, Catherine Charly, and Marguerite Gariépy, accepting for the Congregation.[36] The next day, after the celebration of vespers, in a public religious ceremony that attracted most of the population of Montreal, Jeanne entered her new quarters. She would remain there until her death in October 1714. On the liturgical calendar, this was the feast of Our Lady of the Snows, the anniversary of the baptism of first little Iroquois Marie des Neiges in 1658, an important date for Marguerite Bourgeoys. On 6 August 1695, feast of the Transfiguration of Christ, high mass was celebrated for the first time in the new Congregation chapel. From then on, mass would be celebrated there daily.

Even in seventeenth-century Montreal, which still kept a memory of its mystical origins, Jeanne Le Ber's way of life was perceived as so extraordinary that her first biographers felt they must explain and justify her choice in a way they did not judge necessary when they wrote of Marie de l'Incarnation, Jeanne Mance, and Marguerite Bourgeoys. Across the centuries she has continued to fascinate or to repel.[37] Even outside those who can see in her life nothing but an exercise in morbid psychology, even among those who share her faith, there is criticism. Of course, gestures like that of Jeanne Le Ber have been questioned since Mary the sister of Lazarus "took a pound of perfume made of pure nard, anointed Jesus' feet and wiped them with her hair" and "the house was filled with the fragrance of the perfume," causing Judas to demand, "Why was this perfume not sold for three-hundred denarii and the money given to the poor?"[38] Two objections often raised against Jeanne Le Ber are that she did not renounce her property and that she kept a servant in the person of her cousin Anne Barrois. In answer to the first, it can be argued that Jeanne saw her fortune as a trust and responsibility and that she used it always in favour of others rather than for herself. The clothing she was wearing at the time of her death was so poor that it was found inadequate for her burial. As for Anne Barrois, she acted more as an intermediary with the world outside the recluse's cell than as a servant in the conventional sense.

Another accusation directed against Jeanne Le Ber is that "she seemed to savour the social status of her family ... and always enjoyed prominence and praise for her virtues and talents."[39] It is difficult to find much direct contemporary evidence to support this statement. Some of the extravagant gestures she made in church in her early days were discontinued at once on the word of her confessor. The grand and theatrical ceremony that inaugurated her entrance to her apartment at the Congregation was much more typical of its time than Marguerite Bourgeoys's determined soberness and avoidance of display. What is more, it was not Jeanne herself who designed this ceremony but Dollier de Casson. As has been pointed out, it transformed Jeanne Le Ber's reclusion from an act of private devotion to an act of public worship.[40] Her act became that of the whole Christian community of which she was a part. Jeanne's own silence is perhaps the strongest evidence against the accusation that she sought or even enjoyed admiration.

At the beginning of his account of her life, Abbé Belmont pointed out his main difficulty: usually, he says, when one writes about a holy person, one can use as sources what the person has said and what others have observed about them. Where does one begin when called upon to write about someone who kept a perpetual silence and lived in seclusion? Jeanne Le Ber herself made no attempt to justify her life except when called upon to do so by those in authority. Her only recorded words of explanation were prompted by the visit of two American colonists, probably in 1698:

Two Englishmen having told Bishop Saint-Vallier of their desire to see her in her solitude, he wanted to take them himself. They were extremely surprised to see her in such a small apartment. One of them who was a minister asked her why she put herself to so much trouble when she could have lived in the world with all its pleasures and conveniences (for he was acquainted with her family). She replied that it was a magnet that had attracted her and separated her from all things. He wanted to know what this magnet was that had so separated her from all things. She opened the window where she received holy communion and bowing low as she looked at the altar, "There," she said, "is my magnet! It is Our Lord who is truly and really in the Blessed Sacrament," speaking of this august mystery with such zeal and fervour that he appeared surprised, and it is known that when he went back to his own country, he spoke often of this as of something that had made a great impression on him having seen nothing in the country, he said, more extraordinary.[41]

Jeanne Le Ber chose silence not just for her lifetime but forever: if she had no words for her own time, she left none for the generations to come. Only her bones continue to speak for her: the worn bones of the knees that reflect her many hours spent kneeling in prayer, the marks on the teeth from the many threads she snapped with them. The other tangible evidence that remains of Jeanne is the embroidered liturgical vestments and altar fittings of extraordinary beauty. One of her recent biographers has said that although she cut herself off completely from the beauty of the outside world, she reproduced it in her narrow cell in the profusion of brightly coloured flowers and foliage which she created for the decoration of the altars of New France.[42] These bear witness to the fact that Jeanne was not only a recluse; she was also an artist.

Clearly, Jeanne Le Ber's inspiration was very different from Marguerite Bourgeoys's. Like Marguerite, Jeanne believed that she lived in imitation of the Blessed Virgin Mary, but it was to the inner life of Mary, her life of prayer and contemplation, that she was dedicated. Marguerite's vision of Mary always in relationship with others – responding to the Annunciation by setting out in haste to visit her cousin Elizabeth, attending the wedding feast at Cana because "they were poor people and there was good to be done," active and teaching with the apostles in the early church – is very different from Jeanne's. In fact, as her reference to the presence of the three ways of life in the house of the Congregation makes clear, Marguerite Bourgeoys saw in Jeanne Le Ber an emulator of Mary Magdalen rather than of the mother of Jesus. Describing the entry of Jeanne Le Ber into her apartment at the Congregation, Marguerite wrote: "I was overjoyed the day Mademoiselle Le Ber entered this house as a recluse. It was a Friday, the fifth of August, 1695, at about five o'clock in the afternoon. While the litany of the Blessed Virgin was being sung, M. Dollier, vicar general of the diocese and superior of the seminary, conducted her to the room built for this purpose, in the chapel but outside the main part of the house. He spoke to her exhorting her to perseverance. Like St. Madelaine in her grotto, she never went out and she spoke to no one."[43]

Another striking difference between the two women is reflected in their treatment of their families. Marguerite Bourgeoys had written, "I had the consolation of taking care of my father in his last illness." What did she make of Jeanne Le Ber's treatment of her parents? Jeanne refused to go to her dying mother, even though, at that time, she still lived in her parents' house; nor would she visit her father in his last illness. When her brother was killed, she emerged from her seclusion to provide what was necessary for his burial but not to offer a word of consolation to her father. Her first biographers insist that these were costly sacrifices on her part and that she believed that she could do more for her family through prayer than through conversations with them, but it is perhaps this aspect of Jeanne Le Ber that is most difficult to see as in any way admirable. Yet it is in keeping with some of the more austere theology of the time and may even have been encouraged by her director as a sure test of her vocation as a recluse.

Marguerite Bourgeoys had once considered entry into a contemplative community and saw in prayer both the inspiration and the support of all apostolic activity. She believed that a sister of the Congregation should remain always "in the holy presence of God"; that "the sisters ought to ask in fervent prayer for the graces they need to succeed in their work of teaching girls"; that "the sisters, before applying themselves to teaching in the schools, ought to prepare themselves by prayer."[44] There is no doubt that she was pleased to have Jeanne's constant prayerful presence at the heart of the community.[45] A prayer Marguerite composed in 1698 expresses her gratitude for the presence of the Blessed Sacrament in the Congregation chapel, and she portrays the work of the Congregation as a response to this great favour in a simile drawn from weaving: "Placing ourselves in the company of the Mother of God and the nine choirs of angels, gathering together as so many small threads joined to each other and completely united, we try to accomplish the duties of our state in the education of children in gratitude for God's benefits and with the help of His grace and the intercession of the Blessed Virgin and of the holy angels."[46] Marguerite's certainty about her own vocation made her more accepting of the different vocations of others because she did not feel threatened by them. In addition, she did not see in Jeanne Le Ber the kind of danger that had made her wary of other patronage. Although Jeanne became a major patron of the Congrégation de Notre-Dame, she does not appear ever to have made any attempt to interfere with its inner workings.

In November 1695 the sisters of the Hôtel-Dieu were able to leave the Congregation house and return to their own quarters. The work of rebuilding had been speeded up by a visit from Frontenac, who foresaw a need for the hospital to treat the casualties of war. Before the departure, the two communities signed a "spiritual alliance" drawn up by Marguerite Bourgeoys promising to "bear with each other in the difficulties we may experience and in all the obstacles to persevering in this union that we may meet."[47] Understandably, perhaps, Marie Morin had not quite grasped that when Marguerite Bourgeoys talked about the three states of religious women in the church, she likened the Hospitallers to Martha and Jeanne Le Ber to Magdalen. After describing Jeanne Le Ber's life in the apartment attached to the chapel she had built for the Congregation, Sister Morin observes: "This made Sister Bourgeoys say that the prophecy of her confessor had come true, this woman honouring the contemplative life of the Blessed Virgin, [the Congregation] her life in relation to her neighbours to win souls to God, and we her laborious life serving the sick."[48]

There were three deaths connected with the Congregation in 1695. In March, Edmée Chastel died at the Hôtel-Dieu in Quebec. She had stayed only briefly in the Congregation, but like Marguerite and Catherine Crolo, she had grown up in Troyes and had shared the terrible voyage of 1659 as well as the first days of the community in the stable school. The news of the death of Marguerite Tardy in France in September would not have reached Montreal until the following year.[49] It finally put an end to the idea of a unified reformed community in Montreal. More immediate and touching was the death on 25 November of Marie-Thérèse Gannensagouas. She was not yet thirty years old, and most of those years had been spent at the Congregation, first as a pupil and then as a sister and a teacher at the Mountain Mission. Marie-Thérèse's grandfather had died at the Mountain Mission in 1690 with such a reputation for sanctity that his body, originally buried in the cemetery, had been exhumed and laid to rest in the church of the mission. Marie-Thérèse was buried beside him, and both were later eulogized by Abbé Belmont, who added them to the lines he had composed in honour of Jeanne Le Ber and Marguerite Bourgeoys.[50] But if some faces were disappearing from the Congregation, others were taking their place.

As the war went on, prisoners from the American colonies, such as the Saywards, continued to arrive in Montreal. These were often bought or ransomed from their Native captors and put to work in local households and on the farms until an exchange or return of prisoners was arranged. While most of the men regarded this as a form of slavery, the experience and attitude of some of the women were sharply different. Among the prisoners reaching Montreal in 1694 was a twenty-year-old woman called Lydia Longley.[51] Lydia's grandfather, William Longley, had been among a group of

Puritans who emigrated from England and settled at Groton near Boston about 1650. Lydia must have lost her mother, Lydia Pease, at an early age; her stepmother, Deliverance Crisp, added five more children to the household. The attack of a party of Penobscot Abenaki on the Longley farm, situated about two miles north of Groton, came in the summer of 1694. According to oral tradition, the unarmed William Longley was lured into his field to round up strayed cows and killed there. The raiding party then appears to have attacked the house and brutally killed Deliverance and three of the children.[52] Lydia, her half-brother John, aged twelve, and her half-sister Betty, four years old, were taken into captivity, along with others captured in the course of the day, many of them children. If Lydia ever spoke or wrote about the horrors of the journey that followed, her account has not survived. In its course, she lost or was separated from, the two surviving members of her family: Betty died or, more likely, was killed, perhaps because she cried when told to carry something, and John was taken off in another direction.[53] Finally, Lydia arrived in Montreal, where she was ransomed by Jacques Le Ber and taken into his household.

What did this young woman make of the world into which she had come, alien in language, religion, and culture to the one she had left? She would, of course, have found some English-speakers in Montreal. Several American male captives worked for Jacques Le Ber. At the Congregation were the Saywards, well able to understand and sympathize with an experience that mirrored their own. Some of the French Montrealers must also have spoken a little English because of their trade contacts, and these may have included Jacques Le Ber himself among their number. Lydia, with the skills and experience acquired as she grew up on her father's farm, was a useful addition to the Le Ber household, which had been without a mistress since the death of Jeanne Le Moyne more than a decade earlier. Accustomed to the simplicity and sobriety of the Congregational church to which her family belonged, she must have found the French Catholicism of Montreal somewhat exotic.

At the time of Lydia's arrival, Jeanne Le Ber was in the final year of reclusion in her father's house. Lydia would have witnessed Jeanne's departure for her apartment attached to the Congregation chapel the following August. It has frequently been suggested in Congregation accounts of Lydia's life that admiration for the recluse was the motivating force for the decisions Lydia now took. Perhaps this is true, and certainly Jeanne took an interest in Lydia. But it is likely that another important influence was her contact with the Saywards and visits to them at the house of the Congregation. Like the Saywards, Lydia expressed the desire to become a Catholic. She was received into the Catholic Church on 24 April 1696 by abjuring her heresy and being rebaptized, as was the custom of the time. The parish register records that Lydia had been staying at the Congregation house for the month prior to the baptism, and the *Histoire de la Congrégation* says that on 24 March 1696 she was entrusted to Marguerite Bourgeoys herself for instruction in the Catholic faith.[54] By the special permission of Dollier de Casson, Lydia's baptism took place not in the parish church but in the Congregation chapel so that Jeanne Le Ber could assist at the ceremony from her cell. To her previous Christian name, Lydia, was added that of Madeleine, the name of her godmother, Madeleine Dupont, wife of Paul Le Moyne de Marincourt. Lydia's godfather was Jacques Le Ber, who that year bought himself letters of nobility from the king. It was probably a few months later that Lydia entered the Congrégation de Notre-Dame. She and Mary Sayward became the first women of English descent to enter the Congregation, so that the tiny community had now numbered among its members French women, Native women, and North American–born women of both French and English origin.[55]

In his recent study exploring the difference in attitude between the captive Puritan women and their male counterparts toward their Montreal experience, William Foster contrasts the reactions of Lydia with those of John Gillet, who had proved completely intractable as a workman on the Congregation farm. The men found it exceptionally repugnant to be employed by women. The women found themselves in a society where they could play a more active role in the realm of religion. Foster believes that the very characteristics that attracted the women to the Congregation repelled the men, and he makes the following observation:

For Lydia Madeleine [Longley], that the Congrégation was Catholic, communal, celibate, physically active, and professional had almost the opposite meaning it had for Gillet. The appeal of Catholicism to Puritan women bears emphasizing. The community's special devotion to Marian itinerant life cast the divine presence in a distinctly feminine light. The articulation of the Virgin as a guiding mother gave the community its model for the familial relations of mother, sister, or daughter. Clearly the familial element had strong appeal for those whose original families had been lost or fractured beyond repair.[56]

Several other such women abducted in raids on settlements in the English colonies made their way into the women's religious communities of New France in this and the next century, when the War of the Spanish Succession would put an end to the brief period of truce that came at the end of the seventeenth century.[57]

Meanwhile, Bishop Saint-Vallier was still in France, where Louis Tronson continued to offer advice and to intercede with him about the Congregation rule. When the ships left for New France in the spring of 1697, they carried a revised version of the 1694 rule. In a letter to Dollier de Casson dated 21 April 1697, Abbé Tronson wrote:

I am sending you the rules that the bishop of Quebec had drawn up for the sisters of the Congregation and that you will find much toned down. It seems to me that, in their present state, there are certain articles that should not now cause them any difficulty. For the others, the bishop of Quebec believes he has good reasons to leave them as they are. If the good sisters still have difficulty, they themselves will be able to present to him their reasons for wanting some mitigation. As my incapacities do not allow me to reply to them, you would oblige me by letting them know, and letting them see the memorandum that I am sending to you. In particular, assure Sister Bourgeoys and the superior that their interest will always be a great recommendation to me.[58]

The memorandum to which this letter makes reference contains Tronson's replies to the various objections raised by the Congregation. The arrival of the revised rule presaged the return to New France of Bishop Saint-Vallier himself. When all the pressures brought to bear upon him could not compel him to resign his see, the bishop of Quebec was finally given the king's permission to return to his diocese in 1697. He had promised to act with "prudence," and the first months after his return to Quebec were accordingly months of peace.

Despite the importance accorded her in the letter just quoted where Tronson placed her ahead of Marie Barbier, the superior, Marguerite Bourgeoys continued to feel isolated and useless. She had nothing to do but a little sewing, she says, and was taking her meals with Catherine Crolo, who was no longer able to go to the dining room: "I went to church very rarely for Mass was said near the community. I did not go out or speak to any of the sisters. All this, they said, because of my advanced age."[59] At a moment she dates very precisely as "the night of the fifth to the sixth of July 1697" she decided she must act, even if, like Jonah, the result was that she would be thrown into the sea. She spoke to two of the Sulpicians, who advised her to speak to her superior. She accordingly wrote a note to Marie Barbier but felt that "my words were without unction." So, she says, "I took up my pen in the hope that if I did my best, God's mercy would deliver me from the punishment my lack of fidelity deserved." What she wrote, as in the letters about the rule to Abbé Tronson, was autobiography. She had been asked, when she expressed her concerns about the Congregation, "why I troubled myself about it" and told "that I did not have the responsibility for anything of that kind." The story of her life, she believed, demonstrated why she was convinced that "I will have to render an account of this community before God." She concludes: "I believe that if we wish to keep and to increase the favours of God to this Community and to draw His blessing upon the education of children (without this, it would profit us nothing), we must resolve to destroy all that is contrary to the laws and commandments of the love of God and neighbour in this Community and we must place divine wisdom above human prudence."

Some notes also remain from a retreat Marguerite made in March 1698, when her hope was "the grace to enter once again into that first call to His service which he graciously gave me." She adds, surprisingly, given her age: "This fourth year [since her resignation as superior?] I have been speaking of going to France." She gives no hint of why she wished to make this voyage, whether, as in 1680, it was to look for spiritual guidance away from New France or whether she wanted to confer personally on the question of the rule. It is scarcely surprising that she is forced to add, "This did not succeed."[60]

Glandelet quotes extensively from the correspondance between him and Marie Barbier in the last months of 1697 and the early months of 1698. These passages make clear that Marie was very dependent on his guidance, encouragement, and advice and that her admiration for him was at least as great as his for her. There is no mention in any of the passages of events at the Congregation or of the question of the rule. Rather, their subject is Marie's spiritual problems and her increasingly poor health, with the spectre of cancer now being raised. Of course, Glandelet himself made the choice of the excerpts he chose to quote, but the letters cannot help but raise questions about where real authority was being exercised at the Congregation at this time – this despite Marie Barbier's statement to Glandelet that "although I am in the infirmary, that does not prevent me from performing my particular duties, such as speaking to the sisters and taking part in the chapter and other things. I am at meditation in the morning, and in all I can I follow the community."[61]

In the spring of 1698, Abbé Charles de Glandelet came to Montreal as vicar general to join Abbé de Valens, their confessor, in presenting to the Congregation the revised version of the rule of 1694. He arrived a few days ahead of the bishop himself, bearing a pastoral letter to "our dear daughters in Our Lord, the sisters of the Congrégation of the community of Ville-Marie" signed by Bishop Saint-Vallier on 1 June 1698. The letter reminds the sisters that the rule and the four vows they will make are all means of living in the love of God, as are even the penances and corrections enjoined in the rule. It concludes: "We exhort you, then, by the depths of the love of Jesus Christ, by the tender and maternal heart of the most Blessed Virgin, of whom you call yourselves the daughters and whose virtues you propose to imitate, by the love you must have for your own salvation, to observe invincibly these rules we have given you. We expressly declare that our intention is that you allow nothing to be done against them or to their prejudice; nor that, under any pretext, anything be added or removed without our permission or that of our successors."[62] The bishop himself arrived in Montreal shortly afterward and took up residence at the seminary, where on 14 June he signed a document giving 1,000 livres for the support of the Congregation mission in Quebec.

Beginning on 20 June, Saint-Vallier held several meetings with the Congregation on the subject of the rule. Marguerite Bourgeoys, now in her seventy-ninth year, played an important part in these meetings and in the ceremonies that followed. Glandelet records, "Sister Barbier, very ill then, was marvellously supported and seconded by the venerable older sisters, but principally by Sister Bourgeoys herself, who was present at everything, even though her humility had, for a long time, made her give up the first rank."[63] The opposition expressed by the sisters and the intervention of Abbé Tronson had brought about a compromise in some of the articles of the earlier version of the rule. Although the new version can by no means be considered the document for which the Congregation had originally hoped, the bishop almost certainly saw himself as having shown remarkable generosity and reasonableness. Given the mindset of the time, he was probably correct. Bishop Saint-Vallier was convinced of the necessity of the work being done by the Congregation, but he could not see the way of life that made it possible as anything but temporary. In the revised rule, some of the terminology that had worried the Congregation is gone. The new document is entitled "Reglemens Commun"[64] rather than "Constitutions," and the eighteen constitutions of 1694 with their subdivisions have become thirty-four chapters. The references to St Augustine have been eliminated, though the basis of the Augustinian rule is maintained. The word "solemn," which the sisters had feared would make them nuns and so cloistered, has disappeared, as has the word "cloister" itself. The sisters are called upon to make simple vows rather than solemn promises, and the special vow of obedience to the bishop has disappeared. The permanent boarders are no longer seen as a third category of members of the Congregation. Some provisions of the earlier rule have been removed to the *coutumier*, or customary, a less binding document than that of the constitutions and more easily changed. Certain other provisions, such as those on silence, have been softened, though not to the extent that had been asked. In several places, the words "if possible" have been added.

But what of the main concerns expressed by Marguerite Bourgeoys herself? Her most serious disappointment must have come over the omission from this rule of any statement of the inspiration for the founding of the Congregation. Inevitably, in a rule imposed by a bishop who still saw the lack of cloister in the Congregation as a temporary circumstance of its frontier setting, rather than a part of its essence, there are no references to the *vie voyagère de Marie*, the journeying life of Mary. In the first chapter, which deals with the purpose for which the Congregation was founded, there is mention of the "aid, favour, and protection of Mary," but there is still no hint that the uncloistered life of the Congregation had as its model "the life of Mary when she was on earth." The Visitation of Mary is mentioned only as the patronal feast of the Congregation, and the life of Mary and the other women disciples in the early church makes no appearance at all.

Marguerite's strongly expressed desire, in many ways revolutionary, that all the sisters of the Congregation be equal was not realized. The division of the community into two groups, the members of only one of which would be eligible to hold office, is maintained. With regard to the exaction of a dowry, even Tronson had written in his memorandum: "one cannot demand miracles and must act with prudence for the support of a community that cannot subsist only by the work of its hands in the times we are now in with all the works they are undertaking for the instruction of and charity toward the neighbour."[65] The reference in the constitutions to board to be paid by novices is gone, and some latitude is left as to the dowry.

Marguerite Bourgeoys and her community knew that Abbé Tronson had done the best he could to bring about modifications in the rule, and they could scarcely have wanted a repetition of the scenes, threats, and name-calling of 1694. Most of the sisters must have decided they could live with this rule – most, but not all. Three sisters left the Congregation in June 1698. They were Marie Aubuchon, the daughter of a Montreal merchant, and Marie Genest and Catherine Rochon from Île d'Orléans. The latter two had probably been among Marie Barbier's first pupils. The three women were all in their middle to late twenties and represented a considerable loss to the community.[66] Marguerite Bourgeoys was among those who signed the documents releasing them from their obligations to the Congregation, documents that give no hint of their reasons for leaving. It is, of course, possible that their departures all took place at this time simply because the bishop was there to release them from their promises, although that does not seem to have been necessary in the case of earlier departures. It is more probable that their leaving had something to do with their unwillingness to accept this rule.[67]

On 24 June 1698, twenty-four members of the Congregation signed acceptance of the rule in Montreal, stating: "We accept with every kind of respect and submission the above rules given us by his lordship the most Illustrious and Reverend bishop of Quebec. After reading and examining them several times, we have judged them very proper for the good of our community, and are resolved to practise them with all possible exactitude."[68] Marie Barbier, as superior, signed first, adding to her given name the religious name "de l'assomption," a choice made because the feast of the Assumption of the Blessed Virgin was of great significance to her. One line below appear the signatures of Catherine Charly, *dit* Saint-Ange, who signed "Sr. St. Ange Assistante," and Marguerite Bourgeoys, who signed as she had always done, without any additions. It is only when they signed the document confirming their pronouncement of simple vows the next day that all the sisters took religious names. Those who signed the acceptance of the rule on 24 June 1698 do not constitute a complete list of the sisters in the Congregation at that time. The six sisters on mission in the Quebec region did not sign until 4 August. In Montreal, Catherine Crolo, Perrette Laurent de Beaune, and Catherine Sommillard, Marguerite Bourgeoys's niece, were not signatories, probably because they were too ill to leave the infirmary.

On 25 June 1698 the sisters of the Congregation pronounced public vows of poverty, chastity, obedience, and commitment to the education of persons of their sex. The bishop presided at the ceremony, which took place in the Congregation chapel. After communion, each sister advanced to the altar steps carrying a lighted candle and pronounced her vows in a clear and audible voice. Marguerite Bourgeoys was the fourth in this procession, following Marie Barbier, Catherine Charly, and Marguerite Le Moyne. The sisters retained their baptismal names, to which they added the name of a religious mystery or of a saint. Marguerite Bourgeoys became Marguerite du Saint Sacrement. It might have been expected that she would choose some Marian name or mystery unless it is recalled that her devotion to Mary was closely connected in her mind with devotion to the Eucharist: "Although [Mary] was only a creature, the eternal Father confided to her the sacrosanct humanity of His Word to be nourished and reared in His human life. Even now we can still marvel at her happiness each day at Mass and Holy Communion, adoring Our Lord on the altars, recalling that she contributed to the matter of this holy Body we receive for the nourishment of our souls."[69] Marguerite Bourgeoys had spent her years in Montreal trying to build up Christ's mystical body, the church. At this moment in her life, she also had a sense that, like Christ in the tabernacle, her life was now a hidden life of prayer.[70]

On 26 June the community began a retreat to prepare for the vow of stability, which would make perpetual the four vows they had already made, to be pronounced on 2 July, feast of the Visitation. During the retreat, the sisters also proceeded to the first elections since those following the resignation of Marguerite Bourgeoys in 1693. Marie Barbier was not re-elected as superior, though she remained assistant; instead, the Congregation now passed into the strong and capable hands of Marguerite Le Moyne. Bearer of one of the most illustrious names in the history of New France, she was also descended on her mother's side from the only family among the founders of Ville-Marie in 1642. To this thirty-four-year-old woman now fell the primary responsibility for ensuring that the new rule to which it was now bound would not destroy the basic identity of the Congrégation de Notre-Dame.

CHAPTER NINE

DEPARTURE IN PEACE
1698–1700

Our good Lord has given me this grace:
that all the desires I feel come to an end in peace.[1]

As Marguerite Bourgeoys approached her eightieth birthday and as her life ebbed away, not just a decade but a century was drawing to a close. The Treaty of Ryswick, signed on 1 October 1697, had brought the war between the European powers to an end, at least for a time. Frontenac, still governor though just two years Marguerite's junior, saw the arrival of peace in Europe but died at the end of 1698. Like him, Marguerite would not see the first year of the new century, which would bring the Great Peace with the Native tribes. The treaty that brought to an end the hostilities which had devastated the previous decade was not signed in Montreal until 1701. But the winding down of the war must have brought with it some sense of release. Almost everyone at the Congregation had been touched in some way by this war. Marie Barbier had lost two brothers; Catherine Charly, a brother-in-law; Marguerite Le Moyne, a number of cousins; Lydia Longley, almost her whole family; Mary Sayward, her father; and Jeanne Le Ber, two brothers.

If these were years of endings at the Congregation, they were also a time of beginnings: the beginning of its life as a canonically approved community and the beginning of new leadership. Marie Barbier obviously still had her supporters in the community, for she had been elected assistant, a position to which she was perhaps better suited than to that of superior, if indeed, as she told Glandelet,

she had a gift for inspiring the sisters to confide in her and was able
to console and encourage them.[2] The possibility of friction between
the old and new regimes was reduced when, because of her health,
Marie Barbier left for Quebec in September and remained there all
the winter of 1698–99. Catherine Charly had been elected mistress
of novices, and it would seem that she and Marguerite Le Moyne
worked harmoniously together. The complex, even paradoxical,
combination of qualities characteristic of Marguerite Bourgeoys
has often been remarked. A true daughter of her native Champagne,
land of poets and merchants, she combined the qualities of Mary
and Martha, of mystic and businesswoman. It is possible that her
first two successors, Marie Barbier and Marguerite Le Moyne, each
embodied in a special way one side of the combination that was
balanced in the founder.

Marguerite Le Moyne, who would guide the Congregation
through many of the years remaining to New France, came from a
very successful merchant family. Even her half-sister, Agathe Saint-
Père, who was not a Le Moyne, became one of the most important
businesspersons in New France. But the practical abilities Marguerite no doubt shared with the rest of her family must have been
accompanied by other qualities. Had this not been so, she would
not, at a young age, have been given responsibility for the formation of entrants to the Congregation. There is no evidence that she
shared the social pretensions that made Agathe Saint-Père prevent
the marriage of her half-brother, one of the younger Le Moynes, to
a bride she did not consider socially acceptable. When Marguerite
Bourgeoys died, the first of her virtues that Marguerite Le Moyne
recommended to the Congregation was her humility. If, perhaps, it
was the virtue of which she herself felt most in need, she must have
recognized its importance.

Immediately after her election, Marguerite Le Moyne wrote to
Abbé Tronson to thank him for his intercession in the matter of
the rule and to seek assurance that the Sulpicians would continue
to direct the Congregation. She must also have expressed some dif-
fidence about her fitness for the responsiblities she was now assuming, for in his reply, written in March 1699, he told her: "So now
you are superior ... As you are such by a legitimate election and
through obedience, there is every reason to hope that you will ruin
nothing. Our Lord will help you, and provided that you are faithful, all will go well. You need have no fear that our gentlemen [the
Sulpicians] will cease to render you the services they have given

until this time, as long as you serve God well and that they are useful to you. I am very glad that you are pleased with them; they seem to me to be so with you as well."[3] Tronson ends by asking to be remembered to Marguerite Bourgeoys.

Whether its members were then aware of it or not, Abbé Tronson also undertook another act to protect the Congregation at this time. The Ursulines of Quebec had appealed directly to him for the approval of a foundation of their community in Montreal. Tronson's reply was written at the same time as his letter to Marguerite Le Moyne. Referring to a letter they had sent him the previous October, he says: "To answer you with sincerity, I shall tell you the persons who know the territory find it difficult to believe that two communities of women, who have the same employment, would not be too much for Ville-Marie. All I can do is to write this year to our gentlemen in order to be enlightened on this ... What is important is to understand the will of God, lest as sometimes happens, in the desire to increase and extend the good too much, we weaken and diminish it."[4] These were among Louis Tronson's last services to the Congrégation de Notre-Dame. Like Marguerite Bourgeoys, his life would pass with the century, for he too died in the winter of 1699–1700.[5]

Marguerite Le Moyne was going to need all the encouragement she could get, for almost immediately, the Congregation had a new challenge to face. Bishop Saint-Vallier's endowment for the Congregation missions in Quebec seems to have been given with certain plans for the future not disclosed at the time of its conferral. He appears to have had the intention of splitting the Congregation, so that the sisters on mission in the Quebec area would form a completely separate group from those in the Montreal region.[6] Each group would have its own superior and its own novitiate. Obviously, the bishop expected that he would be able to control the Quebec group more closely. Interested citizens in Quebec were prepared to enlarge the Congregation house there and to assign the sisters an income to help them live. Jamet believed that, for this plan, the bishop had the support of the pastor of Sainte-Famille on Île d'Orléans, François Lamy. Had the bishop been successful, the Congregation might have suffered a fate similar to that of the Filles de la Croix when they were taken over by Madame de Villeneuve.

According to the *Histoire de la Congrégation*, the bishop asked one of his clergy to compose a memorandum advising him of how this scheme could be put into practice. This clergyman, presumably Charles de Glandelet, shows an intimate knowledge of the sisters of the Congregation since he describes what each of those already working in the Quebec region could be called upon to do. He proposes that the superior of the Quebec community should be Marie Barbier, already in Quebec for treatment of her illness. He also suggests that Ursule Gariépy should be her assistant and Marguerite Gariépy, mistress of novices. (Apparently, these positions were to be filled by appointment rather than election.) Besides the house in Quebec, the community would include the missions of Sainte-Famille on Île d'Orléans, of Château-Richer, and of Champlain, an earlier mission which had closed but was soon to be reopened. Besides the sisters already on mission in the area, three more could be sent from Montreal, bringing to twelve the number of sisters in the new community. The writer believes that "provided that the approval of the community at Ville-Marie can be obtained, it would be easy to get the consent of the sisters at Quebec, who are all ready to sacrifice their natural inclination in this matter. This is what they told me when I let them know that we intended to act in concert with their sisters and that they should not fear to see themselves separated in mind and heart from those in Montreal. However, the sisters who are here will find it painful to leave their first community to pass into that of Quebec."[7]

It is impossible to know now how accurately Glandelet, if he is indeed the author, assessed the sentiments of the sisters at Quebec. Far from Montreal and under pressure from their bishop, they may not have found it politic to express their opposition to the plan more strongly. Nor is it certain that Glandelet's obvious confidence in his influence over Marie Barbier was justified. He shows himself very much aware, however, of the source from which the principal opposition would come. He comments: "Although the reasons I advance are plausible, I doubt that Soeur du Saint Esprit [Marguerite Le Moyne], who governs the minds of most of the sisters of the Congregation, especially of the young who were her pupils and who are the majority, would willingly consent to this. They would probably make it difficult to agree that the community of Quebec should be independent from that in Montreal."[8]

Near the very end of the memorandum there is mention of Marguerite Bourgeoys. The writer says that he has sent a loose sheet to Catherine Charly after showing it to the sisters in Quebec, and he

adds, "I believed I had to do it after the answer I gave Sister Bourgeoys in which I had only outlined the reasons that are contained
in the document. Your lordship will judge whether it is opportune
to make it known that she has been informed." Clearly, then, Marguerite Bourgeoys had heard of the plan and had questioned it. It
is peculiar that the loose sheet was sent to Catherine Charly rather
than to Marguerite Le Moyne, the superior. Was this another example of "divide and conquer"? It is fortunate for the Congregation
that the two women worked so well together. How far the bishop
might have gone with his plan to divide the Congregation, with or
without the consent of the community, will never be known. The
peace of the first months after his return to Canada was broken
by a dispute with the Jesuits that took Saint-Vallier back to France
in 1700. He would be prevented from returning to his diocese for
thirteen years, five of them spent as a hostage in England after his
capture on the high seas during the War of the Spanish Succession.

At the Congregation in Montreal, another of the French-born
sisters, Perrette Laurent de Beaune, a member of the recruitment
of 1672, died on 30 October 1698 at the age of forty-five. Then, in
February 1699, Marguerite Bourgeoys lost the last of the companions with whom she had founded the Congregation in 1659. Marguerite and Catherine Crolo were much of an age, and their relationship went back to the days of the extern congregation in Troyes
nearly sixty years before. She was the last person in Montreal able
to remember the young Marguerite and to share all her memories.
Catherine Crolo had run the farm in Pointe-Saint-Charles until
the fire of 1693. Marie Morin wrote of her in 1697, "She was a
woman indefatigable for work, looking on herself as the donkey of
the house. She is still living today, aged over eighty, in great odour
of virtue."[9] Catherine Crolo had taken the religious name Catherine de Saint-Joseph, choosing as her patron the saint who had
provided for the material needs of the Holy Family of Nazareth.
The parish register says that her funeral took place on 28 February
1699 "before all the clergy and a large gathering of people."

Her death could only have increased the loneliness of these days
when Marguerite lived "so humble and retired that just the sight of
her inspires the love of humility."[10] It was followed on 16 August by
that of Catherine Sommillard, the youngest of the three nieces who
had come to Montreal with Marguerite Bourgeoys in 1672, at the
age of only forty-four. She had filled the post of community bursar

as well as founding the Lachine mission, but she must have been ill since before the acceptance of the rule since she was not one of the signatories to it the previous year. The *Histoire de la Congréga-tion* cites a contemporary observation that "the difficult life of the missionary sisters soon impaired their health and obliged them to return to the community in Ville-Marie at the end of a few years of work."[11] Catherine's funeral the day following her death, also attended by "all the clergy and a large number of other people," perhaps gave Marguerite a last chance to see her surviving niece, Louise, and Louise's family.

According to letters written in January and February of 1700, Marguerite Bourgeoys herself showed no sign of her own impend-ing death at this time, though she had been seriously ill the previous year; nor were her mental powers impaired. It is scarcely possible, however, that the deaths of these women left her untouched. She must have been pleased at the reconstruction of the farmhouse at Pointe-Saint-Charles undertaken in 1698. She celebrated one last Christmas in Montreal, perhaps remembering other Christmases, as the aging tend to do. Forty-seven years earlier, in the fort of Ville-Marie, she had shared her first Montreal Christmas with the very young Marie Dumesnil, the first of the would-be brides entrusted to her care. Marie had grown up to give three daughters to the Congregation.[12] One of these had died at the age of twenty and a second at the age of sixteen, and now the life of a third seemed to be in peril. During the night of 31 December 1699 to 1 Janu-ary 1700, the community was awakened with the news that the novice mistress, Catherine Charly, was believed to be dying. She was just thirty-three years old. According to a letter written soon after her own death, Marguerite Bourgeoys was overheard to say when she was awakened with this news, "Ah, my God, why do you not take me rather then this poor Sister who can still serve this little house while I am useless and unable to do anything!"[13] This incident, together with the fact that from that moment Margue-rite Bourgeoys became ill and grew steadily worse while Catherine Charly began to recover, led to the belief in the Congregation that the older woman had offered her life for the younger.

Marguerite Bourgeoys's final illness lasted twelve days, during which she suffered severe pain.[14] In a letter to the sisters on mission outside Ville-Marie written the day of the founder's death, Mar-guerite Le Moyne commented: "Since New Year's evening, when she first became ill, she suffered indescribable agony, at times so intense that in spite of her admirable patience, she could not keep from crying out."[15] The *Histoire de la Congrégation* adds a comment that is a reminder of the shortcomings of the medical practice of that time: "She took without complaint everything the physician prescribed for her or that the sisters who were looking after her gave her, despite the repugnance she felt and the experience that they did nothing but make her suffer more and more."[16]

An unidentified sister of the Congregation wrote immediately after Marguerite Bourgeoys's death, "We have seen in the life of our dearest Mother, Sister Bourgeoys, the truth of the dictum 'as you live so shall you die.'"[17] Certainly, according to the letters that describe her last days and hours, she continued to display the qualities that were apparent in her earlier years. There is evidence of the builder and planner: "Among the other advice that our Mother gave her sisters during her illness, she advised them to profit from the openings Providence could offer them to reconstruct on a larger scale the rooms destined for the sisters, the boarders, and the day pupils, whose numbers had grown considerably since the building of the new house they were then occupying."[18] She also continued to be aware of the feelings and difficulties of those around her: "One of our Sisters told us that two days before our dear Mother died, she was so tired and so overcome with nausea when trying to lift the patient that she had to ask another Sister to replace her. Sister Bourgeoys, noticing her distress, assured her that the illness would quickly pass. Suddenly, sister felt completely well, her nausea disappeared, and she no longer perceived the odour that had made her ill."[19]

Above all, there are signs in these last days of her life that the trials and disappointments of the last decade had not destroyed the joyful spirit of the girl who was once so popular among the young women of Troyes, of the young woman who could laugh with de Maisonneuve and Abbé Souart during the "terrible days" when early Ville-Marie was engaged in a grim fight for its existence. She teased the sisters about taking such good care of her that it seemed they did not want her to go to heaven. And she sang, "Despite the burning fever which consumed her and the suffering she endured, she asked the sisters to sing some hymns, and until the day of her death, she was able to sing with them."[20] After all the doubt and anguish of the last decade, in these final days she was at peace. The word that recurs most frequently in the written accounts of the end of her life is *doucement*, "peacefully"; there is no trace of the fear of rejection by God that had caused her such anguish during the Sister Tardy incident. Whether or not one accepts the suggestion that she offered her life for Catherine Charly, the words that gave rise to that idea reflect Marguerite's readiness to entrust the Congrégation de Notre-Dame into the hands of its younger members and, ultimately, into the hands of God. Finally, on the morning of 12 January 1700, she died "very peacefully" after a final three-hour struggle. Later that day Marguerite Le Moyne wrote: "She died, my dear Sisters, as she had lived, loving God with all her heart and manifesting an ardent desire to be with her Creator."[21]

As was the custom of the time, Marguerite Bourgeoys's funeral and burial took place the next day. Before that final disappearance, however, Marguerite Le Moyne asked her cousin Pierre Le Ber to record a likeness of the founder. Like his sister Jeanne, this youngest son of Jacques Le Ber was both devout and artistic.[22] Pierre Le Ber probably received his artistic training at Quebec, and as the inventory of his possessions made at the time of his death in 1707 demonstrates, he spent most of his time in artistic activity. The account of his creation of the portrait of Marguerite Bourgeoys illustrates the tone of the stories that began to spring up immediately after her death:

Mr. LeBer's son had been asked to paint her portrait shortly after her death. After receiving Communion for her in our chapel, he came prepared to work, but he was suddenly stricken with a severe headache and could not begin. One of the Sisters gave him a tiny lock of our deceased Mother's hair. He placed it under his wig and at once felt so much better that he began to work with ease; he and those watching him were astounded. He continued to carry this relic, and was convinced that, two days later, he was saved from serious injury in a fall which, naturally speaking, should have resulted in a fractured skull.[23]

Although scarcely a work in the grand style of the period, Pierre Le Ber's painting was treasured by the Congregation from the time of its creation. However, it was overpainted in the nineteenth century and not returned to the light of day until the second half of the twentieth, at a time when its qualities evoked more appreciation. At the time of the restoration, one viewer saw in it all the human qualities that we know belonged to the founder: a superior intelligence, strong practical sense, a combination of great resolution and inexhaustible kindness, simplicity, and even, it seems to me, a vague tolerant disillusion ... In spite of the awkwardness of the rendering, the hands with their long fingers have their own eloquence, and even the austerity of the colour of the clothing adds to the quality of the work. One understands in contemplating this admirable portrait how great Marguerite Bourgeoys was and catches a glimpse of the reason for the love and veneration of the whole town for one who had contributed so much to its beginnings and development.[24]

On the evening of the day she died, Marguerite Bourgeoys's body was exposed in the Congregation chapel so that the people of Montreal could come to pay their last respects. "They reverently touched her body with their books and their rosaries and begged for something which had belonged to her."[25] From her cell, Jeanne Le Ber kept vigil during the night. The *Histoire de la Congrégation* says that a disagreement arose between the sisters of the Congregation and the parish about the site of Marguerite's burial. The dispute was settled when Dollier de Casson, always the conciliator, suggested a compromise: the body would be buried in the parish church in the chapel of the Child Jesus, while Marguerite's heart, removed before burial as was the custom in the case of persons of reputed holiness, would be retained at the Congregation. While their desire to have the remains of their founder buried in their own chapel is understandable, such a last resting place would have gone against Marguerite's wish, strongly expressed in writing, that the sisters of the Congregation be buried in the parish church.[26] Her burial in the parish church fulfilled her desire to remain a *fille de paroisse* to the end and beyond.

The funeral took place on Saturday, 13 January, with Dollier de Casson presiding and preaching the homily. Glandelet quotes from a letter written by a priest who attended the funeral: "Sister Bourgeoys died yesterday morning. Her body rests in the parish and her heart is retained at the house of the Congregation. Never were so many priests and religious in the church of Montreal as there were this morning at the funeral of this saintly woman. The Governor General, the Governor of Montreal and a large number of people were present. If the saints were canonized today as they were in olden times, by the voice of the people and of the clergy tomorrow we would celebrate the Mass of Saint Marguerite of Canada."[27] Belief in the holiness of the woman who had just died is also strongly and clearly expressed in the letters of condolence received by the Congregation in the weeks following the death of the founder. "There can be no doubt that she enjoys the lasting glory of heaven. God must have looked on her as one of his most beloved and faithful servants," wrote Bishop Saint-Vallier. The superior of the Jesuits observed: "I am sure she has no need of our intercession ... I have never known a sister so virtuous as Sister Bourgeoys." The superior of the Hôtel-Dieu in Quebec, where Marguerite had stayed on her trips to the capital, assured the Congregation of her sympathy in the loss of one "so dear to you in life and who is venerated now in death." She continued, "We pray for her, although I do not think that she has need of our prayers."

Most of the letters point to qualities their writers had admired in Marguerite Bourgeoys. There is frequent mention of her humility and detachment, of her faith, and of her complete trust in God's providence. They also speak of "her nobility of soul," of her being "blessed with a generous heart, always ready to undertake difficult tasks." The Jesuit superior remarked, "I feel that she was blessed right to the end, for she left this world after a long and fruitful life, having retained her reasoning power, her fervour and her other virtues even to her last moments." Bishop Saint-Vallier added a very personal reflection when he wrote:

Among those virtues, in the practice of which I would like to follow her example, there is one that impressed me in a special way since I recognize that I stand in greater need of it. I refer to the hidden and prayerful life that she led after her resignation from the office of superior. What a precious grace for those who have the responsibility of governing others! I consider it to be one of the surest signs of predestination when Our Lord is pleased to grant such persons a time before death during which they have the opportunity to make amends for the faults they may have committed in exercising authority over others.[28]

The most solemn part of the period of mourning was brought to an end on 11 February, the thirtieth day after Marguerite's death, at the celebration of the mass for what was once known as the "month's mind." Until that day, the lead container in which her heart had been enclosed had been accessible to the people of Montreal for their veneration. One of the sisters observed: "I think that every rosary in town, books of hours, crucifixes were brought to be touched to her heart; if we had been willing to give out in tiny pieces the cloth that we had soaked in her blood, we would have had none left."[29] At that time, the heart was placed in a specially prepared niche in the wall of the sanctuary of the Congregation chapel and the niche covered with a copper plate. The Le Ber portrait was hung above it. The presiding priest on this occasion was François Vachon de Belmont, who preached a sermon based on the text of 1 Corinthians 11: 1: "Be imitators of me as I am of Jesus Christ." In it he chose to speak of three qualities of Marguerite Bourgeoys that were the fruit of her union with Christ and that he recommended for imitation by the sisters of the Congregation.

The first is her "love of the cross," her acceptance of suffering. In this context he places an event that happened during his own first years in Montreal, the fire of 1683, with the deaths of the two sisters that resulted and the poverty and struggle that followed. He then makes what can only be a reference to the Sister Tardy affair and its aftermath: "Distress and travail of the mind succeeded those of the body; and as she endured them with a gentleness and complete equanimity and patience, they truly contributed to making her lowly in her own eyes, but very great in the eyes of God and his angels. The obedience she gave not just to her superiors but to her own daughters is a lesson in practical humility more persuasive than any sermon."[30]

In his development of the second characteristic, zeal for the salvation of souls, Belmont shows an understanding of the Congregation way of life which it would surely have heartened Marguerite Bourgeoys to have heard. He speaks of the inspiration of the Blessed Virgin, which drew Marguerite to face generously the dangers of crossing the sea to work for the education of women and the establishment of schools, and of the fruit of her work among the women and families of Canada. Then he tells the assembled Congregation:

You yourselves, sisters, are the best fruits of her zeal which has given you birth in Jesus Christ. Her zeal made her assemble this community of Christian Amazons to fight the devil and to fight him not in the entrenchment of the cloister but in the midst of the world. It was for that, sisters, that she founded you as secular women of the parish, so that you might be like the most precious part of the flock, the good aroma of Jesus Christ, the healing aroma that purifies the tainted air of the world. She intended that the presence of God would serve you everywhere as an unbreachable refuge and, as scripture says, as a cloister of fire; and that armed in this way, you would go forth, like living tabernacles within which Jesus Christ is hidden, to conquer the world, in working through education to win the hearts of children to him and in edifying older people.[31]

The last characteristic Belmont develops in his sermon is that of Marguerite's courage. Once again, he shows a familiarity with the early life of Marguerite Bourgeoys herself, of the act of faith she made when she set out alone for the New World with nothing but a very small bundle and the hope that what God had not willed in Troyes, he would perhaps bring to pass in Montreal. Belmont is also aware of the comparison she had made of her Congregation to the Apostles:

When I speak of her courage, I speak of her confidence and of her faith. This true daughter of Abraham left her country without knowing where she was going; she threw herself into the arms of the God who called her; she was unshakable in her confidence and believed that he could draw from her nothingness a great and numerous family. Thence came the magnanimity with which she viewed the perils of the sea, the dangers of war, and thence she undertook with invincible steadfastness the works you have seen her accomplish with such glorious success. The Apostles, without eloquence, without worldly wisdom, did what wealth, authority, and power could not accomplish. So it pleases God to confound human wisdom, in choosing the weakest instruments to overthrow the strongest. Sisters, the arm of God has not been shortened. He will do as much for you whom he calls to walk in the footsteps of the holy Apostles like your admirable founder.[32]

The year after this sermon was delivered, François Dollier de Casson died in Montreal and was succeeded as superior of the seminary and seigneur of Montreal by Abbé Belmont, the position that Joseph de La Colombière had once been destined to fill. There can be no doubt this succession made a great difference to the survival of the Congrégation de Notre-Dame. For the Congregation did survive to become one of the oldest communities of uncloistered women in the Roman Catholic Church with an unbroken history. Both the Filles de La Croix and the Filles de Sainte-Geneviève were

suppressed at the time of the French Revolution, a fate the Congrégation de Notre-Dame escaped because Canada had passed from
French to British rule in 1763. The opening years of the eighteenth
century brought their share of epidemics, such as the smallpox that
carried off six sisters in the space of two months in 1702. The century also brought renewed warfare, immense economic hardship,
and eventually conquest and the beginnings of a new regime. In
spite of all these difficulties, the Congregation continued to increase
its numbers and became by far the most numerous religious community of women in New France.

Despite the tendencies that had distressed Marguerite Bourgeoys
in the last decade of her life, the Congregation remained committed
not just to the education of women but especially to the education
of poor women. Among the many testimonies to this fact is that of
the Jesuit Pierre-François-Xavier de Charlevoix, who observed the
work of the Congregation during his visit to Canada in 1721 and
later wrote of Montreal:

A city began to grow up there, the foundation of which was marked by an
establishment which now constitutes one of the fairest ornaments of New
France. Montreal owes it to Marguerite Bourgeoys, that holy woman who
had several years before followed Mr. de Maisonneuve to Canada. With
no other resource than her courage and her trust in God, she undertook to
afford all the young persons of her sex, no matter how poor or destitute,
an education which many girls, even of good families, do not secure in the
best-ordered kingdoms. She succeeded to that degree, that you constantly
behold, with renewed astonishment, women in the very depths of indi-
gence and want perfectly instructed in their religion, ignorant of nothing
that they should know to employ themselves usefully in their families, and
who, by their manners, their manner of expressing themselves, and their
politeness, are not inferior to the most carefully educated among us. This
is the just meed of praise rendered to the Sisters of the Congregation by all
who have made any stay in Canada.[33]

On the subject of the dowry, the Congregation was also as faithful to the vision of Marguerite Bourgeoys as it was permitted to be.
In February 1722, Bishop Saint-Vallier fixed the dowry of entrants
to the Congregation at 2,000 livres. This was in keeping with royal
policy, for the king later that year issued an ordinance intended to

discourage entry into religious communities by setting the dowry at 5,000 livres. In spite of this requirement, the superiors were able to seek and obtain a dispensation from the bishop in the case of those they presented as suitable candidates. They were warned, however, that they would risk losing their right to exact a dowry if they waived it too often.[34]

The years immediately before and immediately after the Conquest were difficult for the Congregation, as for most of the population of New France, and the problems were exacerbated by the loss of the Montreal house and all its contents in a fire that destroyed a considerable area of Montreal in 1768. However, the community rebuilt as Marguerite Bourgeoys had done in 1684. In the ensuing decades the sisters began receiving into their schools children of Scottish, Irish, and English extraction and soon admitted English-speaking novices, mostly of Scottish and Irish origin. In 1843 the bishop of Montreal lifted the ordinance imposed on the Congregation during the French regime which had limited its number to not more than eighty. After that, the number of women in the Congregation continued to swell until it reached its highest point of almost four thousand in the third quarter of the twentieth century.[35] Geographically, it spread to other parts of Canada and to the United States in the nineteenth century and to Japan, Latin America, and Africa in the twentieth, which even saw the establishment of sisters of the Congregation in Marguerite Bourgeoys's native Troyes and in other towns nearby. As the role of women changed in society, so did the education offered them by the Congregation. In the twentieth century the community became very active in post-secondary education. When it opened the first Catholic college for women in Quebec, this was given the name of the founder, Marguerite Bourgeoys. With the growth of coeducation, it came to number persons of both genders among its students, as it had in the days of its origins. At the beginning of the twenty-first century, new members to the community have come most frequently from areas, such as the Latin American countries and Cameroon, where conditions most resemble those in which Marguerite Bourgeoys began the Congregation in Montreal in the seventeenth century.

In 1984, for the first time, the *Constitutions and Rules* of the Congregation included at least some of the inspirational statements she had so wanted to see in the original rule:

The foundation of the Institute goes back to the very origin of Ville-Marie, today Montreal. Saint Marguerite Bourgeoys ... who came to Canada from France in 1653, believed that she was answering a call from God in uniting around her a group of women who would honour the life of the Blessed Virgin. She and her companions considered the Mother of Jesus, in the mystery of her Visitation, as the exemplar of feminine apostolic life: they would imitate the "vie vogagère" of Mary in a commitment to education ... Our Foundress invites us to imitate "the life led by the Blessed Virgin throughout her time on earth." Therefore, especially in the mystery of the Visitation and in Mary's life among the Apostles in the first Christian community, we find spiritual and apostolic inspiration.[36]

Marguerite Bourgeoys was canonized by Pope John Paul II on 31 October 1982. Since that time, many parishes and schools in Canada and the United States have been given her name. Nor is she forgotten in the city to whose beginnings she dedicated her life. The island of Montreal has undergone many transformations since Marguerite Bourgeoys first stepped onto its shores in November 1653. However, in the shadow of the city's skyscrapers, streets, a park, and a school commission bear her name, and her statue stands near the city hall. Fittingly, this statue is not a massive work but a life-size figure accompanied by the figures of a small girl and boy in modern dress who reach out, like her, toward the future. The group is completely approachable to the passers by, as she herself was in her life. It is still possible to identify the location of the stable school on the common in which she began her work of education and to approach it along streets that continue to bear the same names as when she travelled them in Old Montreal. The garden of what remains of her farm in Pointe-Saint-Charles provides a green oasis in the midst of the inner city. The chapel she founded on the banks of the St Lawrence became both the Sailors' Church and the cradle of the English-speaking Catholic community of Montreal in the nineteenth century. As she had intended, it still offers to all who enter it a small haven of peace in a world as turbulent in its way as her own eventful and challenging century.

APPENDIX

REPRESENTATIONS OF
MARGUERITE BOURGEOYS

Marguerite Bourgeoys was never painted in her lifetime, but attempts were made, almost from the moment of her death, to capture her image, the first being the painting by Pierre Le Ber made as she lay on her bier (illus. 1).[1] Since that time, many artists, both within the Congregation and without, have endeavoured to give her a countenance, features, an appearance. They have drawn her, engraved her, and sculptured her. Most have tried to be faithful to seventeenth-century history, to the traditions of the Congregation, to inherited documents and accounts, and to previous works of art. Artists of each generation have also striven to be faithful to the language and spirituality of their own time and to illumine the face of Marguerite Bourgeoys for their contemporaries.

Two representations were produced in the first quarter of the seventeenth century, the Le Ber portrait in January 1700 and a drawing or miniature commissioned by the Sulpicians of Montreal and sent to their confreres in Paris about 1722. This miniature has since disappeared, but it served as the model for an engraving by Charles-Louis Simonneau intended to illustrate a biography of Marguerite Bourgeoys (illus. 2). Although it represents its subject as a serene young woman, the engraving resembles the Le Ber portrait, especially in the upper part of her face and in her headdress. All the nineteenth-century portraits derive from the Simonneau engraving. Both a painting of Marguerite Bourgeoys attributed to Antoine Plamondon and presented to the Congregation in 1851 (illus. 3) and the engraving by Massard created as the frontispiece for the biography published by Étienne-Michel Faillon in 1853 (illus. 4) clearly illustrate this fact. In the eighteenth and nineteenth centuries, religious art was expected to be edifying, austere, and so respectful of tradition that artists copied one another from one epoch to the next. They attempted to portray Marguerite's depth,

1   *Painting of Marguerite Bourgeoys by Pierre Le Ber (Musée Marguerite-Bourgeoys)*

Le portrait de venerable Soeur Marguerite Bourgeois, premiere Superieure des filles de la Congregation de Nôtre Dame établies à Ville-marie en l'Isle de Montreal en Canada, decedée en odeur de Sainteté le douzieme de Janvier 1700.

C. Simonneau Sculp.it

2   *Engraving by Charles-Louis Simmoneau after a miniature sent to Paris about 1722 (Library and Archives of Canada, C-008986)*

3 Painting attributed to Antoine Plamondon and presented to the Congregation in
1852 (Musée Marguerite-Bourgeoys)

MARGUERITE BOURGEOYS,

Fondatrice des Sœurs de la Congrégation de Villemarie,

née le 17 Avril 1620, décédée le 12 Janvier 1700

4 *Engraving by Massard, probably Jean-Marie-Raphael-Léopold Massard, for the frontispiece of Étienne-Michel Faillon's 1853 biography of Marguerite Bourgeoys*

the authenticity of her prayer, and the fullness of her commitment, and their painting had a sacred character not always present in later works. The danger of following earlier models in this manner, however, is that the image may become fixed, static, and remote.

The frontispiece was not the only work created by Massard for Faillon's biography. The two-volume work is illustrated throughout with engravings representing events in the life of Marguerite Bourgeoys and of the Congregation. Later, other figures were often added to portraits of the founder. Frequently, these are children, both aboriginal and of European descent, as in the 1904 painting by a Congregation artist for the fiftieth anniversary of the Villa Maria in Montreal (illus. 5). In the Ozias Leduc painting created for Notre-Dame-de-Bon-Secours chapel in 1909, several sisters of the Congregation can be seen behind Marguerite (illus. 6). In the first half of the twentieth century, Congregation artists created whole series of works illustrating the life of their founder, culminating in a group of paintings for the main corridors of the Congregation mother house in 1950, the year in which Marguerite Bourgeoys was beatified by Pope Pius XII (illus. 7).

The beatification, the last formal step before canonization, inspired many new works of art representing Marguerite Bourgeoys. In keeping with the honour just accorded her by the church, she is shown "in glory": the aim of the artist is to portray the meaning of the event, rather than to produce a naturalistic portrait of how the subject might have appeared in her lifetime. The most striking of these works is the large painting done by the Italian painter Georges Szoldatics for the wall above the left side altar in the chapel of the Congregation mother house, painted earlier but unveiled the morning of the beatification (illus. 8 and 9). Sylvie Daoust's statue, carved for Notre-Dame Basilica at that time (illus. 10), is reminiscent of the recollection and serenity of the eighteenth-century engraving, and the effigy created by M.J. Guardo for Notre-Dame-de-Bon-Secours chapel in 1952 is also an idealized representation of a young woman (illus. 11). Just a decade later, however, changes in the church and in society would lead to changes in the way Marguerite Bourgeoys is represented.

In the mid-nineteenth century the Le Ber portrait had been painted over; by whom and in what circumstances is unknown. The act is often attributed to the influence of Faillon, who began his biography of Marguerite Bourgeoys in the 1830s and is known to have expressed contempt for Le Ber's work. Certainly, the new portrait of a pleasant-faced middle-aged woman (illus. 12) bears little resemblance to the stark, powerful, and primitive Le Ber. In time, the memory of the original Le Ber image was completely lost, and the painting that overlaid it was accepted as his work

5   Marguerite Bourgeoys et les enfants, *painting by S.S.-René (Elmina Lachance), 1904. Used in 1975 for the Canadian postage stamp commemorating the 275th anniversary of the death of Marguerite Bourgeoys. (Musée Marguerite-Bourgeoys)*

6 *Painting by Ozias Leduc, 1909 (Notre-Dame-de-Bon-Secours chapel, Montreal)*

7 *Marguerite Bourgeoys participates in the building of Notre-Dame-de-Bon-Secours chapel; from the series painted by Congregation artists in 1950*

8   Marguerite Bourgeoys en gloire, *painting by Georges Szoldatics*
for the chapel of the Congrégation de Notre-Dame mother house

9   The chapel of the Congregation mother house, 3040 Sherbrooke Street West, in
1950. The paintings in the chapel were later removed, and it is now the library of
Dawson College.

10   *Sculpture by Sylvie Daoust in Notre-Dame Basilica, Montreal*

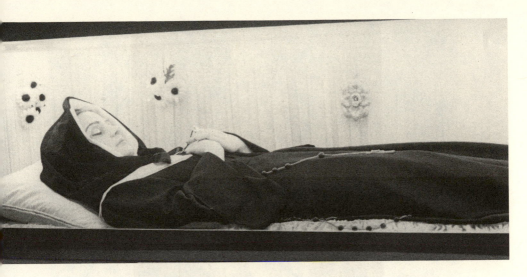

11   *Plaster image of Marguerite Bourgeoys by M.J. Guardo, in Notre-Dame-de-Bon-Secours chapel from 1952 to 2005; now in the collection of the Musée Marguerite-Bourgeoys*

12 Copy of the painting known as the pseudo–Le Ber, made by Jori Smith-Palardy before the nineteenth-century overpainting was removed and the original painting was restored.

more or less officially. But by the early 1960s,[2] artists within the Congregation called this identification into question because of both the style of the painting and the obvious signs of retouching; certain older sisters even remembered instances in which they had witnessed such retouches. In 1962 Jean Palardy, a leading authority on Canadian antiques, was consulted. He confirmed the suspicion that what was visible on the canvas could not be the work of Pierre Le Ber, and he raised the possibility that, beneath the overpainting, the artist's work might still exist and be recoverable. The decision was made to investigate this possibility, and in 1963 Sister Mary Eileen Scott took the canvas to Edward O. Korany, of the International Institute for Conservation in New York, an expert with forty years' experience in this kind of work. Before the restoration process began, the painting was photographed, and a copy of the overpainting, which would then become known as the pseudo–Le Ber, was made by the Montreal artist Jori Smith-Palardy.

The restorer found that the original canvas had been twice repainted and frequently retouched; it was glued to a sheet of cardboard, which was in turn attached to a fibreboard panel. When he x-rayed the painting, he found proof of the existence of another portrait beneath the two repaintings. He was able to discern praying rather than folded hands, a different shoulder line, and a little of the face (illus. 13, 14, and 15). But layers of white lead, impenetrable by x-ray, prevented him from knowing if the entire face was intact. Sister Sainte-Marie-Consolatrice, then superior general of the Congregation, accepted the risk entailed in proceeding with the restoration, and Korany began his painstaking work, taking two hours to clear a single square inch of the canvas, which measured nineteen by twenty-four inches. The restorer had been told nothing about the life of the person on whose portrait he was working except that she was a seventeenth-century religious figure. When asked for his first reaction to the face he had revealed, he answered with one word, "Compassion."

Pierre Le Ber's work returned to light not only at a time when its artistic style could be better appreciated but also when his interpretation of his subject corresponded with contemporary ideas of holiness. The Second Vatican Council had begun in October 1962 and would continue until December 1965. Its discussions and decrees brought about sweeping changes in Catholic life, piety, and religious practice. It urged religious communities to return to their roots and to recapture the authentic spirit of their founders. In the succeeding decades, there was more and more emphasis on the relationship between religion and the struggle for social justice. In Marguerite's case, holiness was sought not in austerities or

13, 14, 15   *Photographs taken at various stages of the restoration of the Le Ber portrait of Marguerite Bourgeoys (Musée Marguerite-Bourgeoys)*

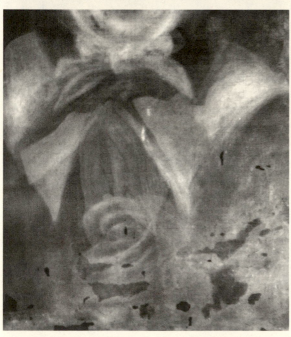

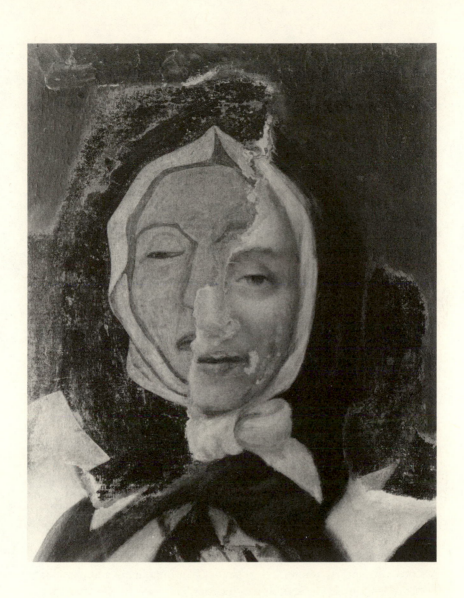

16   Hommage à Marguerite Bourgeoys, *sculpture by Jules Lasalle for Place Marguerite-Bourgeoys, 1988 (Photograph: Carmen Riffou)*

visions but in her relationship with the ordinary people of Montreal in the seventeenth century, among whom she was an unfailingly compassionate presence, and in her dedication to educating the poor. Le Ber's portrait is that not of an idealized saint already enjoying the beatific vision but of an old woman who carries on her face the marks of much suffering. At the beginning of a new millennium, response to the visible illness and death of Pope John Paul II in the spring of 2005 would suggest that a modern audience does not shy away from these reminders of limitation and mortality. Le Ber's work speaks to a time when many believe that a true work of religious art does not provide answers but asks questions and often speaks more of absence than of certitude.

17   *Detail of Lasalle's sculpture of Marguerite Bourgeoys*

In the works created after the canonization, however, Marguerite is usually portrayed in action of some kind. Typical of this approach is the group of statuary created by Jules Lasalle and erected in Place Marguerite-Bourgeoys, just west of the Hôtel de Ville on rue Notre Dame in Old Montreal, in 1988. A life-sized Marguerite Bourgeoys draws two children in modern dress upward and onward toward the future (illus. 16 and 17). In a pastel painted by Victoire Roy in 1992 to commemorate the 350th anniversary of the founding of Montreal, she struggles against the wind in a snowy landscape on her way to "wherever charity calls" (illus. 18).

18   En partence, *pastel by Victoire Roy, 1992 (Musée Marguerite-Bourgeoys)*

On 24 April 2005 Marguerite Bourgeoys's remains were removed from the mother house of the Congrégation de Notre-Dame to Notre-Dame-de-Bon-Secours chapel in Old Montreal. They were placed under the left side altar, where formerly the Guardo figure had lain. The only decoration on the slab of white marble that now covers the tomb is the copper plate commissioned by François Dollier de Casson in 1700 to mark her burial place.

The many representations of Marguerite Bourgeoys tell as much about the people who created them and the times in which they lived as they do about Marguerite herself. To peruse them is to observe not only changing artistic styles but also shifting priorities and values.

NOTES

ABBREVIATIONS

ACND	Archives de la Congrégation de Notre-Dame de Montréal
AJM	Archives judiciares de Montréal
AMMB	Archives du Musée Marguerite-Bourgeoys
ASQ	Archives du Séminaire de Québec
BN	Bibliothèque national, Paris
CMB	*Courrier Marguerite-Bourgeoys*
DCB	*Dictionary of Canadian Biography*
DdeC	Dollier de Casson, *A History of Montreal*, ed. and trans. Ralph Flenley
EMB	*Les écrits de Mère Bourgeoys*, ed. S.S. Damase-de-Rome
HCND	Sainte-Henriette, *Histoire de la Congrégation de Notre-Dame*
HSV	M. Morin, *Histoire simple et véritable*, ed. Legendre
LAC	Library and Archives Canada
RAPQ	*Rapport des Archives de la province de Québec*
RHAF	*Revue d'histoire de l'Amérique française*
RND	Registers of Notre-Dame Parish, Montreal
SCHEC	Société canadienne de l'histoire de l'Église catholique (reports)
WMB	*The Writings of Marguerite Bourgeoys*, trans. M.V. Cotter

INTRODUCTION

1 For a history of the transmissions of the so-called "écrits autographes," see *The Writings of Marguerite Bourgeoys*, xiii–xvi. For a discussion of biographies of Marguerite Bourgeoys, see Simpson, *Marguerite Bourgeoys and Montreal, 1640–1665*, 7–9.

2 Fragments of the handwriting of Marguerite Bourgeoys continued to be distributed as relics until Faillon put a stop to the practice and attempted to recover and reconstitute any that could be found. A relic acquired by the Marguerite Bourgeoys Museum contains ashes from her heart backed by a tiny sample of her handwriting containing the words "Saint Gabriel." This relic must have been made after the fire of 1768 that reduced the embalmed heart to ashes.

CHAPTER ONE

1 *WMB*, 113 (172). Page references to the English edition of Marguerite Bourgeoys's writings are followed by a cross-reference in parentheses to the original French *Écrits de Mère Bourgeoys*.
2 See Simpson, *Marguerite Bourgeoys and Montreal*, 179–82.
3 *HSV*, 75.
4 *HSV*, 74–5.
5 Juchereau and Duplessis, *Les annales de l'Hôtel-Dieu de Quebec*, 144–5.
6 Marie de l'Incarnation, *Correspondance*, 755.
7 Ibid.
8 At key points in Garakontié's speech, he paused, and ceremonial gifts were placed at Tracy's feet. See Faillon, *Histoire de la colonie française en Canada*, 3: 127–8.
9 Ibid., 130.
10 These were directed toward making French colonies self-sufficient, able to provide themselves with food, shelter, and clothing, to produce exports of tangible value, and to serve as markets for French manufactured goods. Talon attempted to develop a diversified economy – the precariousness of depending solely on the fur trade was obvious – hence his attempts to encourage lumbering, fishing, and mining. A three-cornered trading market involving France and its colonies in New France and the West Indies was envisaged.
11 Talon wanted these young women married as soon as possible after their arrival. To this end, an ordinance was passed providing that once their ships had arrived, no bachelor was allowed to fish, hunt, or engage in the fur trade until all the filles de roi had been married.
12 Modern attempts to halt the decline of the population of Quebec pale into insignificance beside the population policies of this period. The government paid special subsidies to men who married before their twenty-first birthday and women before their seventeenth; parents of those who failed to do so without good reason were liable to a fine.

The parents of large families were rewarded: an annual pension of three hundred livres to those who had ten living legitimate children, none of whom had entered the clergy, four hundred to those with twelve such children (Eccles, *Canada under Louis XIV*, 48)

13 HCND, 1: 91, HSV, 156. Marie Raisin's departure would also have meant a financial loss to the Congregation. Besides the sum settled on her by her father at the time of her departure for Montreal, she inherited the estate of her brother Nicolas when he died in 1687, and his executor invested the proceeds for the Congregation, to which Marie had deeded it (AJM, Basset, 30 juin 1688). Marguerite Bourgeoys wrote that in 1659 Edmé Raisin "gave 1,000 *livres* for the trip and for her clothes, of which I took only 300 *livres*. I left him the rest which I did not need. But every year, he sent us 35 *livres* on the 700 *livres* and after his death his son continued it. And at the death of his son, a lawyer to Parliament, besides these bequests, we had an income of 300 *livres* on 6,000 *livres*" (WMB, 36 [62]).

14 Trudel, *La population de Canada en 1666*, 41.

15 Recent demographic studies of clergy and religious in Canada during the French regime show that the average life expectancy of members of the Congrégation de Notre-Dame, although longer than that of the hospital sisters, was shorter than that of the Ursulines. While the shorter life expectancy of the hospital sisters is attributable to their contact with the diseases of their patients, Louis Pelletier suggests that that of the sisters of the Congregation is due to the fact that, "Not living in community, they dedicated themselves to the education of children pretty well all over the colony. They thus lived in conditions that were sometimes very diffcult and injurious to their health" (Pelletier, *Le clergé en Nouvelle-France*, 97–8).

16 To her son, 24 September 1654 (Marie de l'Incarnation, *Correspondance*, 546). This is her first mention of plans to go to Montreal, although Marguerite Bourgeoys was already there waiting for her first pupils to achieve school age, and the cloistered Congrégation de Notre-Dame of Troyes apparently still had hopes of going to Ville-Marie. There is also reference in a letter to Mother Cécile de S. Joseph, 1 October 1669 (853) and to an Ursuline sister of Tours, September-November 1671 (936). The Ursuline account of the 1666 entry of Marie Raisin reads: "The same year in the month of July Sr Marie Raisin de la congrégation Notre Dame entered this house with the intention of becoming a Religious madame our very honoured foundress supplied her dowry her Entry caused a great stir however after several months of trial she got tired of the life and decided herself to leave which she did in the following October" (Archives des Ursulines de

Québec, "Ancien récit" [1666], p.27, lines 15–20). The "Ancien récit" is a document reconstructed from memory by Soeur Anne Bourdon, *dite* de Saint-Agnes, after a fire at the Ursuline monastery in Quebec in 1686.

17 *HSV*, 132–3.

18 Based on the figures supplied in Trudel, *La population du Canada en 1666*, 274–315.

19 For information about Marguerite Bourgeoys's reception of the filles du roi in 1663, see Simpson, *Marguerite Bourgeoys and Montreal*, 165–8. Yves Landry's *Orphelines en France* makes use of the *Registre de la population du Québec ancien* as well as earlier studies to present a treasury of information about these women, who received some form of government aid to assist their passage to and marriage and settlement in New France between 1663 and 1673. At the close of the chapter examining the families produced by the filles de roi, he adds one more argument to those advanced in previous studies against the suggestion that these women were prostitutes: their high fecundity (222).

20 *EMB* contains the statement that the number of women welcomed at the shore by Marguerite Bourgeoys in 1663 was seventeen (257; *WMB*, 178), but the most recent research published by Yves Landry would indicate that the number should be seven rather than seventeen. If figures were used rather than words, it would have been easy for an extra stroke to have been added at some time when the writings were being transcribed.

21 This was Marguerite De Nevelet, who was from the parish of Saint-Madeleine in Troyes, site of the marriage of Marguerite Bourgeoys's parents, and was about twenty-three years old at the time of her arrival in Montreal. It is possible, then, that Marguerite Bourgeoys or one of the other members of her group was already acquainted with her or with her family. Marguerite De Nevelet, whose father is identified as a bourgeois, married Abraham Bouat, habitant, church warden, innkeeper, bourgeois, and merchant, and the two had eight children. She spent the last eleven years of her life as a permanent boarder at the Congregation, where she died in 1720. In his study of the filles du roi, Landry suggests that they fell into three categories: those recruited and transported to Canada at the king's expense, those who presented themselves at the port of embarkation and were integrated into the king's contingents, and those who were neither recruited by the king nor transported at his expense but whose establishment between 1663 and 1673 was probably facilitated by the colonial administrators (*Orphelines en France*, 24–5). Marguerite De Nevelet probably belonged to the third category.

22 For information about the reason for his absence, see Simpson, *Marguerite Bourgeoys and Montreal*, 155–6.

23 DdeC, 339. So completely did these girls identify with the French that when the mother of the younger one tried to take her away, she tore herself out of her mother's hold and ran back to a sister of the Congregation. The Trudel edition of Dollier de Casson's history notes that on 22 November 1672 Pierre Hogue married Marie-Madeleine-Catherine Nachita, a Native woman sixteen years old who had been baptized on 2 July 1672, and that a Marie whose origin is not identified was baptized on 22 July 1671 with Governor Courcelle as godfather. (290n6)

24 *WMB*, 97 (150).

25 *WMB*, 71 (113).

26 *WMB*, 171 (247).

27 See Simpson, *Marguerite Bourgeoys and Montreal*, 115–16, 123–4, 154. For the date at which the chapel was begun, see Simpson and Pothier, *Notre-Dame-de-Bon-Secours*, 35–6.

28 *WMB*, 113 (172).

29 AJM, Basset, "Vente par francois Le Ber et Jeanne Testard Sa femme Aux filles de la Congregaon' avec. Une quictance des lods et Vente par Monsr. Galinier du 24e. 7bre. 1668." The price was 1,258 livres, 12 sols, and 9 derniers, some of which had already been paid in merchandise, including beaver skins.

30 Chicoine, *La métairie de Marguerite Bourgeoys*, 17.

31 Landry, *Orphelines en France*, 62. At least nine of the filles du roi who arrived in Montreal in 1670 were from Paris.

32 *RAPQ*, 1930–31, 64–5.

33 *HCND*, 1: 97–8.

34 See Simpson, *Marguerite Bourgeoys and Montreal*, 127–8, 134.

35 Marie de l'Incarnation, *Correspondance*, 894–5.

36 Ibid., 936.

37 Faillon, *Vie de la soeur Bourgeoys*, 208. Reference is made to this document by the clerk who registered the letters patent of the Congrégation de Notre-Dame at the Parlement de Paris, although he dates it in 1667 rather than 1669. Bishop Laval himself makes reference to it in his approbation of the Congregation in 1676, citing the date 20 May 1669 (*Mandements, lettres pastorales et circulaires des évêques de Québec*, 99).

38 AJM, Basset, "Reconnaissance de Marguerite Bourgeoys à ses compagnes," 14 May 1669. See also *HCND*, 1: 101–3. The woodland would later be exchanged for land in the town and would come to be the site of the Native village on the mountain.

39 See Simpson, *Marguerite Bourgeoys and Montreal*, 149–51.

40 *WMB*, 114 (174); *HSV*, 73.

CHAPTER TWO

1 *WMB*, 113 (172).

2 *WMB*, 36 (63). The preceding sentence is misplaced and refers quite clearly to the third voyage to France. Since it is inconsistent with all that follows, it is more likely the result of an error on the part of a compiler or copyist than of confusion on Marguerite's part, as Faillon suggests.

3 The registration of the letters patent in Paris also lists the supporting documents with dates. The date given for Talon's letter is 17 August 1670, but the intendant only reached Quebec on a return journey from France on 18 August. Is it a mistake for 27 August?

4 Le Blant, "Les derniers jours de Maisonneuve," 277.

5 A half-brother of the famous archbishop of Cambrai, he had arrived in Canada in 1667 while not yet a priest. After his ordination by Bishop Laval in 1668, he became one of the founders of the mission of Kenté (Quinte) on Lake Ontario. He returned to Canada but was forced to leave again after he fell foul of the civil authorities in 1674 and died in 1679 at the age of thirty-eight. A reminder of him remains in the name of Fenelon Falls, on the Trent River in Ontario.

6 *WMB*, 37 (64).

7 *WMB*, 38–9 (67). This payment is probably that referred to by Marguerite when she writes: "When I was in Quebec, a priest of the Seminary for whom we had done some work and to whom we had supplied something or other, asked me how he could pay the sisters. I did not know how much he might owe us. I let him know that if I could have the money in Paris, it would be useful to me. And I thought no more about it; we were on the point of setting sail" (*WMB*, 37–8 [64–5]).

8 Desrosiers, *Paul de Chomedey*, 302.

9 *WMB*, 39 (67). The article of furniture to which she refers caused considerable difficulty for Marguerite's biographers in the eighteenth and nineteenth centuries. Montgolfier thought it was a kind of Indian-style shelter erected in the corner of the garden. Dom Jamet identified it correctly from other seventeenth-century references.

10 *HSV*, 71.

11 Jamet, *Marguerite Bourgeoys*, 1: 366.

12 *WMB*, 38 (65).

13 *WMB*, 39 (68).

14 Montgolfier, *Vie de la vénérable soeur Marguerite Bourgeois*, 107; Faillon, *Vie de la soeur Bourgeoys*, 1: 217–18.

15 See Simpson, *Marguerite Bourgeoys and Montreal*, 52–3, 62.

16 *RAPQ*, 1930–31, 125.

17 Faillon, *Vie de la soeur Bourgeoys*, 1: 219, note.

18 Niel, *Marguerite Bourgeoys et sa famille*, [22].

19 Le Blant, "Les derniers jours de Maisonneuve," 276–8.

20 An original copy of the letters patent belonging to the Congregation remained in the archives of the Congregation until 1922, when it was lent to a relative of a member of the council and never returned. There is another contemporary copy in the Archives de la Marine in Paris. The quotation is from the modernized transcript in HCND, 1: 113–15.

21 Faillon, *Vie de la soeur Bourgeoys*, 219.

22 Niel, *Marguerite Bourgeoys et sa famille*, [24].

23 This information on the family of Marguerite Bourgeoys was assembled by Lucienne Plante and published in a series of articles in the *Courrier Marguerite-Bourgeoys* ("The Family of Marguerite Bourgeoys"). She concludes, "There is still further research to be done in the archives of Troyes, Paris, Évreux and Sens to unearth further facts about Marguerite Bourgeoys' family."

24 Saint-Jean-au-Marché.

25 WMB, 39 (68). Unless the names of Louise and Catherine have been confused here.

26 HCND, 1: 340–1, 343–6; 2: 179–81; 3: 147–8; 4: 357.

27 WMB, 114 (172–3).

28 Montgolfier did take some liberties in giving a context to the fragments with which he was working, even to the extent of creating imaginary conversations. Sometimes his misconceptions were related to an ignorance of conditions in New France a century earlier. For example, he did not know that Louis Frin was Maisonneuve's personal servant. He conjectured that he was someone Marguerite wanted to engage to teach the boys, replacing a young man hired for this purpose who had died. The fact that Marguerite and her companions had taught both boys and girls had apparently been forgotten. See Montgolfier, *Vie de la vénérable soeur Marguerite Bourgeois*, 108.

29 Oury, "Pierre Chevrier, baron de Fancamp," 34. This article contains all the most recent research on the Baron de Fancamp.

30 HCND, 1: 313. For further information on the history of the oak of Montaigu, see Huet, "From Montague to Ville Marie," 22–4.

31 The original act of donation by the LePrestre brothers is in Library and Archives Canada. That act and the attestation of his cure by the Baron de Fancamp are cited in their entirety in Archives de la Paroisse Notre-Dame de Montréal, "Registres des délibérations de la fabrique de la Paroisse de Notre-Dame de Ville-Marie," 29 June 1675. Marie-Claire Daveluy sums up all that is known of the LePrestres in *La Société de Notre-Dame de Montréal*, 234–40.

32 Plante, "The Family of Marguerite Bourgeoys," 26.

33 Montgolfier, *Vie de la vénérable soeur Marguerite Bourgeois*, 108–9.
    No other trace of a Madeleine Senécal has ever been found. However, a
    woman identified as Marguerite DeSenne made a contract of marriage
    with Jullien Hautboys on 22 September 1672. This was dissolved on
    12 October, and on 13 October she signed a contract with Jean Séné-
    cal (AJM, Basset). The two were married two days later, but the mar-
    riage register identifies the bride as Catherine de Sennes (RND). It is
    quite possible that by the time Montgolfier wrote about the events, she
    was remembered by her husband's surname, and the confusion about
    the given name seems to have begun early. Jamet objected very much
    to the appearance of the adjective "coldly" in this story. He found it
    more characteristic of an excessively inhuman view of the saints than
    of anything known of Marguerite Bourgeoys.

34 There is uncertainty about Catherine Boni's origins. She was not among
    the six recruits to the Congregation named by Marguerite Bourgeoys
    as having been received by Bishop Laval in Paris. However, she was a
    member of the Congregation by 1676, when she went to work at the
    Native mission on Mount Royal. Because Montgolfier described Mar-
    guerite as accompanied by eleven women on her journey to Rouen
    and she arrived in Montreal with twelve or thirteen, according to Dol-
    lier de Casson, it has been conjectured that Catherine was a native
    of Rouen who joined the group there without necessarily having the
    intention of joining the Congregation. She is also described as having
    been directed toward Canada by the Messieurs de Saint-Sulpice de
    Paris. Even her age is uncertain, for the census of 1681 put it at thirty-
    nine while the age given in the records at the time of her death in April
    1712 is seventy-five. For another suggestion about her background,
    see chapter 6, note 7, below.

35 The main problem with the date of arrival is that the letters patent
    Marguerite Bourgeoys was bringing from France were not registered
    in Quebec until 17 October 1672. Why the long delay? And since it is
    highly unlikely that she herself stayed on in Quebec for more than two
    months, who presented them for registration? Montgolfier also placed
    during this voyage an incident of a threatened attack by enemy ships,
    and the editor of *WMB* accepts this dating, but I follow Faillon in plac-
    ing this event in 1680.

36 *WMB*, 174–5.

37 Montgolfier, *La vie de la vénérable soeur Marguerite Bourgeois*,
    111.

38 "This good sister has just been for two years in France ... obtained
    her permit from the court, and has come back with twelve or thirteen
    girls" (DdeC, 191–3).

CHAPTER THREE

1 *WMB*, 69–70, 89 (111, 138).

2 *HSV*, 73.

3 The seventeenth-century chapel was completely destroyed by fire in 1754, and the present chapel was built over but not on the foundations of the first in 1772. The site of Notre-Dame-de-Bon-Secours chapel is the oldest in Montreal to have retained its original purpose. Archaeological explorations in 1997 uncovered the foundations of the seventeenth-century chapel as well as evidence of the intensity of the fire that destroyed it. They have also cast light on earlier Native use of the site.

4 Beneath this stone were placed an incribed lead plaque and a metal engraving of the Blessed Virgin. These objects were recovered after the fire of 1754 and placed in the foundations of the eighteenth-century chapel. They were rediscovered in 1945 when the centre wall of the crypt beneath the apse was pierced to provide an exit onto rue de la Commune and can now be seen in the Marguerite Bourgeoys Museum.

5 *WMB*, 114 (174).

6 *WMB*, 167 (240); see also *HSV*, 74.

7 *WMB*, 115 (174). In November 1678, with the approval of Bishop Laval, the chapel was ceded to Notre-Dame parish, to which it would be annexed "in perpetuity." The document of cession, which mentions the sum of 2,400 livres contributed by the Congrégation de Notre-Dame for the building of the chapel, also states that the sisters of the Congregation will continue to take care of the chapel in the future as they have already done in the past (Archives de la Paroisse Notre-Dame de Montréal, "Régistres des délibérations de la paroisse de Ville-Marie," 6 November 1678).

8 Daveluy, *Jeanne Mance*, 245.

9 Cécile's mother was Elisabeth Moyen. Jeanne Mance always remained close to the two Moyen sisters, who had been placed in her care after their parents were killed in a Native raid.

10 These codicils included Jeanne's consent to the removal of her heart, an action that was performed a few hours after her death.

11 The strip of land lay between what are now William Street and René Levesque Boulevard somewhat east of what is now Atwater Avenue. Marguerite Bourgeoys held a piece of land immediately to the north.

12 AJM, "Affaire de l'enfant d'André Michel-St-Michel," 20–1 July 1673.

13 AJM, Basset, 8 July 1674.

14 Louise Sommillard and François Fortin were living in Pointe-aux-Trembles by the time of the baptism of their daughter Françoise in

February 1679 and in Rivière-des-Prairies when Joseph was baptized in November 1687.

15 The most complete account of the whole affair can be found in Faillon, *Histoire de la colonie française en Canada*, 3: 496–513.

16 The Incident of the Corsican Guard, 20 August 1662.

17 *Mandements, lettres et circulaires des évêques de Québec*, 99–100.

18 See Simpson, *Marguerite Bourgeoys and Montreal*, 114–15.

19 *HCND*, 1: 265–6. Anne Meyrand was not yet in Canada.

20 Montgolfier, *Vie de la vénérable soeur Marguerite Bourgeois*, 117.

21 Maurault, *Le Fort des Messieurs*, 14.

22 Montgolfier, *Vie de la vénérable soeur Marguerite Bourgeois*, 116–17.

23 *HCND*, 2: 137; Vachon de Belmont, "Éloges," 188.

24 *HCND*, 1: 289.

25 She was to receive 160 livres as well as a small income connected with other family settlements.

26 Both the will and details of the inventory can be found in Le Blant, "Les derniers jours de Maisonneuve and Philippe de Turmenyes," 278–80, 269–72.

27 *WMB*, 115 (174).

28 This issue was to continue to present a problem for the Congregation, as will be seen in the discussions surrounding the rule the Congregation would accept in 1698. A century later Montgolfier wrote: "Although it was the intention of Sister Bourgeoys to receive sisters into the Congregation free, there was later a declaration of the king that obliged them to exact a dowry of at least 2,000 livres; although some relaxation on this article has been permitted them since then, in whole or in part, according to their prudence and with regard to circumstances of time and persons" (*Vie de la vénérable soeur Marguerite Bourgeois*, 124).

29 *WMB*, 167 (240).

30 AJM, Maugue, "Reception de Marie Barbier en la congregation," 11 August 1679; AJM, Maugue, "Reception de Françoise Lemoyne a la congregation," 24 March 1680. (Although it was accepted by her council in her absence, Marguerite Bourgeoys had to sign the latter document on her return from France.) In 1684 Marie Barbier's parents settled on her 100 livres and a piece of land with a small wooden house on rue Notre-Dame near the hospital, all to go to her after their deaths (AJM, Basset, "Donation Entre Vifs par Gilbert Barbier et Catherine de la Vaux Sa femme en faveur de Marie Barbe leur fille," 20 December 1684.

31 For example, AJM, Maugue, "Donation de personne et biens de Jean Caillou de Baron aux Soeurs de la Congrégation," 20 March 1678;

AJM, Maugue, "Donation de personne et de biens de louis Fontaine a la congrega'on," 13 February 1678.

32 See Simpson, *Marguerite Bourgeoys and Montreal*, 161.

33 WMB, 69 (110). This description corresponds to some extent with that given by Ransonet in the first published biography of Marguerite Bourgeoys, although the fabrics seem to have become more elaborate: "The sisters' habit is very simple. The dress is black serge, falls to their heels is completely closed in the front and has no arrangement in the pleats. The belt is black wool and encircles then twice. The apron is made of black muslin." After describing the linen kerchief and cornet, he adds that "the overcoiffe is made of veil muslin and is long. This modest dress hides a silver cross the sisters wear on the breast" (*Vie de la soeur Marguerite Bourgeoys*, 68–9).

34 WMB, 69 (110).

35 Glandelet says that while she was superior, Marie Barbier would wear "only the silver cross worn by her Sisters" although she was pressured to substitute something more impressive (ASQ, "Receuil," 184)

36 The rule accepted by the Congregation in 1698 described the habit in some detail, even to the extent of specifying what underwear would be worn under it. The floor-length black wool dress with loose pleats encircled twice at the waist by a woven belt, white linen neckerchief and coiffe, and black headdress described in the rule accepted by the Congregation in 1698, remained, with slight modifications, the habit of the community until the 1960s. The advent of starch in 1835 made the cornet much more conspicuous, and later the sisters were prevailed upon by the bishop to transform the black part of their headdress into a veil. The main reason that this and other religious habits were eventually so removed from the dress of other women, especially in western Europe and North America, was that their form remained fixed while women's fashions changed. At least one of the communities founded in the seventeenth century anticipated the problem, for its rule states that the style and fabric in which the habits are to be made is not prescribed "because the manner of dressing most modestly and most simply and even the fabric become so outdated that those who want to continue to keep them would appear singular and would even pass for ridiculous" (Constitutions de la communauté des Filles de Ste Geneviève, 82).

37 HSV, 75.

38 WMB, 174 (252).

39 ASQ, Glandelet, "Receuil," 17–19.

40 AJM, Basset, "Declaration de Soeur Marie Touchard a la reqte de fiacre du Charme," 18 November 1676.

41 *HCND*, 5: 242–7; Sévigny, "Histoire de la Congrégation de Notre-Dame à Laprairie," 5.

42 In 1708 the sisters of the Congrégation de Notre-Dame were forbidden to pronounce vows by Jérôme Phélypeaux de Pontchartrain, then minister of the Marine. In her attempts to have this restriction lifted, Catherine Charly, the superior, sought the intercession of Madame de Maintenon in a letter that contains the following passage: "Our community ... no longer making vows is on the point of finding itself deprived of subjects, either by turning away women who will be dissuaded by that fact, as experience has already shown, or by the inconstancy and discouragement of those who will have come into the community, and who, seeing themselves free to leave, will believe themselves able to make use of that freedom without scruple, as happened in other times before we made vows" (*HCND*, 3: 131).

CHAPTER FOUR

1 *WMB*, 40 (69).
2 Montgolfier, *Vie de la vénérable soeur Marguerite Bourgeois*, 117.
3 *WMB*, 50 (82).
4 *WMB*, 175 (252).
5 Jean Valliquet, *dit* Laverdure, began to molest his younger daughters after the death of his wife. When they reported what was happening to the parish priest, he placed them in the Congregation boarding school. At Valliquet's trial in Montreal, Elisabeth de la Bertache had to testify as to what the girls had told her, and Marguerite Bourgeoys to vouch for her testimony. Valliquet was condemned to death and sent to Quebec, but there the sentence was greatly mitigated. For an account of the procedures, see Boyer, *Les crimes et les châtiments*, 22, 257, 330, 331.
6 *WMB*, 43 (73). In this context, I have translated *flattent* as "soothing" rather than "flattering."
7 *WMB*, 91 (140).
8 *WMB*, 98 (151).
9 *WMB*, 81–2 (125–7).
10 *WMB*, 177 (255).
11 *WMB*, 178–9 (258). I have modified the translation.
12 Glandelet, *Life of Sister Marguerite Bourgeoys*, 93–4; Montgolfier, *Vie de la vénérable soeur Marguerite Bourgeois*, 148.
13 *HCND*, 1: 146–7.
14 Glandelet, *Life of Sister Marguerite Bourgeoys*, 93–4; *WMB*, 3 (19). I have slightly altered the translation to keep it closer to the original French.

15 *WMB*, 9–11 (29). The letter is misdated in the English translation.

16 The version of this letter found in *HCND*, 1: 150–1, is longer than that in Faillon, *Vie de la soeur Bourgeoys*, 255–6. In it Marguerite Bourgeoys appears to have consulted the Ursulines about the conduct of the boarding school and to have decided to follow their example in not allowing the boarders to go out.

17 *WMB*, 40 (69).

18 Roserot, *Troyes: Son histoire ses monuments des origines à 1790*, 110.

19 *WMB*, 5 (22).

20 *WMB*, 176 (254). Also "the thought came to me that I had so many times repeated my promises to God, promises not to give up except by His order" (*WMB* 168 [241]).

21 *WMB*, 40 (70).

22 *WMB*, 40–1 (70).

23 Le Blant, "Les derniers jours de Maisonneuve," 273.

24 *WMB*, 41 (70–1). I have altered the English translation because I did not consider it strong enough.

25 In a letter to Mary Eileen Scott dated 24 August 1959, Professor W.J. Eccles wrote: "I rather think that Laval was not the bigotted tyrant he has been made out to be. The anti-clerical historians made him appear almost an ogre, but somewhat to my surprise, I find that the evidence indicates him to have been a reasonable man, albeit of strong character, and when he dug in his heels I find myself agreeing that he was in the right i.e. the brandy issue" (*AMMB*).

26 *WMB*, 42 (71-2).

27 Salinis, *Madame de Villeneuve*, 276–7, citing a manuscript in the Archives de Roye.

28 Ibid., 374–5, citing P. de Beauvais, "Histoire de l'établissement et des progrès de la Congrégation des Filles de la Croix" (ms.).

29 Ibid., 280–1, citing Archives de Roye, "Aprobation de 27 Juillet 1627."

30 Ibid. Salinis quotes the document and the response by the doctors of the Sorbonne in their entirety, 284–9.

31 *WMB*, 72 (115).

32 Madame Acarie, who established the Carmelites in France, and Madame Saint-Beuve, who established the Ursulines there, were both related to Madame de Villeneuve. The Duchesse d'Aiguillon, Cardinal Richelieu's niece, who endowed the Hôtel-Dieu in Quebec, was also a member of the group.

33 Salinis, *Madame de Villeneuve*, 315, quoting "Vie abrégée de Mme de Villeneuve etc" (ms.).

34 Madame de Villeneuve eventually gained the exclusive right to use the name (ibid., 417).

35 In August 1790, when they were visited by the commissioners of the municipality, the community in Paris numbered 20 choir sisters and 10 domestic sisters. There were 23 paying pupils in the boarding school and 120 extern students in the free school, 80 who were learning reading, writing, and arithmetic and 40 young children learning the elements of catechism. The commissioners approved what they found. In 1791, however, the arrival of a constitutional parish priest and disturbances in the neighbourhood caused the community to disband (Ville de Paris, *Commission municipale du Vieux Paris*, 213)

36 HSV, 75.

37 WMB, 42 (71–2). A biography, *Madame de Miramion: Sa vie et ses oeuvres charitables*, was published by A. Bonneau-Avenant, a descendant of her family, in 1874.

38 AJM, Maugue, "Contrat de marriage de Pierre Chantereau ... et Marie Cordier," 13 November 1680; RND, 18 November 1680.

39 The record is torn, but it establishes that Nicolas Cordier married a Marie whose surname is difficult to decipher in February 1652. Marie Cordier's parents are identified in her marriage contract as Nicolas Cordier and Marie Paujet.

40 Faillon, *Vie de la soeur Bourgeoys*, 2: 263.

41 WMB, 41 (71). The identity of the "Father Charles" to whom reference is made here has never been established.

42 AJM, Bailly, 25 October 1687. Marguerite Bourgeoys does not usually name anyone of whom she says anything detrimental, especially if the person might be known to her readers.

43 WMB, 41 (71). Since Frin's name does not appear in the census of 1663, it seems that de Maisonneuve hired him after his return to France in 1665 and Marguerite Bourgeoys met him first in 1670. His age is given as forty in the census of 1683. Later records indicate that she also hired at least one other manservant.

44 WMB, 40 (69).

45 Montgolfier, *Vie de la vénérable soeur Marguerite Bourgeois*, 110; Faillon, *Vie de la soeur Bourgeoys*, 1: 263–4. As Faillon points out, the problem with situating this event in 1672 is that France and England were not at war at that time.

46 Faillon, *Vie de la soeur Bourgeoys*, 2: 262.

CHAPTER FIVE

1 WMB, 175 (253).

2 Céline Dupré, "Cavelier de La Salle, René-Robert," DCB 1: 172.

3 Quoted in HCND 1: 278–9.

4 HCND 1: 340–1.

5 She is called Catherine Grolleau, and her age is given as seventy-one, but this appears to be the only serious inaccuracy with regard to the Congregation provable by other evidence.

6 An account of the ancestry and family circumstances of these girls, as well as of their future lives, can be found in HCND 1: 175–86.

7 WMB, 101 (155).

8 AJM, Basset, "Testament de Thomas Mounier."

9 AJM, Adhémar, "Testament de Thomas Mousnier."

10 AJM, Basset, "Testament de Thomas Monié."

11 AJM, "Plainte d'Antoine Primot et sa femme contre Barthélémy Le-maistre," April-June 1679.

12 HCND, 2: 183–4; Chicoine, La métairie de Marguerite Bourgeoys, 22–4. ACND contains an account of the inquest conducted by Migeon de Branssat.

13 WMB, 170 (244–5); AJM, Maugue, "Accord entre la Soeur bourgeois and Louis Pichard," 2 June 1681. The accord also illustrates Marguerite Bourgeoys's particular combination of charity and detachment and practical common sense. There will be no attempt to fight the claim of her later contract, and the terms of the earlier contracts will be observed; the value of Fontaine's movable goods is carefully accounted for. At the same time, Marguerite recovers the expenses she has gone to, including the seeding of Fontaine's landholding and notarial expenses. Part of the amount of the estate is written off against the debt owed her by the parish for the sacristy laundry.

14 The account of the inquest is wrongly dated 29 June 1681 (AJM, Maugue), but the burial record signed by Marguerite Bourgeoys and Marguerite Sommillard says 28 September (RND).

15 Jamet, Marguerite Bourgeoys, 2: 590. The supposition is based on the fact that they came from the same area of France as Guyotte himself.

16 Faillon, Vie de la soeur Bourgeoys, 1: 286–7.

17 Jesuit Pierre Cholenec quoted in Béchard, Kaia'tano:ron, 112.

18 Montgolfier, La vie de la vénérable soeur Marguerite Bourgeois, 149.

19 HSV, 239.

20 HCND, 2: 188.

21 WMB, 178 (258).

22 Ransonet, La vie de la soeur Marguerite Bourgeoys, 76.

23 Jamet, Marguerite Bourgeoys, 2: 591.

24 The absence of a record of the burials in the parish registers does not prove conclusively that the bodies were not recovered since there are other cases in which the burial was not recorded but is known from other sources. However, whether or not the bodies were recovered, there would have been some kind of religious service.

25 AJM, Mauge, "Grosse de tous les contrats qui sont en dépôt dans le greffe et tabellionnage de Claude Maugue, concernant les Soeurs de la Congrégation," 23 September 1684. Among the properties added since the list prepared in 1669 before Marguerite Bourgeoys left to seek the letters patent was the considerable donation signed over by Zacharie Dupuy and his wife when they became *donnés* of the Congregation in 1673, as well as a house and land that had been the dowry of Marie and Catherine Charly. With the house for teaching the Native girls at the Mountain Mission went another acre to feed a cow, as long as the sisters continued to teach there. The properties excluded were Île aux Hérons and the Bon-Pasteur fief on Île Jésus. The grant on Île Jésus (now Laval), part of the Dupuy donation, was lost in the confusion when Bishop Laval and the Jesuits exchanged Île d'Orléans for Île Jésus.

26 Quoted in *HCND*, 1: 204–5.

27 Montgolfier, *La vie de la vénérable soeur Marguerite Bourgeois*, 123–4.

28 Archives de la Marine, M. de Meulles à M. de Seignelay, 4 November 1683; cited in Faillon, *Vie de la soeur Bourgeoys*, 1: 309.

29 *WMB*, 181.

30 Glandelet, *Life of Sister Marguerite Bourgeoys*, 82–3.

31 The twentieth was to be the only century in the existence of the Congregation when its mother house was not destroyed by fire. A new mother house, known as the Mountain Mother House, was built near the Villa Maria in 1883 when all the old communities were being pushed out of Old Montreal by expanding commerce. It was completely destroyed by fire in 1893, and the community returned to Old Montreal until 1908, when a mother house on Sherbrooke Street in Westmount was built. That building now houses Dawson College.

32 The land was expropriated by the city of Montreal and the Congregation mother house razed in 1912 in order to extend Saint-Laurent to the river. In April 1913 a sister of the Congregation visited the demolition site and asked the contractor if he had discovered any antiquities. He replied: "We did find something in the foundations ... A worker found a medal of Our Lady of the Rosary carrying the date, clearly visible, of 1692 ... We also found two axes, hammers, and a sabre" (AMMB, "Annales de l'école Bonsecours"; see also Simpson and Pothier, *Notre-Dame-de-Bon-Secours*, 125–7).

33 *L'Île de Montréal en 1731*, 31.

34 *HSV*, 75.

35 Juchereau and Duplessis, *Les annales de l'Hôtel-Dieu de Québec*, 281.

36 Saint-Vallier, *Estat present de l'Église ... dans la Nouvelle France*, 64–5; quoted in Faillon, *Vie de la soeur Bourgeoys*, 1: 355.

37 Letter to Dollier de Casson, 7 August 1684; quoted in Faillon, *Vie de la soeur Bourgeoys*, 1: 351–2.

CHAPTER SIX

1 *WMB*, 82 (126).
2 Eccles, "Brisay de Denonville, Jacques René de," *DCB*, 2: 99.
3 *HCND*, 1: 211.
4 *HCND*, 1: 327–8. Émilia Chicoine points out that the Providence which supported this workshop often acted through the agency of the Sulpicians, whose archives show that they supported several of the women as well as donating a weekly supply of bread (*La métairie de Marguerite Bourgeoys*, 39).
5 Faillon, *Vie de la soeur Bourgeoys*, 1: 186.
6 *HSV*, 250.
7 Quoted in Faillon, *Vie de la soeur Bourgeoys*, 1: 187. Faillon attributes the letter to the governor, but it should rather be attributed to the intendant. The wording in this letter that refers to the Congregation – "*and besides* an establishment of *filles de la Providence*" – with the other puzzling references to this group in the early documents has led Elizabeth Rapley to raise an interesting question. Was Marguerite Bourgeoys joined for a time by one or more members of another new community of secular women? Catherine Boni, who is associated in the *Histoire de la Congrégation* with the recruitment of 1672, is there described as a native of Rouen, where Marguerite is believed to have met her and as having been a "fille de la Providence" before becoming a sister of the Congregation. The Soeurs du Saint-Enfant-Jésus, most commonly called the Dames de Saint-Maur, were founded in Rouen in the 1660s as the Soeurs de la Providence. The community believes that one or more of their members went to the New World, though it does not know their names or their destinations (Rapley, "La Providence"). This is a possibility that invites further study. See 133n9 below.
8 It must be remembered, however, that everything comes from a single source, Glandelet, who has selected what he wishes to quote from Marie Barbier's letters and so given his own bias to her portrait. In the case of Marguerite Bourgeoys, there exist comments from a range of her contemporaries.
9 ASQ, Glandelet, "Receuil," 34.
10 Ibid., 36–7.
11 Luke 9: 3.
12 *WMB*, 97–8 (152).
13 ASQ, Glandelet, "Receuil," 38.
14 Ibid., 40–1.

15 Ibid., 45–6.

16 Ibid., 47–8.

17 The sisters who made public profession in 1698 were Marie-Madeleine Asselin, Marie Gagnon, Catherine Jahan Laviolette, Marie-Louise Létourneau, and Marie Prémont. In addition, two of the three sisters who left the Congregation at that time were from Saint-Famille parish. They were Marie Genest and Catherine Rochon.

18 Ransonet, *La vie de la soeur Marguerite Bourgeoys*, 99–100. If the incident happened at this time, the most obvious source for the story is Marie Barbier, who would have been in Quebec when Marguerite Bourgeoys arrived. Montgolfier repeats the passage almost as it is found in Ransonet but attaches it to one of the later journeys to Quebec (128), as does Faillon. Jamet refused to believe the story or to include it in his biography, giving as his reason that it was not included in Glandelet's *Vie*. Glandelet's omission could, of course, spring from the fact that in his time, and given his approach to his subject, the feat was not considered so extraordinary.

19 Quoted in Noël Bélanger, "Glandelet, Charles de," DCB, 2: 247.

20 "Lettre de MM. Brisacier et Dudouyt 11 juin 1687," quoted in Oury, *Monseigneur de Saint-Vallier et ses pauvres*, 47.

21 Saint-Vallier, *Éstat present de l'Église ... dans la Nouvelle France*, 41.

22 HCND, 3: 348–55; 4: 90–101, 201–5, 368–9.

23 Archives de l'Archevêché de Québec, Rég. A, 512–13. Jamet thought that Saint-Vallier had probably rented the house earlier in the year.

24 Archives de l'Archevêché de Québec, Registre des insinuations ecclésiastiques, vol. A, 279–80, 15 March 1689.

25 Marie Barbier persuaded the girls of La Providence to replace their taffeta headdresses with simpler white linen ones, a practice that later spread to Île d'Orléans. It is very difficult to assess how serious a problem was posed by vanity in female dress at this time.

26 Both Glandelet and Marie Barbier are careful not to describe any of these events as miraculous or attribute them to the means Marie sometimes used, such as a statue of the Child Jesus in the grain attic or a special roll baked for someone who was ill. Instead they are attributed to her complete and childlike faith, and Glandelet quotes the Epistle of James in support.

27 Marguerite Bourgeoys herself made a copy of one of these contracts, which still exists.

28 RND records on the same day the burial of Agathe Pacau Chapacou, aged twenty-two, and identifies her as a "fille de la providence." HCND counts her as a sister of the Congregation. Madeleine Cadieux, who was buried on 16 January 1693, is also described as a "fille de la Providence" in RND, but the letters CND have been inscribed under her

name in the left margin of the register. Émilia Chicoine has examined the question of the identity of the "filles de la Providence" in an appendix to *La métairie de Marguerite Bourgeoys*. She suggests that they might have been members of the extern group of the Congrégation de Notre-Dame living in community and observes that a reference in Tronson's letters seems to raise the possibility they were part of an attempt by Abbé Guyotte to form a community (279).

29 According to the *HCND*, this suggestion was prompted by the visit by Abbé Saint-Vallier to the Visitation convent in Annecy in August 1687 (1: 215–16). However, the references to the subject in Tronson's letters date from 20 May 1687, and he appears to be replying to overtures made by François Seguenot, the Sulpician priest at Pointe-aux-Trembles, overtures that must have been made the previous year.

30 Tronson to Dollier de Casson, 20 May 1687, quoted in Faillon, *Vie de la soeur Bourgeoys*, 1: 372–3. The letter has been abbreviated in the published version of Tronson's letters and this section omitted. There is a microfilm version in LAC, MG 17, A 7.1. In a letter to Abbé François Le Febvre on 5 April 1677, before his first meeting with Marguerite Bourgeoys, Tronson had shown himself more open to the desire of a "Paris nun" to establish a convent of her community in Montreal.

31 The dispute involved the right of the king to collect the revenues of a diocese between the death of one bishop and the registration of the coat of arms of his successor. In this case, Bishop Laval did not officially resign until the eve of Saint-Vallier's consecration.

32 Gosselin, *Vie de Monseigneur de Laval*, 2: 378.

33 Juchereau and Duplessis, *Les annales de l'Hôtel-Dieu de Quebec*, 232.

34 ASQ, Glandelet, "Receuil," 29–30.

35 See Simpson, *Marguerite Bourgeoys and Montreal*, 60.

36 The account is found in ASQ, Glandelet, "Receuil," 5.

37 The details are unknown, but according to Jacques Boulenger, sorcery and magic were much in fashion in the Paris of the 1670s, with scandals that touched even court circles (*The Seventeenth Century*, 191–2).

38 Tronson recommended him to Dollier de Casson in a letter dated 20 March 1680 (*Correspondance*, 2: 191–3). See also Maurault, *Le Fort des Messieurs*, 6.

39 LAC, COL C11A6, 316–18, 4 November 1683.

40 LAC, COL C11A6, fol. 401v, 12 October 1684.

41 His criticism of the Jesuits for their failure to implement the policy was, at one point, a cause of considerable conflict in the colony (Harel, "Le domaine du Fort de la Montagne," 17).

42 LAC, MG 17, A 7.1, 25 March 1686.

43 Notably, the Compagnie du Saint-Sacrement. Madame de Bullion, who in 1650 endowed the Hôtel-Dieu in Montreal, established the Hôpital de la Charité de Notre-Dame des convalescents on the rue de Bac in Paris for those who left the Hôtel-Dieu "without strength, without resources and without employment" (Oury, *Monseigneur de Saint-Vallier et ses pauvres*, 20; quoting Bernard Violle, *Paris, son Église et ses églises*, 391)

44 Oury, *Monseigneur de Saint-Vallier et ses pauvres*, 32, citing Archives de l'Archevêché de Québec, 2: 301.

45 *HCND*, 2: 188. Much of this story is recorded in a lawsuit brought against Marguerite Bourgeoys by Jean Quenet regarding payment of board for his daughter (AJM, Registre du Bailliage de Montréal, 2,9 January, 1691, f. 128).

46 Landry, *Orphelines en France*, 334, 366, 368.

47 Eccles, *Canada under Louis XIV*, 166.

CHAPTER SEVEN

1 *WMB*, 175 (253).

2 Glandelet quotes from a letter written to Marguerite Bourgeoys by Philippe de Turmenyes in 1691. After referring to the war then taking place, de Turmenyes wrote: "Just a few days before his death [Abbé Souart] told me that he had such confidence in God and in the prayers of Sister Bourgeoys, whom he called 'la petite Geneviève du Canada,' that he believed no serious harm could befall either the country or our holy religion. I am telling you this ... to inform you of the last words spoken by this holy man and to make you aware of his esteem and affection" (*Life of Sister Marguerite Bourgeoys*, 157).

3 *WMB*, 179 (258–9). The year is incorrectly given as 1690.

4 *HCND*, 2: 131 gives her name as Marie Tardy, but she always signed herself Marguerite Tardy.

5 Jean Saint-Père killed by the Iroquois in 1657. See Simpson, *Marguerite Bourgeoys and Montreal*, 112–13.

6 His place and date of birth are unknown.

7 Tronson, *Correspondance*, 2: 187.

8 *HCND*, 2: 186. Trouvé never returned to Montreal.

9 Tronson, *Correspondance*, 2: 238.

10 For this letter, dated 20 April 1682, and one to La Colombière written the same day and quoted below, see ibid., 267–70.

11 Faillon, *Vie de la soeur Bourgeoys*, 1: 379–85.

12 *WMB*, 123–4 (184–5). She also says that she has written to Father Pierre Chaumonot, the Jesuit missionary whom she had known from

her early days in Montreal. He was at this time seventy-nine years old
and living at the Huron mission of Lorette.

13 WMB, 167–8 (241).

14 Jamet, *Marguerite Bourgeoys*, 2: 651.

15 Tronson, *Correspondance*, 2: 309. This is an abbreviated version of
the letter, and the numbering of the points has been altered. The sixth
point in the published version is the seventh in the original letter.

16 To Monsieur de Chaigneau, 22 March, 1691, in Tronson, *Correspondance*, 2: 307. This letter too responds to questions raised by the cor-
respondant about the visions.

17 An abridged version of this letter dated 2 March 1691 can be found in
ibid., 301–2.

18 Ibid., 303.

19 The entry in RND, signed by E. Guyotte, reads, "Le 25 juillet a été
enterré un enfant de Fortin agée d'environ 3 ans et un enfant de bois
menu de la riviere des prairies agé de 6 mois."

20 AJM, "Contrat de mariage fleuricour et Soumillard sa femme." The
contract was signed 8 November 1690 under private seal. It was transferred 12 July 1698 and copied 17 March 1699.

21 Tronson, *Correspondance*, 2: 311.

22 HCND, 1: 362–3 identifies a Madeleine Cadieux, whose burial record
appears in RND for 16 January 1693 as a daughter of Pierre Cabassier.
The letters CND appear below her name, and she is identified as a
"fille de la providence."

23 This incident is first recorded in Archives de Saint-Sulpice, Paris,
Montgolfier, "La Vie de la venerable soeur Jeanne le Ber," 183–4.

24 WMB, 27 (49).

25 As late as February 1693, Tronson was writing to Dollier de Casson:
"They have written to M. Turménie to furnish Sister Tardy with whatever she needs to return to Canada. You can see from thence that the
old ideas have not completely disappeared" (*Correspondance*, 2:
322).

26 WMB, 192 (272–3).

27 Montgolfier, *La vie de la vénérable soeur Marguerite Bourgeois*, 129.
Montgolfier speaks of a letter Marguerite Bourgeoys is supposed to
have written congratulating the sisters on sharing the conditions of
the origins of the Congregation, but much of it seems to reflect what
Marguerite says about events after her arrival in Quebec the following
spring.

28 WMB, 194 (276). I have brought the English translation closer to the
original French.

29 WMB, 192–3 (273–4).

30 WMB, 170 (244–5).

31 *WMB*, 193–4 (274–5).

32 *WMB*, 194 (276–7). When difficulties about the payments arose later, they were solved through the use of Marie Raisin's inheritance.

33 *WMB*, 194 (276). I have corrected the English translation.

34 Letter of 4 March 1692, quoted in Faillon, *Vie de la soeur Bourgeoys*, 1: 391–2.

35 *HCND*, which lists Marguerite Tardy's death as the seventeenth in the institute and the first during the Superiority of Marie Barbier, concludes an account of her life with the words: "We have great confidence that this poor sister received a merciful judgment; for she was motivated by illusion rather than guilt, and her fault served only to attain the greater glory of God by the great merit she made our Venerable Mother acquire. Both of them, having been separated in body and divided in sentiment but always united in the love of Our Lord, are now, we hope, reunited in the kingdom of the predestined. There our Venerable Mother, resplendant in glory, and considering the value of those fifty months of internal crucifixion, looks on her sister with delight and lets her hear these words: Felix culpa, O happy fault!" (2: 133–4).

36 This document arranges for the security of an unspecified number of women from a group of *données* described as "the sisters who received the gray habit" (*WMB*, 105 [159]).

37 Cited by Oury, *Monseigneur de Saint-Vallier et ses pauvres*, 73.

38 *HCND*, 4: 85.

39 *HCND*, 4: 85–6.

40 *WMB*, 177 (255). See also Chicoine, *La métairie de Marguerite Bourgeoys*, 25.

41 A group of his parishioners agitated for his return. They went to the bishop and to Dollier de Casson, and Jacques Le Ber sent a petition with forty signatures to Tronson making that demand. Tronson's reply to Dollier de Casson, 7 April 1694, is quoted in Faillon, *Vie de la soeur Bourgeoys*, 392–3.

42 *WMB*, 179–80 (259).

43 *WMB*, 176 (254).

44 *WMB*, 180 (259).

45 Jamet, *Marguerite Bourgeoys*, 2: 738.

46 ASQ, Glandelet, "Receuil," 197.

47 *WMB*, 201 (284).

48 ASQ, Glandelet, "Receuil," 186.

49 Glandelet, *Life of Sister Marguerite Bourgeoys*, 117–18. Glandelet is able to report only one extraordinary act of penance performed by Marguerite Bourgeoys, the wearing of "a cap that had pins on both sides about six inches wide and half an inch thick" (120). Even this

he derives though hearsay rather than direct knowledge. Glandelet's interest in the penances performed by his subjects is clearly demonstrated in his writings on Marie Barbier. That he can report so little about Marguerite Bourgeoys renders very suspect the list of penances and mortifications that appears in Ransonet's biography in 1728: that she always carried with her a nasty powder to add to her food and make it taste unpleasant, that she never sat down comfortably in the refectory, that she never approached the fire no matter how cold the winter, and so on. The cap mentioned by Glandelet has become "a bonnet bristling with pins" (*La vie de la soeur Marguerite Bourgeois*, 114–16).

50 ASQ, Glandelet, "Receuil," 84. Marguerite Le Moyne appears to have been the leader of the opposition to Sister Tardy and her visions and also the source of Marie Barbier's difficulties on her return to Montreal.

51 *WMB*, 67 (107–8).

52 ASQ, Glandelet, "Recueil," 210.

53 Juchereau and Duplessis, *Les annales de l'Hôtel-Dieu de Québec*, 295.

54 ASQ, Glandelet, "Receuil," 162.

55 Ibid., 184.

56 Pitcher, *Artists, Craftsmen and Technocrats*, 96–9.

57 *WMB*, 167 (241).

58 Glandelet, *La vie de la soeur Marguerite Bourgeoys*, 90.

CHAPTER EIGHT

1 Letter to M. Tronson, 1695, in *WMB*, 141 (203).

2 *WMB*, 176, 168 (254, 242).

3 *EMB*, 242. I have tried to give the sense of the French rather than a literal translation.

4 ASQ, Glandelet, "Receuil," 85.

5 *HCND*, 2: 55.

6 Montgolfier's comments about earlier efforts to formulate a rule brought to an end by the resignation of Bishop Laval are not enlightening since they occur in a section of his *Vie de la vénérable soeur Bourgeois* (117–21) that confuses both dates and the actions of Laval and Saint-Vallier.

7 A manuscript entitled "Minutes des Règles des Soeurs de la Congrégation Notre-Dame établies à Ville-Marie" is in the Archives de l'Archevêché de Québec. This includes a copy of the 1694 "Constitutions" corrected and annotated by Louis Tronson (81 CD, SS. de

la Congrégation de Notre-Dame, vol. 1:1). An uncorrected copy of the "Constitutions" is in the Archives du Séminaire de Québec at the Musée de la civilisation de Québec (SME 12.2.4/22). References here are to the latter manuscript.

8 Besides the passage in HSV already cited, there are several references in the letters of Louis Tronson at this time. To Abbé Trouvé he wrote in 1692, "I do not know what this community of La Providence is that M. Guyotte wants to establish for poor little girls." On 14 March 1693 he wrote to Dollier de Casson, "I do not know what M. Guyotte's views are on the *filles de la Providence*"; and to the same recipient later that year, "I do not see the usefulness of the *filles de la Providence* ... I imagine that these are the women under the direction of M. Guyotte." On 7 April 1694 he wrote to Dollier de Casson, "You have not replied to me about the *filles de la Providence* to whom, they say, the Seminary gives fifteen loaves of bread a week" (LAC, MG 17, a 7.1). Émilia Chicoine's hypothesis about an attempt on the part of Abbé Guyotte to found a community still leaves many questions unanswered about the relationship of such a community to the Congrégation de Notre-Dame and its work (*La métairie de Marguerite Bourgeoys*, 279–80). On 26 February 1691 Guyotte deeded a house on rue Notre-Dame adjacent to the land of the Congregation to Marguerite Tardy. She renounced this gift the following year when she had already returned to France (AJM, Adhémar, "Re'on faite par la soeur Tardy a La donnaon q' Mr Guiotte Luy avoit faite passé devant L. Mussot nore de Bezançon," 2 April 1692). Is this the house into which the hospital patients moved after the fire at the Hôtel-Dieu? See also the question raised in chapter 6, note 7, above.

9 Glandelet, *The True Spirit*, 67. I have supplied a phrase missing from the English translation.

10 HCND, 2: 73–4. The sister in question is believed to have been Catherine Crolo, the first of all Marguerite Bourgeoys's companions. If so, the bishop did not show the best judgment in approaching someone whose loyalties went back so far.

11 There are two versions of the "Rémontrances," one of which is more detailed than the other. The longer version is quoted by Faillon, who gives as his source the ACND. This document is also quoted in HCND, 2: 68–85. However, the only document now in the ACND is a copy of the shorter version, of which the original is in the Archives de Saint-Sulpice in Paris (2B/01). It would seem that the shorter document is the revised and condensed version of the first and the one that was sent to Abbé Tronson and to which he added his answers to the objections raised by the Congregation.

12 The complete letter appears on *WMB*, 141–4 (203–8).

13 Marguerite reiterated her insistence on the equality of the sisters in another letter to Louis Tronson dated 30 October 1695 (*WMB*, 153 [221–2]). Elsewhere she wrote, "Formerly the Rules stated that we would never have lay sisters. I made a great mistake when I told the bishop of Quebec that we could not do without them in the future. It is very much contrary to poverty. All the sisters must be equal. Each one must be employed at whatever she is best fitted for. It must be so that the superior could be the cook and the cook, superior if they are capable of it" (*WMB*, 171 [247]).

14 The English translation uses the word "wanderers," but the more shocking term was the one Marguerite intended and had probably been directed toward the community in a pejorative sense.

15 *WMB*, 49–50 (81–2).

16 Faillon here inserts a comment that is true but is not to be found in *WMB*: "The Congregation came to birth in this country and it seems to me that it was the first community formed here. The others were all already formed in France." He adds, "The women of the Congregation even came with no plan for a community," a statement that is true if one uses the term "community" to designate only the type of cloistered community already in existence. Marguerite's own words and the contract of Edmée Chastel, one of her first companions, show that some form of community was envisaged from the beginning. See Simpson, *Marguerite Bourgeoys and Montreal*, 139–42.

17 Faillon, *Vie de la soeur Bourgeoys*, 2–4.

18 *WMB*, 50–1 (83).

19 *WMB*, 52 (84–5).

20 *WMB*, 88 (136).

21 *WMB*, 85 (131–2).

22 *HCND*, 2: 68–9.

23 The Congregation was right in its contention that this rule was not in conformity with its letters patent. In 1708 it came to the attention of the minister of Marine, Louis Phélypeaux de Pontchartain, that the sisters of the Congregation were making vows. He forbade this practice as contrary to the letters patent granted to Marguerite Bourgeoys by Louis XIV. In an effort to have this restriction lifted, Catherine Charly, then superior, was forced to appeal even to Madame de Maintenon. The incident was the result of an effort of the governor and the intendant of New France to ensure that the Congregation would not become cloistered. After this, no further attempts were made to impose cloister on the Community. (*HCND*, 3: 108–38)

24 *HCND*, 2: 71–2.

25 *HCND*, 2: 76.

26 In the days following the fire, the surrounding houses were visited and their inhabitants tactfully invited to return "what they had carried off to save it from the fire" (*HSV*, 252).

27 *HSV*, 242.

28 *WMB*, 144 (207).

29 Vachon de Belmont, "Éloges," 149.

30 An island just south of Montreal, Île Saint-Paul, was divided into three fiefs and conferred on Jacques Le Ber, Claude Robutel de Saint-André, and Jean de la Vigne in 1664. The last of these passed his share to Marie Le Ber, and she passed it on to her brother Jacques. The island became the property of the Congregation in the eighteenth century as a part of the legacy of Jeanne Le Ber. The Congregation farmed the island and maintained a house of rest and retirement for the sisters there until the 1950s, when plans to construct the Champlain Bridge forced the sale of the island, now known as Île des Soeurs or Nuns' Island.

31 Vachon de Belmont, "Éloges," 152.

32 *HSV*, 246.

33 *HSV*, 76.

34 *HSV*, 254.

35 Anne Barrois entered the Congregation in 1702, provided with a hand- some dowry from Jacques Le Ber's will, since her own branch of the family was not much "favoured with fortune." She lived to the age of ninety-one, saw the fall of New France to the British, and died shortly before the fire that destroyed the Congregation mother house in 1768 (*HCND*, 4: 218–23).

36 AJM, Maugue, Basset, "Conventions entre Madlle Jeanne le Ber et les Soeurs de la Congregation de Villemarie," 4 August 1695.

37 An exhibit devoted to Jeanne Le Ber at the Musée Saint-Gabriel in 1995 inspired an editorial in *Le Devoir* by Lise Bissonnette, who saw in Jeanne "the compact nucleus" of Ville-Marie's economic and reli- gious elite.

38 John 12: 3–4.

39 C.J. Jaenen, "Le Ber, Jeanne," *DCB*, 2: 376.

40 Dion, "La recluse de Montréal," 41.

41 Vachon de Belmont, "Éloges," 159–60.

42 Langlois, *The White Orchid*, 106–7. Langlois suggests that she also introduces "otherworldly" vegetation into her designs.

43 *WMB*, 136 (199–200).

44 *WMB*, 90, 70, 71 (139, 112, 114).

45 After the community had retired at night, Jeanne would emerge from her apartment to pray in the chapel. Each midnight she prayed for one

and sometimes two hours. In 1696 she signed a contract with the Congregation providing for permanent adoration of the Blessed Sacrament in its chapel from morning to night prayer (AJM, Adhémar, "Contract de l'Adoration du Saint Sacrament," 10 October, 1696).

46 *WMB*, 209 (293).

47 *WMB*, 157 (228).

48 *HSV*, 76.

49 Tronson wrote to Belmont in April 1697: "The death of Sister Tardy must have disabused M. de La Colombière, I am not surprised that he has now changed" (*Correspondance*, 2: 361).

50 Vachon de Belmont, "Éloges," 187–9. This section is entitled "Brief Recit des actions edifiantes de deux excelentes Chretiennnes iroquoises morte en odeur d'une grande vertu et celles d'un saint veillard huron." The second Iroquois woman mentioned is Kateri Tekakwitha. The third person is François Thoronhiongo, Marie-Thérèse's grandfather. Belmont gives an instance of the efficacy of the old man's prayers in the following story. With the years, François Thoroniongo became blind and was brought to the church each day by a young grandson born after his father returned to the forest. Thoronhiongo used to pray each day for this son, who had not accepted baptism and had not wanted to stay at the mission. In March 1690 the grandson, now a young man, took part in a skirmish against a group of Senecas, one of whom he took back to the Mountain Mission as a slave. His prisoner was recognized by his mother and by others among the older persons at the mission as his father, the son of Thoronhiongo, who had abandoned his wife before the birth of their son. There was a great reconciliation, and Thoronhiongo's prodigal son was baptized before his death, which followed soon after.

51 The most recent and complete account of Lydia's history is to be found in William Foster's *The Captors' Narrative*, which examines the experiences in New France of captives from the American colonies .

52 Foster thinks they must have put up some resistance since the primary object of the raid was said to be plunder and Deliverance and her children would have been "eminently ransomable" (*The Captors' Narrative*, 22).

53 John became a servant to one of the Abenaki chiefs and began to train as a warrior. He was forcibly returned to Groton in 1698 and reintegrated into the life of the town, where he married and raised a family (Foster, *The Captors' Narrative*, 54).

54 *HCND*, 4: 406. The notice of Lydia's baptism in RND gives the name of her stepmother rather than of her own mother.

55 As Protestant converts, neither Lydia Longley nor Mary Sayward would have been an acceptable candidate to the Filles de la Croix,

with whom Marguerite Bourgeoys had stayed in France. Their rule specifically barred the entrance of converted heretics: "One must be particularly careful not to receive any spinster or widow who has been a heretic, experience having shown that even if they are really converted and the venom of heresy entirely gone from their hearts, ordinarily there remains something in their outer actions, or in their manner of speaking that can make an impression on weaker spirits and bring some prejudice to the purity and firmness of their faith" (BN, "Constitutions de la Congrégation des Soeurs de la Croix," 8).

56 Foster, *The Captors' Narrative*, 52–3.

57 After her profession in the Congregation, Mary Sayward was sent to work at the Native mission of Sault-au-Récollet. There she was in contact not only with newly arrived captives but with people abducted at a young age and retained by their Native captors, who expected to assimilate them. Among these were Elisabeth (Abigail) Nims and Josiah Rising, who had both been taken in the Deerfield Raid of 1702, when she was about three and he about ten years of age. Both of them eventually refused to be ransomed and return to their surviving relatives. They married each other, prospered, and produced a numerous family whose name became Raizenne. (She had been given the Native name Touatogoach, he Shoentakouani). One of their sons became a priest, and two of their daughters entered the Congregation. The degree to which the family had prospered is indicated by the fact that the father offered a dowry of 2,000 livres when Marie, the younger of the girls, entered the community. As Soeur Saint-Ignace, Marie Raizenne became the thirteenth superior of the Congregation in 1778.

58 Tronson, *Correspondance*, 3: 360.

59 *WMB*, 162–9 (233–43).

60 *WMB*, 161 (231).

61 ASQ, Glandelet, "Receuil," 169–70.

62 *HCND*, 2: 122–3.

63 Quoted in *HCND*, 2: 126.

64 AMMB, "Reglemens Commun Pour Les Soeurs Seculieres De la Congregation De Nôtre Dame De Villemarie."

65 *HCND*, 2: 82.

66 All three eventually married, Marie Aubuchon in September 1698, Catherine Rochon in August 1699, and Marie Genest in 1710.

67 In the case of Marie Aubuchon, at least, the decision seems to have been a sudden one, for on 22 April 1694 an agreement had been reached between the Congregation and her guardian about her dowry (AJM, Maugue, "Convention entre Le Sieur adhemar au nom de tuteur de Marie aubuchon et La Congregation").

68 *HCND*, 2: 127.

69 *WMB*, 52 (84–5).

70 The tradition in the Congrégation de Notre-Dame that Catherine Charly, *dit* Saint-Ange, took the name "du Saint-Sacrement" in honour of Marguerite Bourgeoys after the death of the latter (*HCND*, 3: 106) is disproved by the signatures on the documents relating to the pronunciation of both the simple vows and the vow of stabilility. On each, Catherine Charly signed immediately ahead of Marguerite Bourgeoys as "Catherine du Saint-Sacrement."

CHAPTER NINE

1 *WMB*, 131 (193); fragment of a letter probably written at the end of 1694.

2 ASQ, Glandelet, "Receuil," 10.

3 Quoted in *HCND*, 2: 167.

4 *HCND*, 2: 169.

5 On 26 February 1700.

6 Bishop Saint-Vallier had already divided the hospital sisters in Quebec when he induced them to take over the Hôpital général. Jamet believed the bishop still wanted to create a community of his own out of the Congregation (*Marguerite Bourgeoys*, 2: 770–4).

7 *HCND*, 2: 171.

8 *HCND*, 2: 171–2. For more than two centuries, the Congregation would insist that all aspirants to the community be trained in a single novitiate in Montreal. This requirement was perceived as essential to the maintenance of unity in a group of which the sisters would be widely separated on the various missions. The situation changed when the community opened a mission in Japan in the 1930s and began to accept Japanese aspirants. In 1955, novitiates were opened in the Quebec region at Beauport and in the United States. There is now no common novitiate.

9 *HSV*, 75.

10 *HSV*, 75–6.

11 *HCND*, 2: 189.

12 A fourth daughter, Élisabeth, whose husband, Joseph de Montenon, had been killed by the Iroquois in 1690, entered the Congregation in 1700. Only one of her children, a son, André-Joseph, appears to have survived childhood. He was ordained to the priesthood in 1713, six months after his mother's death, on the return from captivity of Bishop Saint-Vallier.

13 Glandelet, *Life of Sister Marguerite Bourgeoys*, 144. I have slightly altered the translation to bring it closer to the French.

14 It is possible that Catherine was suffering from one of the sicknesses described in the documents of the time as "malignant fevers." Before the discovery of antibiotic medicines, these often resulted in death, and if Marguerite Bourgeoys contracted the same malady at her advanced age, it would most likely have proved fatal.

15 Glandelet, *Life of Sister Marguerite Bourgeoys*, 143.

16 *HCND*, 2: 191–2. This account claims that she even mortified herself further by taking up uncomfortable positions until the nurse prevented her from doing so.

17 Glandelet, *Life of Sister Marguerite Bourgeoys*, 144.

18 *HCND*, 2: 192.

19 Glandelet, *Life of Sister Marguerite Bourgeoys*, 147.

20 Ibid., 193.

21 Ibid., 143.

22 Also like his sister, Pierre Le Ber was deeply involved with a religious community without actually being a member. He had joined François Charon de La Barre, Jean-Vincent Le Ber Du Chesne, and Jean Fredin in founding the Frères hospitaliers de la Croix et de Saint-Joseph, commonly called the Charon Brothers, which opened the Hôpital général in Montreal in 1694.

23 From a letter written by one of the sisters three weeks after the death of Marguerite Bourgeoys and quoted in Glandelet, *Life of Sister Marguerite Bourgeoys*, 148.

24 Bazin, "Le vrai visage de Marguerite Bourgeoys," 16.

25 Glandelet, *Life of Sister Marguerite Bourgeoys*, 147.

26 In 1767 the remains of Marguerite Bourgeoys were indeed removed from the parish church to the chapel of the Congregation. In the centuries since her death, these remains have continued the *vie voyagère* of her lifetime, moving with the Congregation from Old Montreal to the Mountain Mother House and to two successive mother houses in Westmount. In 2005 they were returned to Old Montreal to Notre-Dame-de-Bon-Secours chapel, which she founded and where the first members of the Congregation celebrated their patronal feast and renewed the promises they had made to God.

27 Glandelet, *Life of Sister Marguerite Bourgeoys*, 145. Louis-Hector de Callière was now governor of New France and Philippe de Rigaud de Vaudreuil governor of Montreal. Glandelet, 150–5, also quotes excerpts from letters of condolence addressed to the Congregation by Bishops Saint-Vallier and Laval; by Louis Ango Des Maizerets, superior of the Quebec seminary; by Martin Bouvart, superior of the Jesuits; by Marie-du-Sacré-Coeur-de-Marie (Fiquenal), superior of the Hôtel-Dieu in Quebec; by Gabrielle de l'Annonciation (Denis), superior of the Hôpital géneral in Quebec; and by Madame Champigny,

wife of the intendant; as well as by Marie-Paule de Blaigny, superior of the Congrégation de Notre-Dame in Troyes. Some of these are quoted below.

28 Ibid., 150.

29 *HCND*, 2: 210.

30 Ibid., 202.

31 Ibid., 203–4.

32 Ibid., 205.

33 Charlevoix, *A History and General Description of New France*, 3: 27–8.

34 *HCND*, 3: 326.

35 The highest number of living members recorded in the Congregation was 3,809 in the autumn of 1965. In the autumn of 2004, there were 1,395 sisters, 5 novices, and 6 candidates.

35 Sisters of the Congregation de Notre-Dame of Montreal, *Constitutions and Rules*, 13–15.

APPENDIX

1 I wish to express my gratitude to Danielle Dubois for sharing with me her knowledge of art history and her insight.

2 AMMB, M. Eileen Scott (Sister Saint Miriam of the Temple), "Report on the Cleaning and Restoration of the Portrait of Blessed Marguerite Bourgeoys by Edward O. Korany," 1964. This document contains the correspondence between Sister Scott and the restorer.

BIBLIOGRAPHY

ARCHIVAL SOURCES

Archives de l'Archevêché de Montréal
  "Minutes des Règles des Soeurs de la Congrégation Notre-Dame établies
    à Ville-Marie"
  12A, Registre des insinuations ecclésiastiques
  Charles de Glandelet. "Vie de la Soeur Bourgeoys." In Procès *ne pereant*,
    139th Session, 13 April 1889, 3184–299

Archives de la Congrégation de Notre-Dame de Montréal (ACND)
  Because of the fires that destroyed the mother house of the Congréga-
  tion de Notre-Dame in 1768 and 1893, the archives have few origi-
  nal seventeenth-century documents. However, they do contain certified
  copies of most known documents pertaining to the life of Marguerite
  Bourgeoys and the beginnings of her Congregation.
  "Constitutions Pour les Soeurs de la Congrégation de nostre dame de
    Ville Marie"
  "Copie des Constitutions composées et presentées par Mgr de Saint-
    Vallier avec les corrections faites par M. Tronson et formant les regle-
    ments acceptées en 1698"

Archives de Saint-Sulpice, Montreal
  P1: 24.B-33. Rousseau, Pierre. "Notice sur Mr de la Colombière"
  S2.60 "Etat des depenses faites par le Séminaire de Montréal pour
    l'entretien de la mission de la Montagne." Four-page memorandum
    drawn up by François Vachon de Belmont, corrected and completed
    by Dollier de Casson about 1698
  T-115/S36 "Memoir de Notre Dame des Neiges à la Montagne." Notes
    compiled by Pierre Rousseau

Archives de Saint-Sulpice, Paris
Marie Barbier, et al. "Remontrance qui est entre les mains de M. Belmont" (ACND, 2B/01)
Étienne Montgolfier. "La Vie de La Venerable Soeur jeanne Le Ber recluse
dans La maison des Soeurs de La Congregation nôtre Dame Decedéé
en odeur de Sainteté A Montréal le 3 octobre 1714"

Archives des Ursulines de Québec
"Anciens récit"
"Constitutions du R.P.J. Lalemant Pour les Ursulines du Canada"

Archives du Musée Marguerite-Bourgeoys (AMMB)
Correspondence between M. Eileen Scott CND and Edward Korany
Correspondence between M. Eileen Scott CND and Alfred Morin
Miscellaneous unpublished articles, essays, and notes by M. Eileen Scott
CND
Alfred Morin. "Antoine Gendret, George Proffit, Marie Nicolas Des-
guerrois"; "Les frères de Marguerite Bourgeoys à Évreux"
"Reglemens Commun Pour Les Soeurs Seculieres De la Congregation
De Nôtre Dame De Villemarie"

Archives de la Paroisse Notre-Dame de Montréal
Registres de l'église Notre-Dame de Montréal
A facsimile of the oldest parts of the registers of baptism, marriage,
and burial was published by La Société des Dix in 1961 under the title
Premier registre de l'église Notre-Dame de Montreal. This repro-
duces the entries from 1642 to 1681. The originals are conserved at
the Archives de la Paroisse Notre-Dame in Montreal.
"Registres des délibérations de la fabrique de la Paroisse de Notre-Dame
de Ville-Marie" (beginning 1657)
"Comptes rendus par les marguilliers" (beginning 1658)

Archives de l'Hôtel-Dieu de Montréal
The oldest extant copy of the deed for Montreal's first school is in the
Archives de l'Hôtel-Dieu: 4A2/3

Archives judiciaires de Montréal (AJM)
Various notarial documents of Basset, Mauge, and Adhémar (full references in the notes)

Archives du Séminaire de Québec (ASQ, now in Musée de la civilisation de Québec)
  Charles de Glandelet. "Receuil touchant la S[oeur Marie Barbier], fille séculière de la Congrégation de Notre-Dame" (SME, 12.2.4/MS-198)
  SME 12.2.4 (formerly "Congregation de Notre-Dame")

Bibliothèque nationale, Paris (BN)
  "Constitutions de la Congregation des soeurs de la Croix" (Mazarin 3.333)

Library and Archives Canada (LAC)
  COL C 11 A, vol. 6 Canada, Correspondance génerale, 1682–84, MM. de Frontenac et de la Barre, gouverneurs, et M. de Meule, intendant
  MG 17, A 7.1 Bibliothèque du Séminaire de Saint-Sulpice (Paris), Correspondance de M. Tronson, 1675–99

Registres de catholicité de Troyes
  Registres de la paroisse Saint-Jean-au-Marché
  Registres de la paroisse Saint-Rémi

PRINTED SOURCES

Alacoque, Marguerite-Marie. *Autobiography*. Ed. Vincent Kerns. London: Darton, Longman and Todd 1961

Allard, Michel, Robert Lahaise, et al. *L'Hôtel-Dieu de Montréal 1642–1973*. Montréal: Hurtubise 1973

Aries, Philippe. *Centuries of Childhood: A Social History of Family Life*. Trans. Robert Baldick. New York: Vintage Books 1962

Ashley, Maurice. *The Age of Absolutism, 1648–1675*. Springfield, Mass.: Merriam 1974

Audet, Bernard. *Se nourire au quotidien en Nouvelle-France*. Québec: GID 2001

Audet, Louis-Philippe. "L'éducation au temps de Mgr de Laval." *SCHEC* 25 (1957–58): 59–78

– "L'instruction de dix mille colons, nos ancêtres." *Cahiers des Dix* 37 (1972): 9–49

Auger, Roland-J. *La grande recrue de 1653*. Société généalogique, no. 1. Montréal 1955. Published in English as *The Colonists Who Saved Montreal*, trans. Dianne Little (Pawtucket: Quintin 2002)

Azzarello, Marie. *Mary, the First Disciple*. Ottawa: Novalis 2004

Baboyant, Marie. "Dollier de Casson." *CMB*, no. 55 (autumn 1995): 14–18

Baillargeon, Noel. *Le Séminaire de Quebec sous l'épiscopat de Mgr de Laval*. Québec: Université de Laval 1972

Bazin, Jules. "Le vrai visage de Marguerite Bourgeoys." *Vie des arts*, no. 36 (Autumn 1964): 13–16.

Beaudoin, Marie-Louise. *Les premières et les filles du roi à Ville-Marie*. Montréal: Maison Saint-Gabriel 1996

Béchard, Henri, SJ. *Jerôme de la Dauversière – His Friends and Enemies*. Bloomingdale, Ohio: AFC 1991

– *Kaia'tano:ron Kateri Tekawitha*. Trans. Antoinette Kinlough. Kahnawaki: Kateri Center 1994

Belin, Christian. "Écriture et oraison au XVIIe siècle." *La Vie spirituelle*, no. 715 (mai-juin 1995): 281–92

Blain, Jean. "L'archevêque de Rouen, l'Église du Canada et les historiens, un exemple de déformation historique." *RHAF* 21, no. 2 (septembre 1967): 199–216

– "Les structures de l'Église et la conjoncture coloniale en Nouvelle-France, 1632–1674." *RHAF* 21, no. 4 (mars 1968): 749–56

Boland (S.S. Marguerite of the Sacred Heart). *The Pearl of Troyes*. Montreal: Canada Printing Company 1878

Bonneau-Avenant, A. *Madame de Miramion: Sa vie et ses oeuvres charitables (1629–1696)*. Paris: Didier 1874

Boucher, Pierre. *Histoire véritable et naturelle des moeurs et productions du pays de la Nouvelle-France vulgairement dite le Canada 1664*. Boucherville: Société historique de Boucherville 1964

Boulenger, Jacques. *The Seventeenth Century in France*. New York: Capricorn Books 1963

Bourgeoys, Marguerite. *Les écrits de Mère Bourgeoys: autobiographie et testament spirituel*. Classés et annotés par S.S. Damase-de-Rome, CND. Montréal: Congrégation de Notre-Dame 1964. Published in English as *The Writings of Marguerite Bourgeoys: Autobiography and Spiritual Testament*, trans. M.V. Cotter (Montreal: Congrégation de Notre-Dame 1976)

Boutiot, T. *Histoire de la ville de Troyes et de la Champagne méridionale*. Troyes: Dufey-Robert 1874

Boyer, Raymond. *Les crimes et les châtiments au Canada français du XVIIe au XXe siècle*. Montréal: Cercle du livre de France 1966

Brault, Jean-Rémi, ed. *Les origines de Montréal*. Montréal: Leméac 1993

Breton, Bernadette. *Marguerite Bourgeoys and the Native People*. Trans. Patricia Landry. Heritage no. 4. Montreal: CND 1992

Brown, Raymond, et al., eds. *Mary in the New Testament: A Collaborative Assessment by Protestant and Roman Catholic Scholars*. Toronto: Paulist Press 1978

Burgess, Joanne, Louise Dechêne, et al. *Clés pour l'histoire de Montréal: Bibliographie*. Montréal: Boréal 1992

Buteau, Hélène, and Daniel Chevrier. *D'audace en memoire: Le lieu dit Lachine un regard archéologique*. Montréal: Art Gestion 2000

Butler, Elizabeth. *The Life of Venerable Marguerite Bourgeoys*. New York: P.J. Kenedy & Sons 1932

Campeau, Lucien. "Mgr de Laval et le Conseil souverain, 1659–1684." *RHAF* 27, no. 3 (décembre 1973): 323–59

Carré, Gustave. *Histoire populaire de Troyes et du département de l'Aube*. Troyes: Lacroix 1881

Caza, Lorraine. *La vie voyagère, conversante avec le prochain Marguerite Bourgeoys*. Montréal: Bellarmin; Paris: Cerf 1982

Chabroux, Evelyne. *Troyes – Marguerite Bourgeoys: la rencontre d'une cité et d'une sainte*. Troyes: Renaissance 1984

Chapais, Thomas. *Jean Talon, intendant de la Nouvelle-France (1665–1672)*. Québec: Demers 1904

Charbonneau, Hubert, et al. *Naissance d'une population: Les Français établis au Canada au XVIIe siècle*. Montréal: Presses de l'Université de Montréal 1987

Charlevoix, Pierre-François-Xavier de. *A History and General Description of New France*. Trans. John Gilmary Shea. 6 vols. New York: F.P. Harper 1900

– *Journal d'un voyage fait par ordre du roi dans l'Amérique septentrionale*. Montréal: Presses de l'Université de Montréal 1994

Charron, Yvon. *Mother Bourgeoys*. Trans. S.S. Godeliva. Montreal: Beauchemin 1950

Chatellier, Louis. *Le Catholicisme en France*. 2 vols. Paris: Sedes 1995

Chaumonot, Pierre-Joseph-Marie. *Un missionnaire des Hurons: Autobiographie du père Chaumonot de la Compagnie de Jésus et son complément*. Ed. Felix Martin. Paris: Oudin 1885

Chicoine, Émilia. *La métairie de Marguerite Bourgeoys à la Pointe-Saint-Charles*. Montréal: Fides 1986

Cliche, Marie-Aimée. *Les pratiques de dévotion en Nouvelle-France*. Québec: Université de Laval 1988

Cloutier, Prosper. *Histoire de la paroisse de Champlain*. Trois-Rivières: Imprimerie Le Bien publique 1915

Constitutions de la communaute des Filles de Ste Geneviève. Paris: Eloy Helie 1683

Cranston, J. Herbert. *Huronia: Cradle of Ontario's History*. [Midland, Ont.]: Huronia Historic Sites Association 1972

Crubellier, Maurice, and Charles Juillard. *Histoire de la Champagne*. Paris: Presses universitaires de France 1969

Cuthbert, Brother. *The Capuchins: A Contribution to the History of the Counter Reformation.* Vol. 1. London: Sheed and Ward 1928

D'Allaire, Micheline. *Les dots des religieuses au Canada français, 1639–1800: Étude économique et sociale.* Cahiers du Québec Collection Histoire. Montréal: Hurtubise HMH 1986

– *L'Hôpital général de Québec, 1692–1764.* Montréal: Fides 1971

Daniel-Rops, Henri. *Monsieur Vincent: The Story of Saint Vincent de Paul.* Trans. Julie Kernan. New York: Hawthorn 1961

Daveluy, Marie-Claire. *Jeanne Mance (1606–1673).* Montréal: Fides 1962

– *La Société de Notre-Dame de Montréal (1639–1663).* Montréal: Fides 1965

Dechêne, Louise. *Habitants and Merchants in Seventeenth-Century Montreal.* Trans. Liana Vardi. Montreal: McGill-Queen's University Press 1992

Demers, Georges-Édouard. "Nomination et sacre de Mgr de Laval." SCHEC 24 (1957): 13–32

Deroy-Pineau, Françoise. *Jeanne LeBer: La recluse au coeur des combats.* Montréal: Bellarmin 2000

– *Jeanne Mance: De Langres à Montréal, la passion de soigner.* Montréal: Bellarmin 1995

Derréal, Hélène. *Une grande figure lorraine du XVIIe siècle: Saint Pierre Fourier, humaniste et épistolier.* Paris: Berger-Levrault 1942

– *Un missionnaire de la Contre-Réforme: Saint Pierre Fourier et l'institution de la Congrégation de Notre-Dame.* Paris: Plon 1964

Desrosiers, Léo-Paul. *Dans le nid d'aiglons, la Colombe: Vie de Jeanne Leber, la recluse.* Montréal: Fides 1963

– *Les dialogues de Marthe et de Marie.* Montréal: Fides 1957

– *Paul de Chomedey, Sieur de Maisonneuve.* Montréal: Fides 1967

Dickenson, John A. "Annaotaha et Dollard vus de l'autre côté de la palissade." RHAF 35, no. 2 (1981): 163–78

Dictionary of Canadian Biography. Vols. 1–3. Toronto: University of Toronto Press; Québec: Les Presses de l'Université Laval, 1966–74.

Dion, Marie-Paul. "La recluse de Montréal." *Église et théologie* 22 (1991): 33–65.

Dollier de Casson, François. *Histoire de Montréal.* Nouv. éd. critique par Marcel Trudel et Marie Baboyant. Montréal: Hurtubise 1992

– *A History of Montreal, 1640–1672.* Trans. Ralph Flenley. Toronto: Dent 1928

Doyle, Sister Saint Ignatius. *Marguerite Bourgeoys and Her Congregation.* Gardenvale: Garden City Press 1940

Drummond, Margaret Mary. *The Life and Times of Marguerite Bourgeoys.* Boston: Angel Guardian Press 1907

Eccles, W.J. *Canada under Louis XIV, 1663–1701*. Toronto: McClelland and Stewart 1964
– *The Courtier Governor*. Toronto: McClelland and Stewart 1959
Escholier, Marc. *Port-Royal: The Drama of the Jansenists*. New York: Hawthorn Books 1968
Faillon, Étienne-Michel. *Histoire de la colonie française en Canada*. 3 vols. Montréal: Bibliothèque paroissiale 1865
– *Vie de la soeur Bourgeoys, fondatrice de la Congrégation de Notre-Dame de Ville-Marie en Canada, suivie de l'histoire de cet institut jusqu'à ce jour*. 2 vols. Villemarie: Congrégation de Notre-Dame 1853
– *Vie de Mademoiselle Mance et histoire de l'Hôtel-Dieu de Villemarie en Canada*. 2 vols. In *Mémoires particuliers pour servir à l'histoire de l'Église de l'Amérique du Nord* (Paris: Périsse Frères 1854)
– *Vie de M. Olier, fondateur du séminaire de Saint-Sulpice*. Paris: Poussielgue-Rusand 1843
[Felix, Sister]. *Monseigneur de Saint-Vallier et l'Hôpital général de Québec*. Québec: C. Darveau 1882
Foster, William. *The Captors' Narrative: Catholic Women and Their Puritan Men on the Early American Frontier*. Ithaca: Cornell University Press 2003
Foley, Mary Anne, CND. "Uncloistered Apostolic Life for Women: Marguerite Bourgeoys's Experiment in Ville Marie." PhD dissertation, Yale University 1991
Fourier, Pierre. *Pierre Fourier: Sa correspondance, 1598–1640*. Recueillie, classée et annotée par Hélène Derréal. 5 vols. Nancy: Presses universitaires de Nancy, 1986–91
Gagné, Lucien, and Jean-Pierre Asselin. *Saint Anne de Beaupré: Pilgrim's Goal for Three Hundred Years*. Trans. Eric W. Gosling. Saint Anne de Beaupré 1984
Gagné, Peter J. *King's Daughters and Founding Mothers: The Filles du Roi, 1663–1673*. Pawtucket: Quintin Publications 2001
Gallet-Morin, Elisabeth. *Jean Girard, Musicien en Nouvelle-France: Bourges, 1696–Montréal, 1765*. Sillery: Septentrion 1993
– et Jean-Pierre Pinson. *La vie musicale en Nouvelle-France*. Sillery: Septentrion 2003
Gauthier, Henri. *Sulpitiana*. Montreal: Oeuvres paroissiales de St.-Jacques 1926
Gauthier, Jean. *Ces Messieurs de Saint-Sulpice*. Paris: Fayard 1957
Gauthier, Roland. *La dévotion à la Sainte Famille en Nouvelle-France au XVIIe siècle*. Lumière sur la Montagne 3. Montréal: Oratoire Saint-Joseph 1996
Glandelet, Charles de. *La vie de la soeur Marguerite Bourgeoys*. Ed. Hélène Tremblay. Montréal: CND 1993. Published in English as *Life of*

Sister Marguerite Bourgeoys, trans. Florence Quigley (Montreal: CND 1994)

– *Le vray esprit de l'institut des soeurs seculières de la Congrégation de Notre-Dame établi à Ville-Marie en l'isle de Montréal en Canada.* Notes rédigées par l'abbé Charles de Glandelet, 1700–1701. Ed. Hélène Tremblay. Montréal: Congrégation de Notre-Dame 1976. Published in English as *The True Spirit of the Institute of the Secular Sisters of the Congregation de Notre Dame*, trans. Frances McCann (Montreal: Congrégation de Notre-Dame 1977)

Godbout, Archange. *Les passagers du Saint-André: La recrue de 1659.* Société Généalogique canadienne-française, no. 4. Montreal 1964

Gosselin, Amédée. *L'instruction au Canada sous le régime français (1635–1760).* Québec: Typ. Laflamme et Proulx 1911

Gosselin, Auguste. *Vie de Monseigneur de Laval.* 2 vols. Québec: L.J. Demers et Frères 1830

Graef, Hilda. *Mary: A History of Doctrine and Devotion.* 2 vols. London: Sheed and Ward 1963

Hale, Horatio. *The Iroquois Book of Rites.* Toronto: University of Toronto Press 1963

Hamel, Charles. *Histoire de l'église Saint-Sulpice.* Paris: Librairie Victor Lecoffre 1900

Hamelin, Eddie. *La paroisse de Champlain.* Trois-Rivières: Les éditions du Bien publique 1933

Harel, Bruno. "Le domaine du Fort de la Montagne." In *Le Grand Séminaire de Montréal de 1840 à 1990: 150 années au service de la formation des prêtres*, ed. Rolland Litalien, 17–21. Montréal: Le Grand Séminaire de Montréal 1990

Harris, Richard Colebrook. *The Seigneurial System in Early Canada: A Geographical Study.* Madison: University of Wisconsin Press 1966

Hatton, Ragnild. *Europe in the Age of Louis XIV.* London: Thames and Hudson 1969

Haughton, Rosemary. *The Catholic Thing.* Springfield, Ill.: Templegate 1979

– *The Recreation of Eve.* Springfield, Ill.: Templegate 1985

Havard, Gilles. *The Great Peace of Montreal of 1701: French-Native Diplomacy in the Seventeenth Century.* Trans. Phyllis Aranoff and Howard Scott. Montreal: McGill-Queen's University Press 2001

Huet, Madeleine. "From Montague to Ville Marie." *CMB* 54 (1995): 22–4

Hunt, George T. *The Wars of the Iroquois.* Madison: University of Wisconsin Press 1960

Hurtubise, Pierre. "Ni janséniste, ni gallican, ni ultramontaine: François de Laval." *RHAF* 28, no. 1 (juin 1974): 3–26

L'Ile de Montréal en 1731: Aveu et dénombrement des Messieurs de Saint-Sulpice. Québec: Archives de la Province de Québec 1943

Jaenen, Cornelius J. "The Frenchification and Evangelization of the Amerindians in Seventeenth Century New France." Canadian Catholic Historical Association, *Historical Studies* 35 (1968): 57–71

Jamet, Albert. *Marguerite Bourgeoys, 1620–1700.* 2 vols. Montréal: La Presse catholique panaméricaine 1942

Jeanne Le Ber: Recluse en Nouvelle France, lampe ardente, sentinelle dans la nuit. Cahier 10. Montréal: Oratoire Saint-Joseph 2001

The Jesuit Relations and Allied Documents: Travels and Explorations of the Jesuit Missionaries in New France, 1610–1791. Ed. Reuben Gold Thwaites. 73 vols. New York: Pageant Books 1959

Le journal des Jésuites, publié d'après le manuscrit original conservé aux Archives du Séminaire de Québec. Éd. les abbés Laverdière et Casgrain. Montréal: J.M. Valois 1892

Juchereau de la Ferté, Jeanne-Françoise de Saint-Ignace, and Marie-Andrée Duplessis de Sainte-Hélène. *Les annales de l'Hôtel-Dieu de Québec, 1636–1716.* Ed. Albert Jamet. Québec et Montréal 1939

Jugements et délibérations du Conseil souverain de la Nouvelle-France. Vol. 1. Québec: A. Coté et Cie 1885

Karch, Pierre. *Les ateliers du pouvoir.* Collection documents. Montréal: XYZ 1995

La Flèche et Montréal, ou l'extraordinaire entreprise canadienne du fléchois Jérôme le Royer de la Dauversière. La Flèche: Éditions fléchoises 1947

Lahaise, Robert. *Les édifices conventuels du Vieux Montréal.* Montréal: Hurtubise 1980

Lambert, Thérèse. *Marguerite Bourgeoys, éducatrice, mère d'un pays et d'une église.* Montréal: Bellarmin 1982

Lamontagne, Sophie-Laurence. *L'hiver dans la culture québécoise (XVIIe–XIXe siècles).* Montréal: Institut québécois de recherche sur la culture 1983

Lanctot, Gustave. *Filles de joie ou filles du roi: Étude sur l'émigration féminine en Nouvelle-France.* Montréal: Chantecler 1952

– *Montréal sous Maisonneuve.* Montréal: Beauchemin 1966

Landry, Yves. *Orphelines en France, pionnières au Canada: Les filles du roi au XVIIe siècle.* Montréal: Leméac 1992

Langlois, Michel. *La grande recrue.* Sillery: Septentrion 2003

Langlois, Yvon. *White Orchid: Jeanne Le Ber.* Trans. Irene Morissette. Privately printed 1997.

Latourelle, René. *Compagnon des martyrs canadiens: Pierre-Joseph Chaumonot.* Montréal: Bellarmin 1998

Le Blant, Robert. "Les derniers jours de Maisonneuve et Philippe de Turmenyes." *RHAF* 13 (1959): 262–79. This article includes copies of de
Maisonneuve's statement in support of Marguerite Bourgeoys's application for letters patent for the Congrégation de Notre-Dame of Montreal
and his last will and testament.

– *La sépulture du sieur de Maisonneuve à Paris.* Montréal: La Société
historique de Montréal 1996

Leclerc, Jean. *Le marquis de Denonville, gouverneur de la Nouvelle-
France, 1685–1689.* Montréal: Fides 1976

Lefebvre, Esther. *Marie Morin, premier historien canadien de Villemarie.*
Montréal: Fides 1959

Leleu, J.-M. *Histoire de Notre-Dame de Bon-Secours à Montréal.* Montréal: Cadieux & Derome, 1900

Lemieux, Denise. *Les petits innocents: L'enfance en Nouvelle-France.*
Québec: Institut québécois de recherche sur la culture 1985

Lewis, W.H. *The Splendid Century.* London: William Sloane Associates
1953

– *The Sunset of the Splendid Century.* London: William Sloane Associates 1955

Maland, David. *Culture and Society in Seventeenth Century France.*
London: Batsford 1970

Mali, Anya. *Mystic in the New World: Marie de l'Incarnation (1599–
1672).* New York: E.J. Brill 1996

Malo, Denise, and Jeannine Sévigny. *Participation of Associates in the
Charism of the Congregation of Notre Dame: A Heritage Rediscovered.* Heritage no. 22. Montreal: CND 1995

Mandements, lettres pastorales et circulaires des évêques de Québec.
Publiés par H. Têtu et C.-O. Gagnon. 6 vols. Québec: A. Coté 1887–90

Marchal, Léon. *Les origines de Montréal: Ville-Marie, 1642–1665.* Montréal: Beauchemin 1942

Marie de l'Incarnation. *Correspondance.* Ed. Guy Oury. Solesmes: Abbaye
de Saint-Pierre 1972

– *Word from New France: The Selected Letters of Marie de l'Incarnation.*
Trans. and ed. Joyce Marshall. Toronto: Oxford University Press 1967

Marsat, André. *La cathédrale de Troyes.* Paris: La Goélette [n.d.]

Massicotte, E.-Z. "Le notaire Fleuricourt." *Bulletin des recherches histo-
riques* 39 (1933): 702–4

– "Où demeura M. de Maisonneuve?" *Cahiers des Dix* 10 (1940): 178–
81

Maurault, Olivier. *Le Fort des Messieurs.* Montreal: Printed at *Le Devoir*
1925

Mitford, Nancy. *The Sun King: Louis XIV at Versailles.* London: Hamish
Hamilton 1966

Molette, Charles. "La dévotion à Marie au XVIIe et XVIIIe siècle dans les congrégations féminines." Communication donnée le mardi, 13 septembre 1983, au 9e Congrès mariologique international tenu à Malte

Mondoux, Maria. "Les 'hommes' de Montréal." *RHAF* 2, no. 1 (juin 1948): 59–80

– *L'Hôtel-Dieu, premier hôpital de Montréal*. Montreal: Hôtel-Dieu 1942

Monier, Frédéric. *Vie de Jean-Jacques Olier*. Paris: Ancienne Librairie Poussielgue 1914

Montgolfier, Étienne. *La vie de la vénérable soeur Marguerite Bourgeois dite du Saint Sacrement*. Ville Marie: William Gray 1818. Published in English as *The Life of Venerable Sister Margaret Bourgeois, Foundress of the Sisters of the Congregation de Notre Dame, Established at Montreal, Canada, 1659*, trans. by a Religious (New York: D. & J. Sadlier & Co 1880)

Morin, Alfred. *Du nouveau sur Marguerite Bourgeoys*. Troyes: Renaissance 1964

Morin, Louis. *Deux familles troyennes de musiciens et de comédiens, les Siret et les Raisin*. Troyes: Paton 1927

Morin, Marie. *Histoire simple et véritable: Annales de l'Hôtel-Dieu de Montréal, 1659–1725*. Ed. Ghislaine Legendre. Montréal: Université de Montréal 1979

Mullet, Michael. *The Counter-Reformation and the Catholic Reformation in Early Modern Europe*. London: Methuen 1984

Le mystère chrétien dans l'église Saint-Étienne-du-Mont. Paris 1995

Niel, J.C. *Marguerite Bourgeoys et sa famille d'après des documents inédits*. Troyes: Renaissance 1950

Nitray, A. de. *Une éducatrice au XVIIe siècle*. Paris: Gabriel Beauchesne 1919

Oury, Guy-Marie. *L'homme qui a conçu Montréal: Jérôme Le Royer, sieur de la Dauversière*. Montréal: Méridien 1991

– *Jeanne Mance et le rêve de M. de la Dauversière*. Chambray: CLD 1983

– *Madame de la Peltrie et ses fondations canadiennes*. Perché: Amis du Perché 1974

– *Monseigneur de Saint-Vallier et ses pauvres, 1653–1727*. Sainte-Foy: Les Éditions La Liberté 1993

– "Pierre Chevrier, baron de Fancamp, co-seigneur de l'isle de Montréal." *Cahiers des Dix* 47 (1992): 11–40

Paris, Charles B. *Marriage in XVIIth Century Catholicism*. Montreal: Bellarmin 1975

Pelletier, Louis. *Le clergé en Nouvelle-France*. Montréal: Université de Montréal 1993

Pellus, Daniel. *Femmes celebres de Champagne*. Amiens: Martelle 1992

Pitaud, Bernard. *Petite vie de Jean-Jacques Olier*. Paris: Desclée de Brouwer 1996

Pitcher, Patricia C. *Artists, Craftsmen and Technocrats: The Dreams, Realities and Illusions of Leadership*. Toronto: Stoddart 1995

Plante, Lucienne. "The Family of Marguerite Bourgeoys." CMB 52 (spring 1994): 25–6; 53 (autumn 1994): 25–7; 54 (spring 1995): 29–31; 55 (autumn 1995): 29–31

Poinsenet, M.D. *France religieuse du XVIIe siècle*. Paris: Casterman 1954

Poirier, Jean. "Origine du nom de la ville de Montréal." RHAF 46, no.1 (1992): 37–44

Poissant, Simone. *Marguerite Bourgeoys, 1620–1700*. Trans. Frances Kirwan. Montreal: Bellarmin 1993

Porter, Fernand. *L'institution catéchistique au Canada français 1633–1833*. Montréal: Les Éditions franciscaines 1949

Les prêtres de Saint-Sulpice au Canada. Québec: Les Presses de l'Université Laval 1992

Quigley, Florence. *In the Company of Marguerite Bourgeoys*. Montreal: Novalis 1982

Ransonet, Michel-François. *La vie de la soeur Marguerite Bourgeois*. Liège: Barnabé 1728

Rapley, Elizabeth. *The Dévotes: Women and Culture in Seventeenth-Century France*. Montreal: McGill-Queen's University Press 1990

– "Life and Death of a Community: The Congrégation de Notre-Dame of Troyes, 1628–1762." Canadian Catholic Historical Association, *Historical Studies* 58 (1991), 5–29

– "La Providence." Unpublished essay

Remiremont, A. de. *Mère Alix LeClerc, 1576–1662*. Paris: Congrégation de Notre-Dame 1946

Renault, J. *Le idées pédagogiques de saint Pierre Fourier*. Paris, P. Lethielleux [n.d.]

Robert, Jean-Claude. *Atlas historique de Montréal*. Montréal: Art Global Libre Expression 1994

Rochemonteix, Camille de. *Les Jésuites et la Nouvelle France au XVIIe siècle*. Paris: Letouzey et Ané 1890

Roserot, Alphonse. *Dictionnaire historique de la Champagne méridionale (Aube) des origines à 1790*. Angers: Éditions de l'Ouest 1948

– *Troyes: Son histoire, ses monuments des origines à 1790*. Troyes: Paton 1948

Roserot de Melin, Joseph. *Le diocèse de Troyes des origines à nos jours (IIIe siècle – 1955)*. Troyes: Renaissance 1957

Rouquet, Chantal. *Troyes à travers les âges*. Troyes: CNDP 1985

Rousseau, François. *La croix et le scalpel: Histoire des Augustines et de l'Hôtel-Dieu de Québec.* Vol. 1, 1639–1892. Québec: Septentrion 1989

Rousseau, Jacques. "Les premiers Canadiens." *Cahiers des Dix* 25 (1960): 9–64

Roy, Pierre-Georges. *Inventaire des greffes des notaires du régime français.* Vol. 1. Québec: Archives de la province de Québec 1942

Roy, Regis, and Gérard Malchelosse. Le régiment Carignan. Montréal: G. Ducharme 1925

Rumilly, Robert. *Marguerite Bourgeoys.* Paris: Spes 1936

– *Marie Barbier: Mystique canadienne.* Montréal: Albert Levesque 1935

Sainte-Henriette, Soeur. *Histoire de la Congrégation de Notre-Dame.* Vols. 1–4. Montréal: Congrégation de Notre-Dame 1910–41

Saint-Marie-Odile, Soeur. "Bibliographie critique de la vénérable Marguerite Bourgeoys." PhD dissertation, Université de Montréal 1949

Saint Marguerite Bourgeoys: Canonization. Montreal: Congrégation de Notre-Dame 1982

Saint-Vallier, Jean-Baptiste de La Croix de Chevrières. *Estat present de l'Eglise et de la colonie française dans la Nouvelle-France.* Québec: Augustin Coté & Cie 1856

Sales, Francis de. *Introduction to the Devout Life.* Trans. and ed. John K. Royan. New York: Harper and Brothers 1950

– and Jane de Chantal. *Letters of Spiritual Direction.* Trans. Peronne Marie Thibert. Selected and introduced by Wendy M. Wright and Joseph F. Power. New York: Paulist Press 1988

Salinis, A. *Madame de Villeneuve.* Paris: Beauchesne 1918

Schwarzfuchs, Simon. *Rachi de Troyes.* Paris: Albin Michel 1991

Scott, Mary Eileen. "The Congrégation de Notre-Dame in Early Nova Scotia." Canadian Catholic Historical Association, *Historical Studies* 20 (1953)

– "The Constant Heart." Play first produced by the Genesian Players at the Gésu Theatre, Montreal, 1951

– "Religious Attitudes in New France and their Political and Social Grounds." Lecture delivered at Thomas More Institute, Montreal, spring 1976

– "Spirit, Purpose and Some Charisms of Mother Bourgeoys." Paper circulated in Congrégation de Notre-Dame, June 1968

– "The Spiritual Legacy of Montreal." Lecture delivered at Mass Rally for Christ, Montreal Forum, 8 March 1971

– *A Spirituality of Compassion.* Montreal: Congrégation de Notre-Dame 1979

Sedgwick, Alexander. *Jansenism in Seventeenth-Century France: Voices from the Wilderness.* Charlottesville: University of Virginia Press 1977

Seguin, Robert-Lionel. *La civilisation traditionnelle de l'"habitant" aux 17e et 18e siècles*. Montréal: Fides 1967

– *La sorcellerie au Canada français du XVIIe au XIXe siècle*. Montréal: Ducharme 1961

Sévigny, Jeannine. "Histoire de la Congrégation de Notre-Dame à Laprairie." Conférence prononcée devant la Société historique de La Prairie de la Madeleine, le 21 octobre 1987.

– *Social and Religious Context of Marguerite Bourgeoys's Mission as Educator*. Trans. Patricia Landry. Heritage no. 9. Montreal: CND 1993

Simpson, Patricia. *Marguerite Bourgeoys and Montreal, 1640–1665*. Montreal: McGill-Queen's University Press 1997

– and Louise Pothier. *Notre-Dame-de-Bon-Secours, a Chapel and Its Neighbourhood*. Montreal: Fides 2001

Sisters of the Congrégation de Notre-Dame. *Constitutions and Rules*. Montreal: Congrégation de Notre-Dame 1984

Sulte, Benjamin. *Histoire des Canadiens français 1608–1880*. Vol. 4. Montréal: Wilson and Cie 1882

Talon, Jean. "Mémoire de Talon sur le Canada au ministre Colbert (10 novembre 1670)." *RAPQ*, 1930–31, 122–39

Taveneaux, Réné, ed. *Saint Pierre Fourier en son temps*. Nancy: Presses universitaires de Nancy 1992

Tremblay, Hélène. "Historiographie de Marguerite Bourgeoys aux XVIIe et XVIIIe siècles." MA dissertation, Université de Montréal 1967

– *Marguerite Bourgeoys and the Education of Women*. Trans. Elizabeth Jane Fraser. Heritage no. 12. Montreal: CND 1993

Tooker, Elizabeth. *An Ethnography of the Huron Indians, 1615–1649*. Washington, DC: Huronia Historical Development Council and the Ontario Dept. of Education through the Smithsonian Institution 1967

Trigger, Bruce G. *The Huron: Farmers of the North*. Montreal: Holt, Rinehart and Winston 1969

Tronson, Louis. *Correspondance de M. Louis Tronson: Lettres choisies, annotées et publiées par Bertrand*. Paris: Victor Lecoffre 1904

Trudel, Marcel. *The Beginnings of New France, 1524–1663*. Trans. Patricia Claxton. Toronto: McClelland and Stewart 1973

– *Montréal, la formation d'une société 1642–1663*. Montréal: Fides 1976

– *La population du Canada en 1666: Recensement constitué*. Sillery: Septentrion 1995

– *Le terrier du Saint-Laurent en 1663*. Ottawa: University of Ottawa 1973

Vachon, André. "Valeurs des sources iroquoises et françaises." *Cahiers des Dix* 40 (1975): 197–222

Vachon de Belmont, François. "Éloges de quelques personnes morte en odeur de sainteté à Montréal, 1722." *RAPQ*, no. 10 (1929–30): 144–89

Verney, Jack. *The Good Regiment: The Carignan-Salières Regiment in Canada, 1665–1668*. Montreal: McGill-Queen's University Press 1991

Viau, Roland. *Femmes de personne sexe, genres et pouvoirs en Iroquoisie ancienne*. Montréal: Boréal 2000

Vie intime de la vénérable mère Alix Le Clerc. Gembloux: Duculot 1923

Vies des Saincts et des festes de Toute. Rouen: Jean Osmont 1635

Ville de Paris. *Commission municipale du vieux Paris*. Paris: Imprimerie municipale 1914

Vincent de Paul, Saint. *Correspondance, entretiens, documents*. Ed. Pierre Coste. 14 vols. Paris: Librairie Lecoffre, J. Gabalda 1920–25

Les Vraies Constitutions des Religieuses de la Congregation de Nostre Dame. Faites par le Venerable serviteur de Dieu Pierre Fourier leur Instituteur, et Chanoines reguliers de la Congregation de nôtre Sauveur, approuvées par nôtre Saint Pere le Pape Innocent X. 2e éd. Toul 1694

Vuillemin, Jean-Baptiste. *La vie de la vénérable Alix Le Clerc*. Paris: Société Saint-Augustin, Desclée, De Brouwer et Cie 1910

Walsh, H.H. *The Church in the French Era*. Toronto: Ryerson 1966

Warner, Marina. *Alone of All Her Sex: The Myth and Cult of the Virgin Mary*. New York: Knopf 1976

INDEX